Dialogues on the Teaching of Literature

It is not growing like a tree
In bulk, doth make man better be.

JONSON

DIALOGUES ON THE TEACHING OF LITERATURE

Bertrand Evans
and
James J. Lynch

BOOKMAN ASSOCIATES
New York

TO ALL THE
LIBENTIAS EVERYWHERE

Preface

On the day after word came that Russia had launched its first Sputnik, the American public launched a crusade for more effective education in the elementary and secondary schools. Quite naturally, the arrowhead of investigation pointed directly at that part of the curriculum which seemed to have failed worst, because it had not got up its Sputnik first—science and mathematics. In the short while since the original Sputnik soared, irate patriots, working through officials of government and education, have wrought wonders in the public school's programs of science and mathematics. In the truly "progressive" community, first grade and even kindergarten children are now learning to read, define, and discuss words like "thrust," "velocity," and "orbital."

Sober heads, however, have been quick to realize that missile science and mathematics alone do not constitute a complete education even for the modern American: there must be improvement also in the quality of instruction in the science of "human relations." Hence, across the land, the curricular area somewhat loosely defined as "Social Studies" has lately gained prestige and respectability second only to that accorded the true science, which is dedicated to the modern equivalent of getting there "fustest, with the mostest."

In the midst of this excitement, the presenters of the following dialogues were so fortunate as to discover an ancient manuscript which seemed to them to argue superbly on the side of their personal convictions: that the education of the human being as human being is a more urgent necessity in today's civilization than at any previous time in man's history; that the profoundest fault in American schools at present is their failure to prize highly enough and to provide wisely enough for this kind of education; and that a principal cause of this fault is the domination of the schools by Professional Educationism.

These Dialogues do not concern themselves with science, or

with social science, but with literature. They insist that literature, wisely chosen, arranged, and presented in the schools, can do much toward educating human beings to take the humane point of view. Their contention is well summed up by Harvard President Nathan C. Pusey's recent memorable statement that works of literature, "because they proffer the living, vivid acquaintance with the adventures of the human spirit, can strengthen the humanity that lies in a man and needle it into fullest growth."

The Dialogues present a reasoned statement on the teaching of literature. They insist that mere "reading materials," as the Educationists properly call them, though they may contribute to other worthy ends, can offer nothing toward the great end. Similarly, they insist that literature itself, taught by ill-considered means toward either scholastic or social-studies ends, will contribute little or nothing toward the great end. If a work of art is to accomplish in the student reader's being what at best it may accomplish—the needling of his humanity toward its fullest growth—all activities undertaken by teacher and student, from the first approach to the final activities after reading is completed, must be consonant with one another and directed toward the primary end.

In that it discusses in some detail the inevitable problems of Why, What, and How, this book of dialogues is remarkably like any modern textbook on "The Teaching of Literature in the High School." But it is unique both in its point of view and in its form. Here the widely divergent points of view of the several persons who are peculiarly interested in the teaching of literature in the schools—the teacher, the parent-taxpayer, the professor of literature, and the professional Educationist—are faithfully presented, and to these are added the opinions of a humanely oriented scientist and those of the spokesman for the anonymous author— Elanchius.

To be wholly successful, a book on education must reach not only teachers, but also the growing number of lay people who are concerned for the education of their children. The usual book on the teaching of literature, written in conventional textbook style, is rarely read by those not required to read it for professional reasons. Perhaps these Dialogues of Elanchius, because they are conversations, will invite the attention of all who have a stake in the matter.

A word more, on the place and time of the Dialogues: their setting is vaguely remote in both—who knows where or when? Perhaps their very remoteness will add a dimension of interest; more importantly, perhaps it will help the reader to escape from what Eliot has called "the stranglehold of the present." Possibly by examining an intricate problem in a remote, uncertain time and place, we may all gain truer perspective on that problem as it exists in the present—and thus come, in Arnoldian terms, to see things as they really are. Such is the hope of the translators of these ancient dialogues.

J.J.L
B.E.

Berkeley, 1960

PRINCIPAL SPEAKERS

LIBENTIA, *a young teacher of literature*

PULVIUS, *a literary scholar*

VULPIUS, *an educationist*

QUINTUS, *a parent and taxpayer, also a shoemaker*

EMPIRICUS, *a scientist; formerly a military officer*

and

ELANCHIUS

Contents

PART I

WHY SHOULD LITERATURE BE TAUGHT?

PART II

WHAT WORKS OF LITERATURE SHOULD BE TAUGHT?

PART III

WHO SHOULD BE TAUGHT LITERATURE?

PART IV

HOW SHOULD LITERATURE BE TAUGHT?

BIBLIOGRAPHICAL NOTE

The following text is offered as a translation of a rare manuscript entitled "The Dialogues of Elanchius."

PART I

WHY SHOULD LITERATURE BE TAUGHT?

The Question Unrecognized

Persons of the Dialogue

PULVIUS GRAMMATICUS   LIBENTIA MAGISTRA   VULPIUS MATERIES

Scene: The house of Libentia

Libentia: —to find the key. When I was in your class, Pulvius, you used to say that students who came to you were inadequately prepared to carry out your assignments. Now that I've finished my first year of teaching, I'm afraid you won't find my graduates prepared any better.

Pulvius: Why not, Libentia?

Libentia: Because of the confusion in my own mind. I don't really know what I'm trying to do.

Vulpius: You should have no doubts, Libentia. As my student, you learned that optimum success in teaching results from the teacher's aptitudes for utilizing tested techniques for promoting worthwhileness through continuous learner activities.

Libentia: But there's the rub! I think the original cause of my confusion was that your ideas, Vulpius, and yours, Pulvius, contradicted each other so often. When I was a student in your classes, I was troubled because my two principal advisers disagreed. And now, as a teacher and therefore in still greater need of counsel, I am even more troubled by the fundamental contradiction of your points of view. Whom shall I believe?

Pulvius: Do you mean that you do not know *what* to teach?

Vulpius: Do you mean you tend to feel that your thinking as to *how* to teach is confused?

17

Libentia: Neither exactly. Before my school reopens this fall, I want to be surer than I am now about several things. I must find the answers not only to the questions "What should I do?" and "How should I do it?" but also to the question "How should I arrive at answers to these questions?"

Pulvius: The answers are evident enough. You teach the best that has been thought and said in the world, and you teach it because it *is* the best.

Vulpius: Don't be unrealistic, Pulvius. Young learners have individual differences, as to interests, needs, and maturation levels. Any thinking that tends to hold that Libentia should expose all her students to homogeneous materials is unscientific.

Libentia: Do you mean, Pulvius, that I should teach the best that has been thought and said to *all* my students?

Pulvius: I did not say that. But there are *some* who can read documents of the highest order. If you fail to provide these with a knowledge of the classics, you make it impossible for us to maintain proper standards later on.

Vulpius: Wait a minute, Pulvius! Libentia and her fellow teachers have the obligation of providing worthwhile learning activities for *all* our youths, not just the few who will continue on in their formal educational career. It would be undemocratic if she discriminated in favor of a selected group of gifted individuals.

Pulvius: But our democracy requires properly trained leaders.

Libentia: You have agreed, for different reasons, that I should not teach literature to *all* my students. But, then, should I teach it to *any?* Pulvius says I must teach it to the few; Vulpius says that would be undemocratic. It seems then that I must teach literature to nobody but must instead find substitute "reading materials" to give to all.

Vulpius: Of course.

Pulvius: No! Why, literature has held a place in the program of studies since formal schools were established.

Libentia: But you can't mean that literature should be kept in the curriculum simply because it has always been there! Hasn't it some kind of *value?*

Pulvius: Certainly. By subjecting our future leaders to the discipline of literary study, we give them the kind of rigorous training which their later duties will require. Moreover, consider the vast treasury of knowledge that is literature! Is this cultural storehouse, which has been filling from the most ancient times onward, now to stand—unused?

Vulpius: But let me remind you that such learnings look to no practical outcomes regarded as worthwhile for present-day social utilization by the thinking of we in the profession. You tend to set an unrealistic value on your traditional content, Pulvius. You forget that these are changing times. But our researchers in the field have made available to us during the past half-century numerous empirical findings as to such significant areas as learning processes, the slow learner, the non-reader, the whole child. In short, these realistically approached and excitingly revolutionary researches as to the differences between individuals in these areas have demonstrated conclusively that individual learners have differences.

Pulvius: What! Is that a way of saying that since students are not all alike they must have different kinds of education? What has happened to the position you took a moment ago? You argued that all students must be treated alike. Now you maintain that since children are different they *cannot* be treated alike.

Vulpius: The individual learner must be educated as to his individual needs and capacity.

Libentia: Gentlemen, I am sure that you wish to help me. But you confuse me. Pulvius believes that literature is for a select group, as a discipline and as knowledge.

Pulvius: Right!

Vulpius: Poof!

Libentia: And you, Vulpius, seem not to believe that literature has real value for *any* students. Democracy in education, as you define it, would prevent your allowing some students to read "the best" if others could not. You would therefore use a kind of reading tailored to the individual.

Vulpius: Of course. That is the only realistic way of confronting the realities of the classroom situation.

Pulvius: Bah!

Libentia: I don't want to give it up if there is some reason why it should be taught—even though only to a few. And if there *is* a reason, how am I to decide which students should study literature? Are they those who will continue their education? Should I then separate them from the rest and see they are carefully instructed in the content and forms of literature?

Vulpius: Ah! Your questions have moved into the area of grouping—a field in which I can speak with assurance. Grouping is obviously your answer, as it affords the greatest workability. Research tells us that adequate provision for individual differences require—

Pulvius: Grouping? You were calling it segregation a few years ago. But whatever you call it, how can you reconcile it with your statements about democracy in education?

Libentia: Gentlemen, gentlemen! You keep reaching the same deadlock. But what about all my other questions. For instance, what am I to do with students who not only will not read "the best" but resist reading anything?

Vulpius: Why, provide them with other activities, of course.

Libentia: But what kind?

Vulpius: Those that appeal to their interests, naturally, and in which they have skills.

Libentia: Even though these activities have nothing to do with books?

Vulpius: Of course. Books have no monopoly on real life realities.

Pulvius: We know, Vulpius, that more than books is needed to make the full man. But Libentia's work in the school is with books.

Vulpius: Not at all, Pulvius. It is with children. We in the profession have taken this approach ever since the findings of researches demonstrated the realistic concept of the student-centered curriculum.

Libentia: But I must have something to *teach* them! If, as Pulvius says, that "something" is in books, then *which* books? Just how shall I choose, from among the thousands that have been written, the mere handful that I have time for? And how can I answer this question until I know *why* I should be using books at all? How do I discover that? You see—I don't even know where to begin.

Pulvius: I fail to understand your uncertainty in the selection of documents. Those books should be chosen that are the best, and the best are those that remain after time has winnowed out the chaff.

Vulpius: As usual, you speak of "best" as if it were an absolute concept. But our findings demonstrate that you are unrealistic. What is best for one individual is not best for another. This concept has to be defined in relative terms as to individual differences—needs, interests, aptitudes, reading skills, and maturation levels of different individuals.

Pulvius: What! There is no such thing as one book's being superior to another? Have you no respect for the authority of literary criticism? The most ancient of philosopher-critics established criteria—

Vulpius: Ancient! There you go, Pulvius, utilizing the doctrine of some individual who for all I know or care may have been dead a thousand years, before any empirical researches had been conducted as to the needs of modern individuals in these changing times. We in the profession desire the best for young learners also, but our findings confront the realities of the present-day school population.

Libentia: I see that you both think I should use only the "best"—but you mean quite different things by it. For Pulvius, it is what generations of critics have pronounced distinguished. For Vulpius, it is what professional research has found best adapted to the specific needs, interests, and abilities of each child. If you hold such opposing views of what the "best" is, must you not also hold different views of the purpose it is to serve? Until I find the *right* purpose, how can I define "best"? How can I even be sure that the "best" in *any* sense is needed? Is there something which, above all else, needs to be done, and can be done for my students by their reading? If so, what is it? And is it the same thing for all students? And will the same books best serve this purpose for all students? Gentlemen, I am at wit's end.

Vulpius: Your situation is normal, Libentia. Obviously, you are now experiencing a felt need for definite enabling objectives which will enable you to formulate realistic utilizational plans for the achievement of worthwhile outcomes. I can provide you with any number of bibliographies of studies which enumerate a great many objectively validated objectives. But wait. I usually carry a supply of such materials with me in this bag. Let me see. This? No, this one is a list of "devices which work." This? No, this is a list of techniques for evaluating criteria as to pupil responses to listening experiences.

Pulvius: Great heavens! What next?

Vulpius: Ah! Here is a list of objectives compiled by some of our vigorous young researchers. Let me read you a few that most realistically confront the trend of the modern school curriculum of today: "To inculcate dynamic and worthwhile allegiances." Good, very worthwhile. Here is another: "To make practical certain everyday speech patterns." Good, very practical. Now, here are some more: "To see that there is a bond between men and animals," "To enjoy the world of make-believe by seeing that mystery and fantasy hold sway," "To put the student on guard against defeatism and propaganda," "To learn how to convert the written word into speech," "To develop the language arts, skills of reading, writing, speaking, and listening—"

Pulvius: What! No smelling?

Vulpius: "To see that nonsense takes the place of sense," "To learn the differences in the importance of word pictures in reading materials," "To gain experience in pre-planning to meet the responsibilities of adjusting—"*

Pulvius: Hold, Vulpius! No more. What have these to do with literature?

Libentia: I have asked myself the same question many times. There are hundreds of lists of such objectives—any of which would provide the teacher with more than enough to do. The

---

* The reader will discover that Vulpius' objectives are not exaggerated if he examines the list of twenty-five such items, compiled from questionnaires returned by school officials, and included in James R. Caldwell's "The Teaching of Literature in the High Schools of California," *The Educational Forum* for January, 1946.

trouble is that there are so many! And are any, or all, or none of these objectives "right"? Are some more important than others? If so, how shall I decide? Frankly, I feel more uncertain with all these statements than I would feel with none.

Pulvius: I cannot think that the loss would be insupportable if the ocean opened and swallowed them.

Libentia: Have you some objectives that are more helpful?

Pulvius: It is not my wont to call them objectives, but I can define with some exactness the kinds of knowledge important for students who enter my classes. They should be well grounded in the facts of literary history. They should know the characteristics of the various forms of poetry, drama, and prose, and should understand the conventions and traditions which pertain to each. They should be acquainted with the names and biographies of the principal authors. They should be able to define the temporal bounds of the major periods of literature and to characterize the productions of each period. They should be able to describe a given specimen in terms of its age, its genre, and its author. They should—

Vulpius: These dry bones are unrealistic, Pulvius. Your thinking extends only to the fraction of the total school population who continue their formal education. Besides, such learnings do not provide worthy outcomes even for *these* individuals. For all the others they are, of course, absurd.

Libentia: Gentlemen, we have again made a complete circle. I continue to believe it impossible to decide whether literature is for all, for the few, or for none *until we have found what it is that literature can and should do for its readers.* This is the question for which I must find an answer.

Pulvius: Possibly an acquaintance with the genres, periods, and techniques of literature would have some value for all your students, Libentia. But I must repeat: I am concerned only with the few who proceed to my classes.

Vulpius: If the dry bones you listed a moment ago represent the worthiest outcomes your "literature" can achieve, we need not be distressed if the total pupil personnel achieve none of them. It is now evident to me that you would not really be favoring your select few by giving them these bones to experience.

Libentia: Well, at least Pulvius has made it clear that he finds nothing in literature indispensable to *every* child's education. Do you agree, Vulpius?

Vulpius: There is no empirical evidence tending to prove that literature is indispensable to *any* young learner. But of course all youth must be given access to and a degree of facility with reading materials. However, these reading materials must be prepared by specialists in devising texts suitably graded as to readability and adapted as to vocabulary range, maturation level, and need and interest quotient of individual learners.

Pulvius: What nonsense! Do you truly mean that instead of works of art composed by creative genius you would offer the concoctions of self-styled reading specialists? My gorge rises at the thought. No merit can possibly reside in such stuff. What can be expected of the young scholars who come to me for serious application to literary documents when you have confronted them only with such—such masterpieces of insipidity? By all the majestic deities, I will not have it!

Libentia: But Vulpius, like you, has offered an answer to my question. His "reading materials" can at least be read by all students with a minimum of effort.

Pulvius: But, however easy they may be, they do not deserve *any* effort.

Libentia: Still, it is an answer. Between you, you have given me two choices: to present Vulpius' reading materials to all my students, or to present literature to Pulvius' select few and "reading materials" to the others. But I would like to believe that there is a third choice. If there is something in literature that is truly indispensable, then surely it is indispensable to *all* and I must find how to give the experience of it to all.

Vulpius: The findings of our researches require that you dismiss your third choice. The realities of the modern school environment tend to prove conclusively that we must adjust the learning materials utilized to suit the interests, needs, and capacities of individual learners. You will remember that, in my course in "Curriculum Construction for the Modern School of Today," I stressed many times that the teacher must take individuals where she finds them. It is unrealistic to attempt to adjust young learners to what Pulvius calls "literature." Reading materials must be adjusted to them.

Pulvius: Your selection neglects our future leaders, Vulpius. Do what you will with the others, but give these rigorous discipline in literary documents.

Libentia: Et tu, Pulvius! Even you would deny me the third choice!

Vulpius: Now that you have had experience in the field, Libentia, surely you cannot entertain any illusions that your third possibility has empirical validity. Your service in the actual classroom situation will have confirmed the findings of researchers that in the present-day school population there are individual differences.

Pulvius: I would not put it in those terms, Vulpius. But I will agree that the literary discipline may be unsuited to the inferior intellect. You once referred scornfully to the "cake-theory" of education as undemocratic. But I say, let those eat the cake who can. We cannot deny it to some merely because others have no taste for it.

Libentia: Your agreement that literature contains nothing truly indispensable tempts me to give up trying to teach literature to any except those students whose plans for the future lead them to request it. This is plainly the path of least resistance—one, I'm sorry to say, that many of my colleagues have taken. But if I give up, will I not betray a trust? I *would* have given up last year but for some words I once heard Elanchius speak. They went something like this: that the best teacher is not life but the distilled experience of the most sensitive and observant human beings, and that this experience is preserved only in the best books that have been written. If there is truth in these words, is it right to deny this experience to any student?

Vulpius: Unrealistic nonsense! Who is this Elanchius? He sounds to me like some visionary philosopher.

Pulvius: I also fail to place the name.

Libentia: Elanchius is an old and dear friend whose counsel has never failed me. And it is true, Vulpius, that he is not without vision and that he has the philosopher's wisdom. Indeed, he is so very wise that I have sometimes thought—but no matter. I hope you will soon meet him. I had invited him to join us this evening, but he could not come. He asked me to call on him tomorrow morning. Perhaps you will both be good enough to accompany me.

Pulvius: Gladly.

Vulpius: I should like to talk to your paragon. Some of the findings of we in the profession should be illuminating to him.

Libentia: Then shall we meet here tomorrow at sunrise and go together?

Vulpius: Sunrise!

Pulvius: An appalling hour!

Libentia: Not so for calling on Elanchius.

The Question Recognized

Persons of the Dialogue

LIBENTIA MAGISTRA

PULVIUS GRAMMATICUS   VULPIUS MATERIES

ELANCHIUS

Scene: The house of Elanchius

Libentia: Here we are—just as the first rays of the sun fall upon the door.

Pulvius: Note that shield there with the striking head of—

Libentia: Wait! I hear a step.

Vulpius: Your paragon approaches.

Elanchius: Enter, Libentia, and welcome. And these are the friends you spoke of?

Libentia: Yes, Elanchius. May I present Pulvius Grammaticus and Vulpius Materies?

Elanchius: Gentlemen, I am honored. My door is always open to Libentia Magistra and her friends.

Libentia: Pulvius and Vulpius were good enough to talk with me at some length last evening.

Elanchius: Ah! And you had a pleasant evening?

Libentia: Yes indeed, Elanchius.

Pulvius: But highly inconclusive, I fear!

Elanchius: I am sorry for that, Pulvius. But wise conclusions are not easy to reach when the questions are as complex as those which are troubling Libentia; they must sometimes be sought by winding paths. Tell me, Libentia, did it appear to you that some particular obstacle stood in the way of your search?

27

Libentia: There seemed to be some question—which perhaps we never really recognized—that always stopped us at a certain point.

Elanchius: Well, then. Perhaps we should start afresh. You told me that you were not satisfied with your first year of teaching. What was the cause of your dissatisfaction?

Libentia: When I began teaching, I thought I knew what my proper role was. But I became less sure every day. And now I'm not sure at all.

Elanchius: Ah! It is the self-satisfied teacher for whom we should fear! But you are aware of your perplexities.

Libentia: Too often last year I felt that I was reaching none of my students. The atmosphere of the school seemed more appropriate for a carnival than for a place of learning.

Vulpius: May I point out that recent research in the field tends to demonstrate that extra-curricular activities—they should more properly be termed co-curricular—are a vital aspect of the learning process. They develop realistic learning situations that are worthwhile in the maturation process and constitute empirically valid implementation for achieving common learnings by non-subject-minded students.

Pulvius: But Libentia's work is with literature! Your remarks are no more relevant now than last evening. Non-subject-minded students, indeed! Then they are not students at all.

Libentia: Are we already meeting the same obstacle that blocked us yesterday? We could not decide, Elanchius, whether the study of literature is for everybody.

Elanchius: Better to stop there than to answer unwisely and rush on to other questions. Otherwise, all subsequent answers might prove false. But tell me, what were your differences of opinion?

Libentia: Pulvius insisted that the small group of students coming to him be thoroughly trained in literature; he did not insist that others study it. Vulpius denied that literature is appropriate for most students but also argued that it is undemocratic to favor a small group.

Elanchius: I see. And you could not accept either of these answers?

Libentia: No, I could not—because I remembered some words that you once spoke.

Elanchius: That I spoke?

Libentia: Yes. You said that the study of literature is indispensable. If it *is* indispensable, then it must be for *all* students and not just for the few who go on to Pulvius.

Elanchius: Then as you see it, much depends on how the teacher answers the question: Is the study of literature truly indispensable?

Libentia: It seems to me that everything depends on it!

Elanchius: And did you ask this question of Pulvius and Vulpius?

Libentia: I did. Although they disagreed on everything else, neither believes that all students need to study literature. Their agreement on this point seemed to confirm my worst doubts.

Elanchius: And have these doubts overcome you?

Libentia: No, not yet!

Elanchius: Then let us examine this question, not precipitately, but earnestly and deliberately—and above all, honestly. Gentlemen, I am sorry that my need to discover the precise nature of Libentia's problem has required me to neglect you so long.

Pulvius: No apology. Your manner of questioning has interested me immensely.

Vulpius: Now as to your question, Elanchius, as to whether what Pulvius—as well as yourself, I suspect—calls literature fills a felt need for all youth. I am, of course, willing to discuss it with you. However, I must say at the outset that I do not anticipate any worthwhile outcomes being achieved. Mere commonsense conclusions are worthless as to these areas. Empirical studies of researchers in the field have already tended to demonstrate conclusively that the answer is in the negative: "literature" does not fill a felt need for all. Although some opinionated teachers refuse to utilize the facts accumulated through realistic surveys and controlled experiments in actual classroom situations, the fact is that pupil personnel in the changing school population of today have different needs, interests, aptitudes, and maturation levels. What is adapted to one individual is not suited to another.

Therefore the view that any one type of learning experience, such
as a particular body of reading materials, is adapted to *all* youth
is mere opinion, and therefore unscientific.

Pulvius: If I remember correctly, Vulpius, Libentia's question concerned *literature*, not "reading materials"—and she asked
whether literature is *indispensable*, not whether it is "adapted."

Elanchius: Thank you, in any event, Vulpius, for this full
and unqualified exposure of your position. That children differ
in the ways you mention, no reasonable man will deny. Doubtless,
Libentia observed significant differences last year. What were
your students like, Libentia?

Libentia: Like, Elanchius? or unlike? Vulpius' description
is accurate. They differed in intelligence, interests, tastes, abilities, ambitions, backgrounds—in these ways no less than in
height, weight, color of hair, and dress. Many, but not all, were
children of artisans and tradesmen. A few came from homes in
which books and the arts are as much a part of life as kitchen
utensils, work, sleep, and food. Many more came from homes
which find no place for art in any form, but only for the daily
necessities of survival and for entertainment of a louder and more
glaring kind. A few will go on to Pulvius; of the others, most of
the girls will marry within a few years and become housewives,
while the boys will find work, often in the occupations of their
fathers.

Vulpius: An admirable summary of the facts, Libentia. It is
vital that the teacher have available such data, compiled through
empirical surveys of the community socio-economic pattern. The
student population should next be structured according to the
findings of a battery of tests, including personality-adjustment
and social-acceptance sequences, so that accurate profile charts,
in the hands of counselling and guidance specialists, will be
available for utilization by the teacher.

Pulvius: I should think, Libentia, that such chores as these
would steal time from genuine subject matter.

Libentia: They do.* But after my experience last year and my

---

* The substance of Libentia's problem appears to have been dissipated
in the following solution: "If the teacher considers the evaluation program

conversation with you and Vulpius last evening, I am no longer sure what my "genuine subject matter" is. I am told that I must be aware of all the differences among my students, must adjust subject matter according to these differences, and must even replace traditional subject matter when it is considered not sufficiently adaptable. When I began teaching, I hoped that I could give all my students an acquaintance with literature. But I have been prevented by all this systematized concern with socio-economic patterns, personality assessments, individual differences, and the like. If I could be sure of the indispensability of literature, I would continue the struggle. But if I cannot be sure, how can I oppose the professional authorities who tell me to replace literature with readings chosen merely because they are adapted to students' differences? Elanchius, what should I do?

Elanchius: That we must determine, Libentia! Now you have acknowledged that there are differences among students. Is it for that reason that you question whether literature can be indispensable to all?

Libentia: Both my brief experience and the concurrence of Pulvius and Vulpius make me fear that I must accept this conclusion.

Vulpius: It is the only conclusion that confronts the teaching situation realistically.

Pulvius: Your idealism is commendable, Libentia, but you must admit the truth of the adage that one cannot make silk purses from sows' ears. Just be sure that you *do* make them from silk!

Elanchius: Libentia was right—neither of you believes that literature is indispensable. And if it were true that children are characterized *wholly* by their differences, I should have to agree.

---

as an assignment to be added to an already full-time teaching schedule, necessitating more than the usual amount of record keeping after school hours, then rightly he may consider it a heavy additional assignment. If, however, evaluation is considered in its broader aspects as a regular part of the educational program, the time required for observing, reporting, and routine record keeping should become a regular part of the school day." "Evaluating Pupil Progress," *Bulletin of the California State Department of Education*, Vol. XXI, No. 6, April, 1952, p. 162.

But appearance is often deceptive. Conclusions based on appearance may prove faulty when the deeper reality is perceived.

Libentia: I am cheered already.

Elanchius: Well, then. Libentia, you have acknowledged that there are differences among children, some of which are conspicuous, some subtle, but in either case real, and all, for one purpose or another, significant. No doubt even "identical" twins differ somewhat. We may, then, hold it for a truth that no two persons are completely alike. Now tell me: is the converse also true?

Libentia: That no two persons are completely unlike?

Elanchius: Yes.

Libentia: That must also be true. All persons have some resemblances to all others. All breathe. All require food. All—

Elanchius: Though you searched to the ends of the earth, you would find no two persons who were wholly dissimilar. It must follow, then, that among the children in your class there are none.

Vulpius: Research says—

Pulvius: Go to, Vulpius; *homo* is a name common to all men. *Liber* is a name common to all children.

Elanchius: Then if no two persons are completely unlike, it follows that all have something in common. Hence, can it reasonably be said that the children in your classes are characterized wholly by their differences?

Libentia: It cannot!

Elanchius: Then does it follow that the education of every child must differ in all respects from that of every other?

Libentia: No! Since all have something in common, they must have some education in common too!

Elanchius: Patience, Libentia. Our task is only begun. If the education of each child need not differ in *all* respects from that of every other child, then the *possibility* exists that some subject matter is indispensable to the education of all. We have not established this as a fact, nor have we shown that the subject matter of literature, in particular, is indispensable. But we have reached the point where we can begin to ponder the question. Gentlemen, I know that both of you have much on your minds, and I shall soon become your willing listener. But will you permit me first to inquire further into this question?

Pulvius: I remain more intrigued than impatient.

Vulpius: And I recognize the desirability of further observations as to the trend of your thinking before making available the realistic research findings as to this area.

Elanchius: Thank you! And now, Libentia, we said that although your students have differences of which you are aware—and properly so—yet they are in other ways alike, and you named some of the more obvious of these. Now tell me: is it possible that in teaching your students you should keep in mind their *similarities* as well as their differences?

Libentia: I feel that I should. But I cannot put my feeling into words.

Vulpius: Even if you could, Libentia, your words would only be anecdotal, and certainly not as impressive as the findings of empirical studies as to individual differences.

Pulvius: I doubt that anything could be that impressive!

Elanchius: Now, Libentia, among the ways in which children are like one another, do some seem to you more significant than others?

Libentia: Well, let me think. They all breathe, eat, sleep, wear clothing—

Elanchius: All these are things that they *do* in common. But can you think of any ways in which they *are* in common?

Libentia: They *are*? Let me see. They are not all artisans' sons, although many are. They are not all equally—I'm sorry, Elanchius!

Elanchius: Well, let us start with that. They are not all artisans' sons, but suppose for a moment that they were. Would you then think of them primarily so? Would you teach them *as* artisans' sons.

Libentia: Why, no, I would think of them, and try to teach them, just as I do now—as children.

Pulvius: I said it! *Liber* is a name common to all children.

Elanchius: And in saying that you think of them as children, Libentia, do you not come close to naming an essential thing they are, or *have*, in common? Now, tell me—

Libentia: Wait, Elanchius! You have made me remember what you told me once—that my task was to teach my students not as artisans' sons or tradesmen's sons or even as citizens of our democracy, but as *human beings*. Is not their humanity the most essential thing they have in common?

Elanchius: So I believe, Libentia. *And at this moment in history the necessity to believe so has greater urgency than ever before!*

Libentia: And especially the teacher must believe so!

Elanchius: Therefore, let us consider further. Now, tell me, just what means, or subject matter, will serve the purpose of teaching students as human beings?

Libentia: Elanchius, your question is hard!

Elanchius: Then let us rephrase it. And, since the answers to all our subsequent questions about teaching must follow from the answer to this one, let us call it the *antecedent question*.

Pulvius: Antecedent question? Excellent, Elanchius, excellent!

Elanchius: Moreover, Libentia, since you are a teacher of literature, shall we phrase the question so that it will pertain directly to your work?

Libentia: That will help me most.

Elanchius: Well, let me see. What can be done for students as human beings? By what means can this be done? Those are the parts of our question. And now—ah! Here is our question: *What is it that literature, because of its intrinsic nature, can do for its readers which needs to be done for them because of their nature as human beings?* There! Will that suffice?

Libentia: If we can answer that, we will have found the main reason for teaching literature. And when we have found that, I shall have a starting point for answering all my other questions.

Vulpius: Let me indicate that the assumptions of your questions are based on mere opinions—first, that some totally visionary outcome can be achieved in the whole child, and second, that what you call "literature" contains component factors utilizable to achieve them.

Elanchius: Ah! We should be dishonest if we assumed that our question is an answer and not a hypothesis.

Pulvius: Vulpius is unfamiliar with hypotheses, Elanchius. He deals only in answers. And, speaking of answers, what *is* the one to your question?

Elanchius: It cannot come all in a breath, Pulvius! It will require time, and patience, and all our efforts.

Libentia: I am as eager as Pulvius to find this answer. But first I have a favor to ask.

Elanchius: What is it, Libentia?

Libentia: That we go no further just now. There is in our town one J. Quintus, who keeps a shop. He has children in my school and is much interested in my work. In fact, my final responsibility is to him! I should like to have him with us when we work out our answer.

Elanchius: I agree, Libentia, for I too know the gentleman— in a sense. By all means, invite Quintus to join us. Will you need much time?

Libentia: Only long enough, I hope, for him to arrange to leave his shop.

Elanchius: Well, then. Let us part for the present, and meet later by the fountain in my olive garden. You will find the place if you turn right at the gate and follow the winding path.

Pulvius: At noon, Elanchius?

Elanchius: At high noon, Pulvius.

The Question Answered

Persons of the Dialogue

LIBENTIA MAGISTRA

PULVIUS GRAMMATICUS

VULPIUS MATERIES

J. QUINTUS

ELANCHIUS

Scene: In the garden of Elanchius

Libentia: Here is the olive grove, Quintus, and, as I remember, the fountain is just beyond the next bend where you see that strange white wisp.

Quintus: Looks like dust or mist—can't make out which. Hey, now it's gone.

Libentia: And there sits Elanchius on the bench. I see that the others have not yet arrived.

Quintus: So that's Elanchius. Come to think of it, I've seen him walking through the market place. Never knew his name, but struck me like a fellow I'd want to meet.

Libentia: You will like him, Quintus.

Elanchius: Greetings, Libentia. Quintus, you are welcome.

Quintus: Glad to know you, Elanchius. Was just saying to Libentia, I've seen you more than once going into Vestigius' bookshop across from my place. Say, nice layout you got here.

Elanchius: Thank you, Quintus.

Libentia: Quintus was busy in his shop, Elanchius, but he was good enough to come.

Quintus: Yeh, Libentia said you were talking about our school here. Thought I'd like to get in on it. Got a kid there. Fine lad too, if I do say so myself. Fine school too. Latest thing.

Anyhow, the boys in my shop take care of things. Won't hurt to leave 'em on their own for a while.

Libentia: Ah, here come Pulvius and Vulpius.

Elanchius: Gentlemen, are you acquainted with Quintus?

Vulpius: I know Quintus, of course—as a consultant to him and his group in structuring an educational plant that reflects the latest findings as to the needs and dynamic configurations of the community. I am pleased that you have decided to participate in our little workshop, Quintus.

Quintus: H'are yuh, Vulpius! Should've guessed you'd be here. Yeh, Vulpius's been a mighty big help. Saw to it we put up the latest thing in school plants. Nothing's too good for our kids, I always say. And Vulpius always knows just what's good for 'em. Knows how to get it too. Every time we've got a new problem somebody says, "Get Vulpius!" We've come to think we just couldn't get along without him. Say, don't know this other fellow, though.

Elanchius: This is Pulvius Grammaticus, a very distinguished literary scholar. Pulvius, it is well that you meet Quintus.

Pulvius: How do you do, sir.

Quintus: Scholar, hey? Little out of my line. Glad to meet you—er—Pulvius, is that the name?

Elanchius: Well, then. Quintus, did Libentia tell you why we wanted you to come?

Quintus: Said you were talking about the school and sort of leading up to something important she thought I ought to be in on. Was in on the hiring of Libentia last year. Want to give her a hand any way I can. We've asked her to stay on next year too.

Libentia: But if I am to continue to teach, I must answer some questions that I could not answer last year.

Quintus: How's that again? Mean you might back out on us after all?

Libentia: I hope not. But unless I find answers to these questions, it is best that I resign.

Quintus: That bad, eh? Let's see, you teach 'em about books, don't you. What's the matter—too much work?

Libentia: No, not only that. It was mainly that I became less and less certain of myself last year. The range of possible things to do is so wide, and time is so short! I came to realize that I must find a means of determining priority. First things must come first—but what things *are* first? Is one thing to do just as good as another? Or is—

Vulpius: Obviously, Libentia, the teacher should choose the projects that work best. You surely have seen my comprehensive summary of suggestions for teachers who, like yourself, are in need of further inspiration and guidance. I happen to have a copy with me. Ah, yes, "Ideas Which Work." Here, Libentia, you may have this. You will find them workable.

Pulvius: Just happen, quoth he!

Libentia: But perhaps I should choose from among the many possibilities not that which "works best," but that which "has always been done." Or perhaps I—

Pulvius: One can do worse, Libentia, than seek the security of tradition.

Vulpius: Surely you are not serious, Libentia. If the selection of materials and methods is determined on the obsolete basis of traditionalists like Pulvius, you would set back by at least fifty years the dynamic results which we researchers have been enjoying.

Quintus: Why don't you two quit interrupting and let Libentia finish what she's got to say? Like to get to the bottom of this, myself.

Libentia: I was going to add, Quintus, only that perhaps I should not choose at all, but should just take the first possibility that occurred to me. Last year I had no real basis for the hundreds of decisions I had to make in my teaching. When I was working with my class, I did not really know why I was doing one thing rather than another.

Quintus: Hmm—When we rehired you, we didn't know all this, Libentia. Heard you'd been doing a good job. But now, maybe—

Elanchius: Pray do not suppose, Quintus, that Libentia is the poorer teacher because of the confession she has just made.

Quintus: But if she doesn't even know what she's doing—

Elanchius: It is not that, precisely. Libentia has been asking herself basic questions, which all good teachers will ultimately ponder. She is seeking a *principle* when she asks how she can be sure that what she chooses to do in her classroom is *the best possible thing to do*. Indeed, she has brought us back to the very question we posed this morning and called the "antecedent question."

Quintus: Yeh! She said you came up with a big question this morning and she wanted me to hear the answer to it. Don't think I quite get that "antecedent" business, though.

Elanchius: By the antecedent queston, Quintus, we mean that on which depend all subsequent questions—in this case, all the questions about material, method, and every other aspect of her work which confront Libentia as a teacher of literature.

Quintus: Got to answer the first one before she can get anywhere with the rest of 'em, hey?

Elanchius: Libentia's dilemma is that even when she succeeds completely in some task with her pupils she cannot be sure that the task itself is the right one. Therefore we must find how to enable her not merely to choose but to choose wisely among the many possibilities. Because none of her decisions can be wise unless they are made in the light of the antecedent question, it is only by answering this question that we can provide her with the basis for certainty which she seeks.

Quintus: See why that question's got to be answered, all right. Follow you that far. But why'd you call it—uh—what you did?

Elanchius: Antecedent?

Quintus: Yeh.

Pulvius: Did you study grammar in school, Quintus?

Quintus: Drilled on it for years.

Pulvius: Do you recall the distinguishing characteristics of the pronoun?

Quintus: Pronouns, hey? Let's see—part of speech, personal pronouns—can't seem to remember anything else.

Pulvius: Do you recall how the pronoun was defined? Or any particular thing that always used to be said about the properties of pronouns?

Quintus: Can't say as I do right off.

Libentia: What Pulvius is getting at, Quintus, is that a pronoun must refer to something else. Do you remember what the word is called to which is refers?

Quintus: Hey, its antecedent. Those drills are coming back. Pronouns always got to have antecedents. That's what the rule said, anyway.

Elanchius: And why do you think there is such a rule? Suppose I used a pronoun with no antecedent. If I were to say merely, "He sat by the river," would you need to know something further?

Quintus: Well, guess I'd want to know who the "he" was.

Elanchius: Of course. So "he" without an antecedent might refer to any man or boy of the present or the past—or even to a dog. But if you and I have just been talking about Vatarius the poet, and then I say, "He sat by the river," you know who it is I mean. So you see how essential to a pronoun is its antecedent. Just so, when Libentia sets her students at certain books and activities without having answered the antecedent question, she will be no more certain that these books and activities are the proper ones than we would be that our "he" was a man and not a dog if no antecedent had been mentioned.

Vulpius: I propose that we terminate this discussion of traditional grammar. I must remind you that in the modern approach to language communication skills, developed by our colleagues in linguistic science, these concepts are no longer utilized by we in the profession.

Pulvius: "By we"—Ha!

Elanchius: Now, Quintus, is it clear to you why the antecedent question must be answered if Libentia's later decisions are to be wise?

Quintus: Got ya there. But wait a minute. Know what? You haven't told me just what this antecedent question is.

Elanchius: The question, like its answer, must be approached with care, Quintus. Tell me now: I believe that in your shop you make shoes.

Quintus: Sure do. Best shoes, sandals, boots there are.

Elanchius: Now tell us some things that a shoemaker must know if he is to make good shoes.

Quintus: Got to know a lot. What stuff to use and where to get it. How to cut it up and put it together just so. Lot of things.

Elanchius: And how does the shoemaker know which materials are best?

Quintus: He'd better know, if he's going to stay in business! Stuff has to be the toughest and lightest and best looking stuff he can get hold of.

Elanchius: But *why* the toughest, lightest, and most attractive? Why not the weakest, heaviest, and ugliest?

Quintus: You kidding? Only a fool'd make shoes like that. Nobody'd buy 'em.

Elanchius: Even so, will you tell us *why* the shoemaker should choose materials of the kind you describe, rather than of the kind I have described?

Quintus: Because they make the best shoes, of course!

Elanchius: But *why* do they make the best shoes?

Quintus: Aw, come on. You talk like you don't know what shoes are for.

Elanchius: But *why* do I sound like one who does not know what shoes are for?

Quintus: Because if you knew what they're *for*, you'd know what stuff makes the best ones.

Elanchius: And if I did not know what they are for might I choose the worst possible materials?

Quintus: More likely than not. More stuff won't do than will.

Elanchius: And might I also design and shape the materials so as to render them further unfit for their purpose?

Quintus: You sure might. Like as not you'd turn out something you couldn't get on a foot—even a horse's.

Elanchius: Then your advice is that if I undertook to make shoes I should first ask myself "What are shoes for?"

Quintus: You'd better!

Elanchius: And in the entire process of making these shoes, I should never once forget this question, and its answer?

Quintus: You'd better not!

Elanchius: Then may we not say that for a shoemaker, "What are shoes for?" is the *antecedent question?*

Quintus: Hey! That's where we were awhile ago, only we

were talking about Libentia's business then—books instead of shoes. I get you now.

Elanchius: Now, Quintus, it is one thing to pose a question, another thing to answer it. What is your answer to the shoemaker's antecedent question?

Quintus: Why, the thing shoes are for is to protect people's feet and look good too.

Elanchius: Then we have both posed and answered the antecedent question without which a shoemaker would be helpless to decide how to select and shape his materials.

Pulvius: Very neat, Elanchius.

Vulpius: I must point out to you both that you are being unscientific. You have been speaking of feet as though they were an absolute concept. In taking this approach you have ignored the empirical data as to individual differences. Let us consider your own example. Although I am of course not a shoemaker myself, as you know, I will point out that individual differences as to feet must be taken into account in the making of shoes. Some feet are long, some short; some are wide, some narrow; some have a high arch, some a low one. Furthermore, men's feet differ from women's feet and adults' feet from children's feet. Some feet tend to be normatively structured, while some vary from the norm by having variations. Then too, shoes differ as to the status of the wearer. The calloused foot of the workingman requires a different kind of shoe than the gentleman's, who tends to select shoes having a higher adornment factor.

Quintus: That's the ticket, Vulpius. Really showed your stuff.

Elanchius: Indeed he did! And you are quite right, Vulpius, in observing that human feet are not alike in all respects, and doubtless Quintus takes the many differences into account. But now let us ask him whether it is his practice to vary the *quality* of his materials and workmanship. Quintus, do you, for example, use inferior leather in making shoes for children?

Quintus: Nobody'd better say I do. Shoes I make for kids get genuine neat's leather. Spend as much time making 'em too.

Elanchius: And is the quality the same whether the shoe is wide or narrow?

Quintus: Makes no difference.

Elanchius: And whether the arch is high or low?

Quintus: Makes no difference either. Nothing like that makes any difference.

Elanchius: In short, individual differences of the kinds named by Vulpius, being irrelevant to the *essential purpose* of shoes, do not affect the quality of their material and workmanship.

Quintus: Right!

Elanchius: Good! We can now return to Libentia's question.

Libentia: Perhaps Quintus himself, after this conversation, can state the antecedent question which we posed this morning. Quintus, if the first question for you as a shoemaker, is "What are shoes for?" what is the first question for me, as a teacher of literature?

Quintus: That's not so tough. Got to be "What's literature for?"

Elanchius: And is it clear that unless Libentia first answers this question she will be as helpless to select and present her materials wisely as you would be to select and form yours?

Quintus: Guess she could even do worse.

Libentia: I may have *done* worse last year, Quintus. But now this morning, before you joined us, we succeeded in refining my question beyond the essential statement that you have just made. Elanchius concluded by phrasing the question thus: "What is it that literature, because of its intrinsic nature, can do for its readers which needs to be done for them because of their nature as human beings?"

Quintus: Hey! That looks tougher than "What is literature for?" Tougher than "What are shoes for?" too—that's for sure.

Elanchius: Yes, Quintus, for literature is more complex than a shoe, and the human spirit is subtler than the human foot. Our question, therefore, will not be answered easily. But Libentia must have the answer.

Quintus: Vulpius here'll make short work of that. He's got the answer to any question you can think of. Say, you wrote up a big survey for us a few years ago, Vulpius. That got anything in it about this business?

Vulpius: Ah! That survey was titled, as you will no doubt

recall, "Preliminary Findings Leading to a Tentative Report of an Educational Needs Survey for the Pre-Planning of a Modern Educational Center for Utilization by *All* the Youth of the Community." In passing I may mention that this survey has been very influential. The statistical breakdown as to vocational outlets community-wise, the range of economic and social strata and the anticipated future school population expansion, together with allied educational needs factors, demonstrated conclusively the need for developing an educational plant to train workers in certain skills and fit others for gainful occupations in other categories. I need not recapitulate the empirical data contained in the report, as I happen to have several copies of it with me. I shall be happy to present each of you with one.

Quintus: See there. Told you Vulpius has got all the answers.

Pulvius: A ponderous volume, Vulpius! It must contain a vast quantity of—pages. I shall gladly bear the document to my study. I have just the place for it there!

Elanchius: But are we not now seeking an answer which falls outside the scope of Vulpius' report? Since we shall soon have to break off our talk until a later time, perhaps we should return to the subject of immediate consideration.

Libentia: Elanchius, in defining the antecedent question as we have done, have we not already approached the answer?

Elanchius: Pray, go on.

Libentia: Well, first of all, our statement of the question implies that the study of literature should be directed toward the education of the human being not as worker, artisan, housewife, parent, or even as citizen, but *as human being*.

Quintus: Hold on there, Libentia! Take me with you!

Elanchius: Libentia's remark is one that will require examination, Quintus. Libentia, do you mean that the study of literature has no relation to the education of workers, artisans, housewives, parents, and citizens?

Libentia: No, indeed. The report which Vulpius has just given us is chiefly concerned with that kind of education, but—

Elanchius: When you say "that kind of education," do you imply the existence of more than one kind?

Libentia: Does not our antecedent question itself imply that there are at least two kinds?

Elanchius: It does. And if one of these—that which trains the student to perform certain tasks essential to the community—might be called "education for *doing*"—

Quintus: Hey! That's good! Got to have a lot of that in the schools. Lots of things have to be done right here in this town, just like Vulpius' report showed. Got to teach the youngsters how to do 'em. There's a dozen jobs right in my own shop that take special know-how. Besides that, some lads need to learn how to run the town's business, and others ought to learn how to pick the ones that'll know how to do it best. Whole lot of other things the school ought to teach 'em, too. I'll give you an idea of what I mean. If I had my way, I'd make a law so the school'd teach these kids how to drive the family cart without running over everybody. Just last night—look here—see this bump on the top of my head?

Pulvius: The point of your argument is well raised, Quintus.

Elanchius: And, Pulvius, do you also agree that "education for doing" is a suitable name for the kind of training Quintus has mentioned?

Pulvius: "Doing" is appropriate, but I question whether this sort of thing deserves to be called "education." I also doubt that such matters should be included among the disciplines of the general school.

Elanchius: I understand you, Pulvius. But setting aside for the present the questions whether we should say "training" rather than "education" and whether the general school or institutions of special character should prepare in these ways, do you agree that each generation must somehow be taught to perform the diverse tasks imposed by the nature of our society?

Quintus: Be a fool if you didn't, Pulvius.

Pulvius: Nevertheless, I—

Vulpius: My "Tentative Report of an Educational Needs Survey for Pre-Planning," as it is called for short, tends to demonstrate that occupational and sociological youth needs must be confronted by forward-looking planning in achieving a realistic

curriculum. Pulvius, if you utilized your time in reading empirically compiled research reports instead of delimiting your interests to classical authors, your attitudinal responses would not
be so negativistic. All teachers of youth must see that their own
life-adjustment quotients are maintained at optimal levels. Ivory-
tower thinking has no place in education for today's changing
world.

Quintus: That's good, Vulpius. That's good.

Pulvius: Ivory tower! Vulpius, let me tell you that there are
more things in heaven and earth—

Elanchius: Gentlemen, gentlemen! Let me finish the question
I was in the act of phrasing. Now, once more. If the kind of education which prepares citizens to perform certain necessary tasks
may be called "education for doing," what name will describe
a kind that is directly concerned not with particular tasks, but
with human beings?

Pulvius: Since we are primarily interested in defining the
purpose of the study of literature, I propose "education for
knowing."

Quintus: Knowing what, Pulvius?

Pulvius: Why, for the student of literature, knowing about
literature, of course. There is much to be known about literature.
There are many literary genres, each with well defined characteristics. There are many periods of literature, each with—

Elanchius: Then the ultimate purpose of the study of literature is the acquisition of knowledge about literature?

Vulpius: That is exactly what he would say.

Elanchius: Unquestionably, "education for knowing" is important, for man must have knowledge of many things. And
several subjects taught in Libentia's school are properly considered as education of this kind.

Libentia: But, Elanchius, is the study of literature of this
kind? One must still ask, "Why *have* knowledge about literature?"
Hence, the real question is still unanswered.

Elanchius: You have brought us back sharply to this question, Libentia. Since you find "education for knowing" an inappropriate designation for the study of literature, do you wish to

propose something else?

Libentia: Why not "education for being"?

Quintus: Hey! Education for being what?

Libentia: For being a human being, Quintus! Since the kind of education which we are trying to name is concerned with the human being *as* human being, should we not call it "education for being"?

Quintus: Education of the human being for being a human being! That's about what you said awhile back. What is this, Libentia—a riddle? Besides, we're all human beings to start with anyway.

Elanchius: The quickness of your assertion suggests that you take pride in being human—and therefore that you prize those qualities of mind and spirit which distinguish man from beast. And since you prize them, must you not also prize those studies which, properly conceived and administered, look toward the perfection—however distant that may be—of that in us all which is peculiarly human?

Libentia: Does not one of the poets, Elanchius, ask what a man is, if the chief good and market of his time is but to sleep and feed?

Elanchius: So he does, Libentia, and answers his own question: "A beast; no more." And not only he but all poets ultimately mark the line that separates man and beast. For poetry itself, one of them has said, is the breath and finer spirit of humankind, and in being so argues man's kinship with the infinite which extends above him rather than with that which ranges below. Perhaps you remember another poet, Libentia, who said that poetry collects the brightest rays of human nature, touches them with majesty and beauty, multiplies all that it reflects, and endows it with the power of propagating its like wherever it may fall.

Libentia: I do remember him, Elanchius. And I remember that he asks, "What were virtue, love, patriotism, friendship— what were the scenery of this beautiful universe which we inhabit; what were our consolations on this side of the grave—and what were our aspirations beyond it, if poetry did not ascend to bring light and fire from those eternal regions where the owl-

winged faculty of calculation dare not ever soar?"* Oh, Elanchius!
Last year I labored in a school directed by owl-winged calcu-
lators, so zealously committed to the training of mere doers of
things that the human spirit, far from being ministered to, was
compelled to struggle just to survive at all! The most terrifying
fault of the Vulpian school is that it makes the education of the
human being irrelevant and unlikely!

Elanchius: Gently, Libentia, gently!

Quintus: What's that, Libentia? Making cracks about our
school? Why, Vulpius'll tell you we've got the most up-to-date
educational plant anywhere in the country. Right, Vulpius?

Vulpius: That is an empirically demonstrable fact, Quintus,
Our approach to community educational needs determination was
based on realistic confrontations of present-day school population
realities as to community opportunities and needs. You will find
tabulated in my "Preliminary Findings Leading to a Tentative Report of an"—

Pulvius: Please, Vulpius!

Elanchius: Libentia and gentlemen, the afternoon has grown
hot, even here under the olive trees. But let us not suspend our
talk until we have put into words the answer to our question.
Perhaps we have now come near enough that what remains is
but to phrase it. Do you wish to try, Libentia?

Libentia: Well, we have asked what it is that literature, because of its intrinsic nature, can do for its readers which most
needs to be done for them because of their nature as human
beings. Our question, setting literature and reader side by side,
asks what the former can best give that the latter supremely
needs. Is not our answer *that literature contains a potential for
the humanization of the reader?*

Elanchius: And by "humanization" do we mean the enhancement—the urging toward perfection—of those inner qualities
which most significantly distinguish man from beast and best
evince the reality of his kinship with the divine?

Vulpius: I must remind you, Elanchius, that your utilization
of terminology is unscientific. Before your solution could be

---

* The reader will note that the sentiments expressed by Elanchius and
Libentia here parallel exactly those of Shelley in *A Defence of Poetry*.

accepted as valid, professional research would require empirical data demonstrating that the conceptual content of your term is measurable as to its validity.

Elanchius: We may debate the precise term we use, Vulpius, but about the qualities that are implied by "humanization" we can have no quarrel, either among ourselves or with the poets and philosophers of the past; and surely if man ever fails to identify and prize these qualities his future is dark indeed.

Vulpius: Nevertheless, I shall want to interrogate you on empirical grounds. Your utilization of terms is indicative of the unfortunate lag between professional specialist research findings and non-credentialized layman concepts, which I regret to say are held even by some classrom teachers. Moreover, for our next workshop session, I will invite as consultant a fellow scientist to give you the benefit of his thinking. His field is not exactly in my area, but the methods utilized in his research have been adopted by we in the profession *with amazing results*. Indeed, the great advances apparent even to the layman in the modern school plant of today are due to our adoption of the specifics of scientific technique.

Elanchius: By all means, ask your friend to come, Vulpius.

Quintus: Say, what's this about meeting again? Thought we figured out the answer Libentia wanted. She's supposed to teach literature so it'll humanize these kids. What's there left to do?

Elanchius: We have only begun, Quintus! Vulpius says that he will challenge this answer, and perhaps his friend will do so, too. From your description of him, Vulpius, I suspect that he is a true scientist.

Vulpius: I shall mainly desire to question your opinion that reading materials can "humanize"—to utilize your own terminology.

Elanchius: Very well, Vulpius. So you see, Quintus, our very first answer must be tested, and if we are forced to abandon it, we shall have to seek another. Only after we have agreed upon an answer to our antecedent question, can we assist Libentia in solving the problems which confront her daily as a teacher. The teacher must make many decisions, Quintus, and if she cannot make them wisely she will make them unwisely.

Quintus: Hey! Looks like I'll be out of the shop awhile.

Libentia: Shall we meet again this evening, Elanchius?

Elanchius: By all means. And if we are to enjoy a long talk, we should meet soon after our evening meal. Hence, our meeting place should be central.

Pulvius: Then I suggest we meet at the true center of things—the library. There we can talk without likelihood of interruption!

Elanchius: Good, Pulvius. It cannot be far removed from any of our homes.

Vulpius: It is not close to mine. However, I can manage.

Quintus: I'll take a quick run past the shop, grab a bite to eat, and get there soon as any of you.

Pulvius: The east portico, Quintus, between the main columns.

Elanchius: Until evening, then.

The Answer Questioned

Persons of the Dialogue

LIBENTIA MAGISTRA   J. QUINTUS
VULPIUS MATERIES   EMPIRICUS MARTIALIS
ELANCHIUS

Scene: The portico of the library

Quintus: Said I'd beat you all here. Just about did, too.

Elanchius: You are prompt, Quintus. Do you not agree, Libentia, that the view from these steps inspires the beholder with a sense of calm assurance?

Libentia: Here all seems serene. But wait—is not that Vulpius approaching?

Elanchius: So it is, moving there among the shadows with the friend he promised to bring.

Vulpius: Libentia and gentlemen, meet Empiricus Martialis, a personality of whom you have no doubt heard. He is especially prominent in these days.

Quintus: Heard a lot about you lately. Glad to have you in on our talk.

Empiricus: I am pleased to be here.

Elanchius: We are all pleased that you are here.

Vulpius: Empiricus, as a fellow scientist you can make worthwhile contributions to our discussion of a meaningful curriculum for present-day youth.

Quintus: Well, let's get down to business. Say, where's that scholar fellow who was with us before?

Libentia: Pulvius will not join us this evening. He found that

51

he had a prior engagement to read a paper before a learned society.

Empiricus: I had hoped to meet him. Do you know the subject of his paper?

Libentia: His title is "The Relative Frequency of the Iambus and the Trochee in Extant Sepulturic Inscriptions." He regretted the necessity of being absent this evening and has assured me that he will join us later.

Vulpius: That title motivates one of the questions I shall ask this evening, Elanchius.

Elanchius: By all means, let us hear it.

Vulpius: You have advanced the claim, Elanchius, that the purpose of utilizing reading materials in the classroom is for learner humanization. What empirical data have you compiled to demonstrate this assertion? What evidence have you that individuals experiencing reading materials are more fully "humanized" than others? Pulvius himself is a case in point. Can you realistically contend that Pulvius, who has delimited his whole experience to reading materials, is more fully "humanized" than someone who has never experienced any reading materials? That paper he is reading is evidence of what I mean. Are there any worthwhile values in this type of endeavor? I repeat—is it demonstrable that reading materials "humanize" individuals? Citing Pulvius, quite the contrary is more realistic, since obviously he has failed to achieve a desirable life-adjustment pattern.

Libentia: But, Vulpius, are you being fair to Pulvius in citing him as evidence that literature has no power to humanize?

Elanchius: You speak of adjustment, Vulpius, but adjustment to the ways of a particular society in a particular time is not at all synonymous with humanization. If Pulvius is not "adjusted," yet he is not inhumane. He has already given evidence in our conversation that his nature is composed of admirable qualities, whatever may be his superficial faults or inadequacies.

Quintus: Sort of queer, all right, but seems a nice fellow.

Libentia: I am sure, Vulpius, that you might have chosen a more appropriate example for your purpose from among Pulvius' colleagues. I remember one or two whose aggressive self-seeking was obvious even to their students. One in particular—why, his social graces hid the soul of a snake!

Elanchius: Rather than identify a particular colleague of Pulvius' who seems to have been unaffected by any humanizing force in his studies, Libentia, may we not simply agree that it is possible for a man to make a name for himself as a scholar and critic— even to be a specialist in a poet famous for his profound knowledge of and warmth toward humanity, and yet remain a calculating, coolly grasping, ruthless self-seeker?

Vulpius: I agree, of course.

Elanchius: By offering such a colleague instead of Pulvius, we have greatly strengthened your argument. Indeed, confronted by ample evidence that men can be literary scholars and yet be inhumane, we must either find a reasonable explanation or abandon our noble claim for the power of literature.

Libentia: We spoke of the humanizing force as a *potentiality* within literature. We did not assert that literature would necessarily humanize every reader or even every dedicated literary scholar.

Vulpius: By their fruits you shall know them! That is, one must tend to evaluate the worthwhileness of specifics by their outcomes. Obviously, reading materials have had a more optimum opportunity to achieve their maximal desirable outcomes in the case of Pulvius' colleagues than in the non-atypical case who contacts them only while his maturation processes are being conditioned by the education system.

Elanchius: But are you sure, Vulpius, that literature has really had a fair chance to affect such literary scholars? Presumably, they have studied it for the same purposes that were named by Pulvius this afternoon. Do you remember them?

Vulpius: Why, he indicated that his aims and objectives as to reading materials are to acquire information about types, periods, and authors.

Elanchius: But is acquisition of such knowledge the purpose which *we* have defined?

Vulpius: No, you and Libentia asserted that reading materials "humanize" and should be utilized for that outcome.

Elanchius: Then there is a notable difference between the purpose for which Libentia would have her students read literature and that for which a scholar may have studied it?

Vulpius: Admittedly.

Elanchius: And must we not suppose that the *purpose* for which literature is read influences the effect it will have?

Empiricus: As you know, I am not a literary man. But my training leads me to agree. Indeed, purpose, in this context, is likely to determine result.

Elanchius: Then is it reasonable, Vulpius, to expect that literary scholars will *necessarily* have been humanized by literature, if they have read for another purpose?

Vulpius: I defer to Empiricus. I suppose it is not.

Elanchius: Then can it be concluded that because literature has not subdued the inhumane propensities of certain scholars it lacks power to humanize?

Empiricus: No, such a conclusion would be untenable. I have been keenly interested in your questioning, Elanchius, and quite approve your conclusion. However, I shall be interested to learn whether you intend this conclusion, which is negative, as proof of your positive assertion.

Quintus: Can't say as I get you there, Empiricus.

Elanchius: We should be in error, Quintus, if we failed to heed Empiricus' word of caution. We have concluded that literature does not necessarily lack humanizing power merely because it has failed to humanize some scholars. But we shall be illogical if we assume that because it has not been proved to *lack* humanizing power it therefore *possesses* it.

Quintus: Now I get you. Be like saying the earth has to be round because nobody's proved it's not.

Empiricus: True, Quintus. By making clear that potentiality is not to be measured by its apparent failures, Elanchius has freed us to consider the validity of the hypothesis itself—that literature contains power to humanize. You will agree, Vulpius?

Vulpius: Oh, of course, Empiricus.

Quintus: Good! Let's get down to cases.

Libentia: Gentlemen, what kind of proof do we require? Must we find a certain number of obviously admirable human beings of whom it can be said that all were humanized by the study of literature?

Empiricus: That would indeed be proof!

Vulpius: But impossible, and therefore not worthwhile. If effects are not measurable, it is assumed by we in the profession that none have been achieved. Therefore, education should not endeavor to achieve effects that are not measurable. On the other hand, we view as worthwhile any classroom activities which result in measurable effects.* The field of evaluations has developed amazingly in recent decades, making available batteries of tests on the comprehension and appreciation of reading materials, for example, which have been worked out in terms of broadly extrapolated norms and grade-level averages.

Elanchius: Do any of these tests reveal whether literature has the power to humanize?

Vulpius: They furnish statistical evidence as to the individual reading interests of boys and girls and thus determine the reading areas which realistic teachers must confront.

Elanchius: But are there tests which measure the effects of literature upon the student?†

Vulpius: As I said, the field of tests and measurements is an expanding area which will require increasing teacher participation. There are, for example, tests which explore children's meaning vocabulary growth and others which measure individual reading readiness.

Elanchius: But do any serve *our* purpose?

---

* This logic, so characteristically Vulpian, may also be discerned in modern educational theory; for example, in T. B. Edward's "Measurement of Some Aspects of Critical Thinking," *Journal of Experimental Education* (March, 1950): "Ability to do critical thinking is a valid objective of the schools in that it is possible to isolate techniques of critical thinking and test for the acquisition of skill in the use of techniques." The objective is valid because it is possible to test whether it has been attained!

† Today's professional answer is evidently known: "From the research point of view . . . the effects of reading are an uncharted wasteland in an otherwise well-mapped territory. We have discovered many facts about eye-movements in reading, reading interests and tastes, and methods of reading instruction—but we don't know much about what reading does to people." David H. Russell, "Some Research on the Impact of Reading," *English Journal*, October, 1958.

Vulpius: Others test student ability as to work-type reading and informational reading range. A recently developed scale measures reader listening ability. Besides these, which are of course only samples of the many available, our researchers have developed batteries of general evaluative devices which—

Quintus: Boy! Guess your tests are set up to find out all there is to know about reading.

Libentia: But none of the tests I have ever heard Vulpius describe, numerous and varied as they are, seeks to discover whether any force contained in literature can actually affect the student's deeper nature and enhance his human qualities.

Vulpius: The evaluative instruments formulated by we in the profession as to pupil responses to reading materials confront the real realities realistically, Libentia.

Empiricus: It seems then that because your tests—which were devised for other purposes—find no trace of a humanizing effect, you conclude that literature contains no force capable of producing it. It would follow, therefore, that Libentia should teach literature only for the purposes that your tests can weigh and measure!

Libentia: And give up the purpose we have identified? To do so would be to forfeit the possibility of its attainment! But even if the possibility is remote that literature can refine the humanity of my students, I must not rule it out.

Elanchius: No, you must foster it. But now let us return to Vulpius' statement that if effects of literature are not measurable they are non-existent. Vulpius, would you hold it for a general principle that only *measurable* effects are real?

Vulpius: As I indicated, the educational testing field is constantly moving into new areas, so that soon many additional kinds of learnings will be subjected to measurements. Hence, it is probable that all the desirable learning outcomes will be capable of empirical measurement.

Empiricus: Your reply hardly answers Elanchius' question, Vulpius. Yet it would seem possible to answer it categorically. Obviously, many effects exist which are not and may never be subject to quantitative demonstration.

Vulpius: Oh.

Empiricus: Although the scientist is primarily concerned with measurable phenomena, he knows that outside his laboratory, if not within it, effects exist which defy measurement. I am reminded of a remark made by a colleague. "Science," he said, "deals with but a partial aspect of reality, and . . . there is no faintest reason for supposing that everything science ignores is less real than what it accepts."*

Vulpius: But—

Empiricus: Your error is really twofold, Vulpius. You apply scientific methods where they are not strictly applicable and you then conclude that what is not measurable does not deserve attention.

Vulpius: Oh.

Empiricus: One word further, Vulpius. Though I am not well acquainted with your subject, Libentia, I would assume that particularly in the field of literature certain effects of profound human significance might exist which are not subject to precise measurement. Do not treat too harshly, Vulpius, those who come to you with a theory based on a limited study. They might not be right. They probably have no scientific truths. But often they will have a story to tell that might start us off on a line of thought which will lead to mighty things.†

Elanchius: Let me thank you for your forthright statement that effects can exist which cannot always be measured. Do you accept this statement, Vulpius?

Vulpius: Of course I would not quarrel with a fellow scientist, as I pride myself on belonging to a profession which has achieved its present eminence by utilizing science methods.

Elanchius: Then we all agree that effects which cannot be

---

* The words of Empiricus' friend parallel almost exactly those of J. W. N. Sullivan in *The Limitations of Science* (New York: The Viking Press, 1933), p. 234.

† The preceding four sentences parallel almost exactly some remarks of J. Robert Oppenheimer to the American Psychological Association convention in San Francisco, September 4, 1955.

measured exactly can exist. Does it not therefore follow that literature may produce such effects?

Empiricus: It does.

Elanchius: And may not one of these be the humanization of the reader?

Empiricus: How strong that possibility is depends upon the nature of literature. If literature itself has no uniquely human qualities, then, obviously, the possibility that it can refine such qualities in the reader is negligible. But if, on the other hand, literature and the quintessentially human qualities have close affinity, it follows that the possibility is strong.

Libentia: Thank you for that, Empiricus! For, you see, the common bond of literature and human beings *is* their humanity! Literature is born of human concern for humanity. Its matter is humanity. Even its form may be said to be human, for it expresses human desire for order and design. The poet spoke truthfully who said that literature is the breath and finer spirit of humanity. Therefore, when you assure me that literature may have power to humanize if it has close affinity with things human, you strengthen the belief which helped me withstand the forces of discouragement last year.

Quintus: That's the stuff, Libentia.

Empiricus: Indeed, my own reading, although limited, disposes me to believe, with you, in the close affinity of literature and humanity.

Vulpius: But, quantities of reading materials utilized in the present-day school—thanks to the realistic approach of we in the profession—not only do not contain these aspects but were not devised to contain them.

Elanchius: True, Vulpius—most true! But we are speaking of *literature*, not of devised readings. And now let us consider where we stand. We have asked what is the highest function that the study of literature can serve and have answered, humanization. We have inquired whether literature can humanize and have concluded that because of its close affinity with humanity it is reasonable to believe that it can. But though we now make this claim, we must, of course, in our conversations hereafter, continue to test its validity.

Empiricus: I am willing, until we can examine our hypothesis more closely, to accept this conclusion. But having done so I must immediately challenge the entire proposition from another point of view, which you may find quite shocking.

Elanchius: I guess what you have in mind, Empiricus, and I agree that it must be said. But before we leave our immediate question, may I make two points clear: First, we have not asserted that literature is the *only* way, or necessarily the *best* way, by which the inner natures of human beings can be refined. Second, we have not implied that literature cannot or should not serve other purposes also. Perhaps I need not have made these qualifications explicit, but it is better to labor the obvious than to risk misunderstanding.

Quintus: Got to be sure things are clear.

Elanchius: And now, Empiricus, you were about to question our conclusion.

Empiricus: Thank you, Elanchius. I was not present when you decided that literature must be taught for the purpose of humanizing; however, I have agreed that literature may indeed contain vital humanizing forces. *But now I must question whether these should be released to affect Libentia's students.* I shall put the question bluntly: Is humanization desirable—*especially in these times?*

Libentia: Oh, Empiricus!

Empiricus: You are shocked, Libentia. Let me explain why I ask the question. You all know that the world is filled with wars and the rumors of wars; and not only with wars but with incessant struggle of every kind—at home, on the street, in the marketplace. In such a world, survival often seems the highest good—and upon what does survival chiefly depend? Does it not depend upon a physical competence that is more bestial than human? In these times, therefore, are not crucial aggressiveness and shrewd self-seeking the only indispensable qualities? In such a world, how will one fare whose *human* qualities have been nourished instead of these? Indeed, how will a nation fare?

Quintus: Looks like you got something there, Empiricus. We make softies out of our kids, and then what happens? They get run over by everybody else's kids.

Empiricus: I am afraid so.

Libentia: Oh, no, Empiricus! Must I teach my students to be brutes because only brutes can survive in the world as it is?

Elanchius: Empiricus has raised an ugly question, which demands a wise answer. Do not despair, Libentia, even before we have sought this answer. And let us not blame Empiricus for his challenge, either, but thank him; for he requires us to be clear-sighted in our vision of the world which your students must enter, and realistic in determining what kind of education will best serve both them and the world.

Vulpius: Quite so! Quite so! In confronting the problems of present-day educational planning realistically, an objective preposition must be taken as to youth. The student-centered curriculum is a worthwhile development which utilizes youth needs to achieve life adjustment. That is, our concept of life adjustment is the process of adjusting youths to confront life realistically.

Empiricus: I cannot be certain, Vulpius, that this is precisely what I had in mind.

Elanchius: Well, then. Perhaps we can deal best with this crucial problem by phrasing it as a question. I propose this: Should education be primarily a matter of adjusting youth to life in the world as it is?

Empiricus: I accept your phrasing.

Elanchius: Then let us seek the answer. Quintus, you are a man of the world. Perhaps you can help us. You have a son, have you not?

Quintus: You bet I have. Strapping chap, soon be old enough to help in the shop.

Elanchius: And how do you wish him to be educated?

Quintus: Want him to get the best there is—all he can of it too.

Libentia: But what *is* the best?

Quintus: Why, what'll help him hold his own in the world.

Elanchius: In the world as it is?

Quintus: Of course. Not any other, is there?

Elanchius: Would you say that Empiricus' description of that world is accurate?

Quintus: Come to think of it, guess it's dead right.

Elanchius: And is it the kind of world you wish your son to live in?

Quintus: Well, maybe not. But that's how it is. Might as well face it.

Elanchius: I agree that we cannot ignore the fact. But would you improve the world that your son and your son's son will inherit if you could do so?

Quintus: Wouldn't I though! But things are the way they are. Won't have my boy getting trampled on. Got to learn to stand on his own two feet, and fight it out if he's got to.

Vulpius: A realistic confrontation! Aggressiveness has long been recognized by we in the profession as a worthwhile goal in the developmental process of the total child personality toward socially accepted behavior patterns.

Elanchius: Your concern for your son's welfare in a world of tooth and claw is natural and proper, Quintus. Yet I detect in your remarks a degree of reluctance to approve of the world as it is. Are you then not entirely satisfied that an education which furnishes your son also with tooth and claw is the best that can be given him?

Quintus: Well, I'd like—but what good's it to talk about it? Little as I like to say it, if it's got to be done, it's got to be done.

Elanchius: But why do you hesitate? Why do you dislike to make the choice that you have just made?

Quintus: Mighty ugly, that "tooth and claw" business. Guess it's the way things are, though. Just a way of saying what Empiricus said. Tooth and claw, hey? Well, if everybody else's got 'em, my boy's got to get 'em, too.

Elanchius: Yet you hesitate, as though you suspected that by directing your son's education to this end you might be forfeiting something more estimable. What is it?

Quintus: Don't quite know. But you're right. No use trying to fool myself—or you either—about that.

Elanchius: Perhaps you hesitate to approve of education that merely equips your son to compete in the world as it is because your mind holds some vision of the world as you wish it might be?

Quintus: Don't hold much with visions myself, but don't think everything's right the way it is either.

Elanchius: Just what, do you think, has caused the world to be as Empiricus described it?

Quintus: Well, looks like the main thing wrong with the world is the people in it. Some of 'em are just not all they should be.

Elanchius: But what should they be? Or how should they be different?

Quintus: Well, they ought to be better.

Elanchius: Better?

Quintus: Yeh! Better!

Elanchius: But in what sense do you mean "better"? Do you mean better money-makers? Better artisans? Better shoemakers?

Quintus: Lots of people could stand improvement there, all right. Probably could myself. But that's not the "better" I'm talking about. Got nothing to do with it. Nothing at all.

Elanchius: But you said earlier that you wanted your son educated to survive and prosper. Now do you mean that you want something more for him?

Quintus: Course I want him to survive and prosper. But that's not the whole of it. Maybe if other people didn't go along trampling the other fellow all the time I wouldn't even think my son ought to be fixed up with these teeth and claws you talked about. Then maybe I'd want him to get a lot more of this other kind of education.

Elanchius: Other kind?

Quintus: Yeh, the kind that'd make him better.

Elanchius: But remember that you have not yet defined "better" for us.

Quintus: Well, I mean something different than being just better at trampling the other fellow. I mean better at—better for—better inside. Sort of more human, if you know what I mean.

Elanchius: Human! Indeed I do know, and there you have spoken one of the most important words in the vocabulary of any

language. But we have not finished. You say that you would
prize most a world in which people were more human. Now do
you think that such a world can ever be?

Quintus: Can't say as I expect to find it when I get up tomorrow morning. No reason I shouldn't say it'd be a good idea,
though.

Elanchius: But if the time is to come at all, will it come just
as a matter of course? Or must effort be made to bring it?

Quintus: Well, in my business things don't just happen. Shoes
don't make themselves. That leather'd just keep on looking like
a big piece of hide if you didn't work it up.

Elanchius: But how are we to bring about a world of better
human beings?

Quintus: You got me there. Only one thing—got to keep
headed that way or we'll never get to it. All of us got to work at
it. Hey! That means the schools, too!

Elanchius: Indeed it does. Education must be concerned
not merely—as you said at first—with training people to survive
and prosper in the world of tooth and claw, but with the creation
of better human beings—and through them, of a better world.

Quintus: I'd say the schools better not ever forget that's the
biggest job they've got.

Vulpius: Just a moment! Do you infer that the total school
pattern should be adjusted to fulfill this goal? Let me remind
you that objective findings tends to demonstrate conclusively
that individuals differ as to interests, needs, aptitudes, and capacities, and therefore it is the thinking of we professionals that
education must recognize multiple objectives and aims.

Elanchius: No one denies that the necessary functions of
education are many. *But ultimately all these are really means to
a single end.* A friend whose vision I greatly respect has said,
"Faith in machinery is our besetting danger. Often in machinery
absurdly disproportioned to the end which the machinery, if it is
to do any good at all, is to serve; but always in machinery, as if it
had a value in and for itself. What is freedom but machinery?
what is population but machinery? what is wealth but machinery?
what are, even, religious organizations but machinery?—Now almost every voice is accustomed to speak of these things as if they

were precious ends in themselves, and therefore had some of the characters of perfection indisputably joined to them."*

Libentia: I am acquainted with your friend, Elanchius, and admire him greatly.

Elanchius: He sees things clearly, and sees them whole, Libentia. Well, then. And are not some functions of education mistaken for ends when in fact they are means, or machinery?

Vulpius: Whatever field of endeavor your friend has proficiencies in, Elanchius, is he familiar with present-day curriculum planning trends? We in the profession find it unprofessional to seriously consider the thinking of non-credentialized critics.

Elanchius: I commend the frankness of your statement, Vulpius. But now, should we not remind ourselves of the question which precipitated our present discussion?

Quintus: Good idea. After that workout you gave me, I forget where we started.

Elanchius: Well, then. Let us return to Empiricus. Sir, you have been silent for some time, although I noted that on two occasions you seemed ready to speak. You agreed, I recall, that literature may contain the power to humanize; but then you voiced an emphatic doubt that, the world being as it is, any effort should be made to release this power—a doubt that humanization is in fact a desirable end. Since that time, Quintus and I have come to a conclusion exactly opposed to yours—that the schools are obligated, above all else, to strive for humanization. Will you be good enough now to open your mind to us, withholding nothing? If in your opinion Quintus and I are in error, do not spare our feelings, but tell us wherein our reasoning is false.

Empiricus: Let me first confess that I might never have spoken as I did but for a hope that you could prove my argument false. When I challenged your conclusion that humanization is a desirable purpose of education, I did so less as the scientist than as the human being who is perplexed by problems that lie outside the scientist's laboratory. Both your questioning of Quintus and

---

* The words of Elanchius' friend exactly parallel those of Matthew Arnold (*Culture and Anarchy*), who, the reader will recall, devoted years to the inspection of schools.

the words quoted from your friend have reassured me. I was impressed by Quintus' recognition that, in the workaday world with which he is so thoroughly acquainted, such matters as the artisan's greater technical efficiency and his increased ability to earn a livelihod are insufficient. It is a conclusion toward which I myself have struggled by means of much painful—and assuredly quite unprofessional—self-questioning. Science has given us more efficient means for *doing* than we have ever had before. But unless we know how to set the direction of these means, can we truly value them? When man first learned to use the wheel, he discovered that he could travel more rapidly from place to place; but if man uses his chariot to grind his fellows into the earth, have these wheels brought him nearer perfection as a human being? These are questions that lie outside the province of the scientist, for it is not his function to determine the ultimate ends of man. If he attempts to do so, he has no more authority than one who is quite ignorant of scientific knowledge—and should enjoy no greater influence.

Elanchius: Would that all your colleagues were of like mind, Empiricus! Are you not cheered, Libentia, by what Empiricus and Quintus have said? They agree that—*even* in these times!—you are right in seeking to refine your students' natures.

Libentia: Yes indeed! But you said, "*Even* in these times." Should we not say, "*Especially* in these times"? For in our world that Empiricus has described, the forces which brutalize man are so many and so powerful that the necessity to marshal all possible humanizing forces against them is urgent. I am especially grateful to Quintus and Empiricus and those they represent because, until now, I have felt alone and helpless against the arguments of those who regard education as catering to the superficial differences of human beings. Now I have authority for believing that my teaching must mainly concern the *similarities* of human beings—that is, those qualities which make them all human.

Elanchius: There will be more for us to say, Libentia. But now it grows late and we must agree how to spend our time when we meet again. For I assume that we shall meet again.

Quintus: Count me in, Elanchius. This little talk tonight has got me all keyed up, just like Libentia.

Elanchius: Then I propose that we next turn our attention to the question, which books will best serve Libentia's purpose as a teacher of literature?

Libentia: That would help me.

Vulpius: The assembling of suitable reading materials is always an area of interest to we specialists in the field.

Elanchius: Then, because we shall be speaking of books, let us meet within the library here tomorrow morning. And let us hope that Pulvius will be able to rejoin us then, for we shall need his great knowledge.

PART II

WHAT WORKS OF LITERATURE SHOULD BE TAUGHT?

The Answer Disregarded

Persons of the Dialogue

LIBENTIA MAGISTRA

PULVIUS GRAMMATICUS   VULPIUS MATERIES

J. QUINTUS   EMPIRICUS MARTIALIS

ELANCHIUS

Scene: Within the library

Libentia: And that was what we concluded last evening, Pulvius. The conversation reassured me, for Empiricus and Quintus came to accept our conclusion that books have power to humanize and that humanization is properly my transcendent purpose as a teacher. You were spoken of, and I often wished that you were present.

Pulvius: I am sorry that the prior obligation required my presence elsewhere. I judge that your discussion was most interesting.

Libentia: I found it exciting, and this morning's conversation should be no less so.

Pulvius: I think it will be lively, since, as you say, our subject is to be the selection of literary texts for study in the preparatory school. Our points of view will no doubt be diverse!

Libentia: I discovered long ago that your views and those of Vulpius differ!

Pulvius: Speaking of Vulpius, I see him and the others entering from the portico. Is that your Empiricus with them? Although I have not met him, I respect his field of knowledge, which he is said to approach with the caution and precision that betoken the

69

disciplined intellect. Even more to his credit, I believe, is his recognition that mastery of his own field does not necessarily provide him with solutions to the problems of other fields.

Libentia: Last evening Empiricus himself denied to science the authority to determine human ends. But here they have all arrived. Greetings, gentlemen.

Elanchius: Good morning, Libentia. Ah, Pulvius, I am glad that you have rejoined us. Empiricus, have you met our distinguished literary scholar?

Empiricus: Unfortunately, we have not formed a real acquaintance because of the distance by which our fields seem to be divided. Although I have often heard Pulvius named—and, I may say, with respect—so completely have we been restricted to our respective cubicles that communication between us has been hampered.

Pulvius: Too true, Empiricus.

Elanchius: Perhaps your meeting today will lead to a closer association. But notice Quintus there among the rows of books. He appears bemused.

Vulpius: Here, Quintus! What do you find that appeals to your interests so much among those reading materials?

Quintus: All these books! Never knew there were so many. Vulpius, how come we don't have more books in that new school plant you laid out for us? Got a lot of everything else. Best of it that money could buy, too. How come no more books?

Vulpius: Times have changed, Quintus. We in the profession know that books are not the only instrumentalities that further the learning processes. Children differ. In the changed school population we find many activity-oriented individuals, for whom we have provided non-book type facilities.

Quintus: Yeh, you said that when you were planning our school for us. Still, all these books are mighty impressive.

Elanchius: Impressive in more ways than one! They hold something that one would not willingly part with. And as for their great number, what you see in this room is but a fraction of the total in existence. Even so, could you read all that are here in your lifetime?

Quintus: Ho! Big joke! Couldn't get a tenth of 'em read through even if I didn't do anything else.

Elanchius: And if these books are perhaps only a hundredth part of all that exist, must not the total reach a staggering number?

Quintus: Staggers me, anyway.

Elanchius: Well, then. Since you could read only a negligible part of the total, would you not want a means of choosing?

Quintus: Come to think of it, guess I'd have to have one.

Elanchius: What means would you use?

Quintus: Fact is, never thought of that before. Never had to. Just read whatever was handy. Guess if I had more books, though, I'd have a problem.

Elanchius: And the more you had, the greater would be your problem?

Quintus: That's so.

Elanchius: And given the privilege of choosing from among all the books in existence, would you not find that a wise principle of selection is a necessity?

Libentia: If I knew a stronger word than "necessity," I would use it here. I cannot tell you how helpless I felt last year, knowing that although the number of books in existence is enormous, the number my students could read was minute. If I had then had a principle of selection which I could believe in, I would have been a better teacher. During the whole year the problem of selection baffled me. Obviously, I could not teach at all without making choices. But I could never be sure that my choice was the best—or even good. The realization that I had such a short time to affect my students' natures made me wish for a means of making certain that my choices were wise. I knew that as a teacher of literature I could draw upon the world's noblest resources. But the hours were so few! Was I choosing what could do most in the limited time? Or was the basis of my choice as absurd as if I had chosen by the color of the jacket or the number of pages?

Elanchius: Your wish to make the most of time is laudable, Libentia. Given brief access to a storehouse of stones, rare, less rare, and common, one would take care to choose only the most precious. As the curriculum becomes increasingly crowded and reduces the time that is given to literature, it is necessary to sharpen the instrument of selection so that no time is wasted on the inferior. It is therefore curious that in some of our schools the contrary is true; for, as the time given to literature diminishes, more and more of the inferior is allowed to claim attention.

Libentia: And therefore, gentlemen, you can help me most by defining a principle by which to select the books most deserving of attention in the time I am allowed for literature. Given this principle, Quintus, I shall be a better teacher for your school than I have been.

Elanchius: And perhaps a wiser teacher of literature than most schools have had.

Quintus: That's the ticket. No teacher's too good for our kids. So let's figure out how to pick the right books. I'm no expert myself, so I'll go along with whatever Libentia and you fellows say.

Elanchius: Well, then. Pulvius, all of us will concede that your acquaintance with books exceeds ours. Will you therefore suggest a principle by which Libentia can choose books wisely from among the many?

Pulvius: Clearly, books must be chosen so that they represent accurately and fully the subject matter Libentia is to teach, namely, literature. Literature exists within certain frames. For example, the time-frame. Every literary text stands within a historical context. Hence works must be chosen to illuminate this context.

Vulpius: There you go again, Pulvius—making the reading materials program a survey of museum pieces.

Pulvius: I detect scorn in your remarks, Vulpius. But the teacher should represent the various ages in man's written record. Certain books reflect more faithfully than others the characteristics of the age which produced them. Obviously, then, historical representativeness is a sound principle of selection.

Elanchius: Would you then include certain books merely as specimens of their historical epochs, whether or not they possess any intrinsic merit as literature?

Pulvius: It is certainly the teacher's responsibility to represent all periods adequately.

Libentia: Then in choosing books I must be careful not to leave any gaps in the chronological representation of literature?

Pulvius: Certainly. For otherwise your students would have gaps in their knowledge of literary history.

Elanchius: If Libentia adopts this principle of selection, she will, at least, have a sure guide to a sufficient number of books. But let us not yet conclude our quest.

Pulvius: Of course not. For, as I said, literature exists within several frames, of which time is only one. Books must be selected also to illustrate particular genres and modes of literature. It is unthinkable that a teacher of literature should deserve that title if she fails to set before her students specimens of tragedy, comedy, ode, epic, romance, fable—and so on. And also of various modes, as the satirical, the pastoral, the lyrical, the pastoral-lyrical, the lyrical-elegiac—

Quintus: Hey, never heard most of those names!

Elanchius: Are there yet other frames that Libentia should remember in choosing her "specimens"?

Pulvius: I have named only the most obvious. It is also necessary, of course, to represent the characteristics of major authors in their early, middle, and late periods. With most authors a specimen or two will suffice for each stage. Further, since geographical matrix has significant influence upon litera-ture, it is necessary also to select books that accurately reflect their respective national and regional origins, and, conversely, illuminate the stages of the nation's growth.

Elanchius: Evidently, from your exposition, books are to be chosen for their representation of particular periods, forms, authors, and countries. Although a program based on this prin-ciple would be somewhat crowded, the teacher of literature would always know, at least, what works she must choose and what must be her emphasis in teaching them. Libentia, are you satisfied with Pulvius' principle of selection?

Libentia: I know that it is a highly respected one. But before we conclude that it is the best, should we not hear other possi-bilities?

Quintus: Wait a minute, Libentia. Don't know much about these things myself, but your friend Pulvius here's laid out something you can really get your teeth in. You been complaining you never knew just where you stood last year. If you see how to go ahead the way Pulvius said, maybe you ought to. At least it's a program. You'll know where you are.

Libentia: True, Quintus. Even so, I should like to hear others speak.

Elanchius: Vulpius, for one, seems impatient to have a word. Vulpius, I take it that you are not happy with all that Pulvius has said. Have you a different principle in mind?

Vulpius: Fortunately, yes. I am shocked that even you, Pulvius, can retain such outmoded concepts as you have just instanced. To utilize your patterns of thinking in the modern education program would set curriculum construction back by fifty years. Your concepts evidence your ignorance as to the findings of specialists in such curriculum planning areas as learning processes, group dynamics, and individual differences. You ignore the realities as to modern needs and the changing pattern of the total school population of today. Your program imposes a predetermined system upon individual learners and has no correlation as to concepts of dynamic structuring utilized in community and social living. Your selection of traditional materials utilizes only outmoded reading materials which have nothing to communicate to modern youth. Moreover, for today's child-centered curriculum your undemocratic prescriptiveness—

Pulvius: I scarcely expected my proposal to gain your approval, Vulpius. You and I live in different worlds.

Elanchius: We now know your opinion of the literary study that Pulvius cherishes, Vulpius. May we now hear your own proposal?

Quintus: Always like to hear Vulpius talk about these things. He's an expert on 'em all.

Vulpius: A cardinal principle as to the selection of reading materials is the utilization of the latest empirical findings compiled by specialists in the reading materials selection area. Reading materials must be adapted to the felt needs, immediate interests, and reading readiness levels of individual youths as these have been tabulated by experts. Obviously, no prescribed list of your "classics," Pulvius, patterns with these realities.

Empiricus: It seems then, Vulpius, that in the final analysis you would make the child's own preferences the chief factor in the process of selection.

Vulpius: Definitely. The child makes the curriculum. Reading material selection involves intercorrelating the readability quotients of individual materials with the reading levels, interests, and needs of individual youths.

Pulvius: And just how, pray, is this feat accomplished?

Vulpius: Readability quotient determination involves consulting readability scales devised by specialists in the readability scale structuring area. Such scales are based on empirical examination of data as to vocabulary range and difficulty, sentence length, prepositional phrase count, and personal reference word utilization. These scales have been objectively standardized and all coefficients, quotients, averages, norms, and variables scientifically established.

Empiricus: Can you be certain, Vulpius, that your data are of the kind to which truly scientific analysis can be applied?

Pulvius: I second the implication of your question, Empiricus. But I suggest also that a book might satisfy every demand made by such tests and yet possess no literary merit at all. Vulpius never worries about that!

Libentia: But I do, Pulvius. Surely I must demand that the books my students read possess *something* more than mere "readability."

Elanchius: Before we either accept or reject Vulpius' argument for selecting books according to the reading levels, interests, and needs of students, should we not ask him to describe these more fully for us?

Vulpius: As the individual learner is the central factor in modern curriculum construction, reading levels, interests, and needs of individual youths are of course the vital factors. Let me now consider these aspects in order. Reading readiness specialists have developed batteries of evaluational instruments of demonstrated efficiency which fix the reading level of the individual youth precisely.

Pulvius: Fix indeed! You accused *me* of imposing a system upon the child. But now you encase him in a strait-jacket woven of his own deficiencies!

Vulpius: Fancy figures of speech, Pulvius, but hardly relational thinking. We in the profession are more realistic.

Empiricus: Yet what Pulvius means is quite clear. Mind you, I am not persuaded that your data—those concerned with either the book or the child—are measurable with scientific precision. But let us assume for the moment that they are. Now if you take such great pains to match *precisely* what you called the readability quotient of the book with the reading level of the child, do you not thereby, so to speak, halt the child in his tracks?

Libentia: I have actually seen that happen, Empiricus. In some classes at my school, after the child's reading level has been statistically fixed, the teachers seem determined to hold it at that point, for they insist that the student read only what has been graded to his level.

Quintus: Hey! Maybe that's what's the matter with my own kid. He's been in school a lot of years now. But he's still reading things not much harder than he did quite awhile before. Seems fed up with it too. Won't try anything else either.

Vulpius: Evidently none of you understand the developmental reading concept that has been developed by developmental reading experts.

Pulvius: What in the name of the ever-living deities is developmental reading?

Vulpius: To utilize terms that communicate to the non-professional, developmental reading takes the child at his own level and channels him on by means of scientifically determined difficulty reading materials gradations. We term this Reading-Ladder progression.

Empiricus: Then you do *not*, after all, match the readability quotient of the book precisely with the reading level of the child, but allow him a certain degree of headroom.

Vulpius: Definitely. In moving into each new reading level area, unfamiliar words and concepts are scientifically fed into the reading materials which the individual youth contacts.

Empiricus: I marvel, Vulpius, at the precision of instruments which can determine not merely the reading level of the child and the readability quotient of the book, but also *the exact interval by which the latter exceeds the former!*

Vulpius: The readability formula developed by developmental reading specialists is one of the many marvels resulting from the scientific approach to readability formulae development.

Pulvius: An eighth wonder, I should say! And does your formula tell whether the book is a *good* one? Or does that little detail matter? But tell us, Vulpius, does it ever happen that you are unable to find a book whose "readability quotient" represents the exact degree of difficulty required?

Vulpius: Definitely.

Pulvius: And what, pray, do you do then?

Vulpius: Then our reading materials specialists compile the materials themselves, thus achieving the desired degree of difficulty.

Pulvius: And such concoctions are used instead of literature? I am struck dumb.

Empiricus: I am disturbed for another reason. Vulpius' conception of "progress" in reading suggests that the value of a reading program lies in the mere movement from one level of difficulty to another.

Libentia: Exactly! But such progress is valueless in itself. I want my students to read for the effect that literature can have on them.

Elanchius: These criticisms must give us pause. But Vulpius has yet to speak of two of the three pillars which support his principle of selection—that is, students' interests and needs.

Vulpius: Ultimately, the immediate interests of individual youths provide realistic reading material selection criteria. Moreover, vast quantities of objectively accumulated experiential data tending to demonstrate that interests differ, are available. These studies prove conclusively, for example, that boys differ from girls. These objective investigations are of course definitely based upon realistic researches as to what children actually do read.

Empiricus: Then your reading lists include only the books which the children themselves say they are interested in reading.

Vulpius: Definitely. Our lists of reading materials pattern with the realities of adolescent reading responses.

Empiricus: And such lists are actually in use?

Vulpius: Their utilization is widespread. As it happens, I have one with me, based on the latest findings. Ah, here it is.

Empiricus: It appears that you give books little opportunity to extend interests, since you choose them according to students' existing interests. But something else mystifies me here. When you spoke of reading levels, you said that books should be chosen for their degrees of difficulty. Are not your own two principles of selection in conflict?

Vulpius: Naturally, interests are altered in the natural maturation process.

Empiricus: Vulpius, the chief claim that you have made for your program is that it is scientific. But unless the progression in students' interests is as rigidly controlled as the progression in difficulty, and synchronized with it, your program is, in fact, not scientific, but haphazard.

Libentia: But even supposing that Vulpius' program were scientifically sound, would it not miss the point entirely? In literature some of my students found new interests which they would never have found in books chosen because they appealed to existing interests.

Elanchius: Again, serious questions have been raised, Vulpius. But before we consider them, will you describe the remaining pillar of your principle of selection?

Pulvius: Ah, "felt needs"!

Quintus: Good! Vulpius really knows his stuff about that— er—them.

Vulpius: No principle of reading material selection can be valid or can even be adopted which fails to realistically utilize the felt needs of youths.

Elanchius: If so, these needs must first be identified. Can you enumerate them for us?

Quintus: This is the part I always like best. Tell 'em Vulpius!

Vulpius: Professional researches tell us that there are four basic needs which reading materials must meet. First of all, the learner must achieve the reading proficiency level suited to his anticipated social and occupational needs. Second, since he has need to learn information related to his needs, he must acquire reading proficiency in those materials containing data relational to this purpose. Third, since he will not utilize all his time for vocational and citizenship activities, he must be prepared to pursue worthwhile leisure-time activities—among which activities is, of course, reading. Finally, and most importantly, as every individual is a member of a varying number of social constructs— such as, the family, the community, the state—he must achieve facility in making realistic adjustments structured to the functional needs of such social units and in making the approved social responses to them.

Pulvius: By all the unregimented deities!

Empiricus: You are even more definite in categorizing the needs of students than you were in discussing their interests and levels of difficulty.

Quintus: Told you he knew his stuff about 'em.

Empiricus: Earlier this morning when Quintus remarked on the number of books in this room, Elanchius pointed out that of the almost unlimited number in existence only an infinitesimal fraction can be read by a child in his school years. I was struck by the truth of his comment that the instrument of selection must therefore be an exacting one. Do the needs which you have enumerated provide such an instrument?

Vulpius: Definitely. As it happens, I have a list with me, compiled by student needs specialists.

Pulvius: But you have already mentioned a list of books based on interests. Do you mean that you have two lists?

Vulpius: Two! Why, I have three. You forget the list arranged according to difficulty levels.

Empiricus: But are not your lists identical? You have repeatedly assured us that you were scientific in compiling them. But however scientific your methods, they are useless if they result in three lists. For we are in need of a principle by which to select the best possible list—which obviously must be a single one. Here, let me examine your lists. Pulvius, would you care to look on?

Quintus: Bet they'll be plenty impressed—hey, Libentia?

Libentia: I shouldn't be surprised.

Pulvius: Why, no title appears on more than one list!

Empiricus: Yes, here is one. But merely by the operation of the laws of chance there should be at least two or three.

Elanchius: The discovery which you two have just made suggests that a fallacy of fundamental character exists in Vulpius' approach to the problem of selection. Therefore, let us make a new start in our quest for the wisest principle of selection. Do you remember, Libentia and gentlemen—

Pulvius: By all the learned deities! This is most extraordinary!

Elanchius: What is it, Pulvius? Why do you stare so intently at Vulpius' lists?

Pulvius: Just a moment. There, I've reached the end of them, and do you know, I did not recognize a single author or title!

Empiricus: How can that be? I have long known you by reputation as a distinguished literary scholar, whose knowledge of the world's literature is second to no man's. Not being a literary man, I did not think it significant that I failed to recognize any of these titles. But when you say that you have never heard of them, I can conclude only that you are jesting.

Pulvius: These titles are as strange to me as if they had come from outer space. I will take an oath on it. Where do you get your books, Vulpius? From another planet?

Vulpius: Instead of limiting your acquaintance to traditional materials compiled before this century, you should familiarize yourself, Pulvius, with the many worthwhile reading materials currently being prepared to communicate to youth in this changing world of today. But as a matter of fact, modern curriculum planning *does* utilize some traditional materials. In deference to traditionalists, curriculum experts often include certain of your "classics." So you can see that your charge is not altogether valid.

Libentia: Nevertheless, when I began teaching last year, I soon found that in most of my classes I was not permitted to use such classics as I had studied when I was preparing to teach. Once I planned to use a certain masterpiece, but a friendly colleague told me that such a departure from the prepared curriculum would get me into trouble. So instead of the books I had read in Pulvius' classes, I used those on Vulpius' lists—none of which I had read before.

Elanchius: Were you allowed to teach no literature at all?

Libentia: As Vulpius said, some literature remains in our curriculum—but it is confined to a few classes that are elected by students.

Vulpius: So you see, Pulvius, certain youths do experience your "classics"—even though it regresses from research findings of our specialists to do so. These youths are the "select few" that later matriculate in your classes. If we professionals who are in contact with the realities were free to devise the reading program for these learners as well as the others, they would also enjoy the benefits of professional research findings. They too would then experience both work-type and creative-type materials scientifically adjusted to their reading levels, interests, and needs. What can today's youths achieve from your "classics" except traditional learnings which tend to be obsolete and unfunctional? As long as you demand these readings for your "select few," we who are conversant in the field cannot fully meet the needs of the total school pupil personnel. But fortunately, the structuring of an enriched curriculum for the large majority is controlled by we professionals.

Elanchius: In a word, the majority are given books to read like those on your three lists.

Vulpius: Definitely! But we are handicapped precisely at this juncture, as Libentia inferred when she complained that the teacher-education program did not familiarize her with adolescent-type reading materials. Obviously, as education experts have long felt, the teacher-preparation curriculum should be revamped to familiarize teachers with the reading materials that they will utilize in the classroom situation.

Pulvius: What? Require *my* students to read the trash on your lists? Indeed, sir!

Libentia: Gentlemen, I must correct an impression which I unfortunately gave. When I said that I was required to teach books different from those I studied under Pulvius, I certainly was not complaining that *his* list of books should be changed!

On the contrary, though I was not permitted to teach literature to most of my students, my own study of it made me a better teacher—even of such books as are on Vulpius' lists. I would not have been prepared as well if I had read such books instead of literature!

Empiricus: Let me be positive that I understand you, Libentia. You say that you are not complaining about your studies with Pulvius. Yet you say that you were required to use books of a different order with your own students. Evidently it is your meaning, then, that the latter books are the ones that need to be changed.

Elanchius: Well, then. Let me return to the question I was about to ask just as Pulvius discovered that the books on Vulpius' lists were unknown to him. You remember that when we first met we posed what we called the antecedent question.

Quintus: Ought to! Had plenty of trouble with that word "antecedent" myself. Finally caught on though.

Elanchius: And do you remember the question itself, Quintus?

Quintus: Let's see. Guess the whole thing was why should Libentia teach literature at all.

Elanchius: And do you remember our answer?

Quintus: Yeh, you said a kind of a riddle—something about literature educating human beings as human beings.

Elanchius: Right. We agreed that the ultimate purpose in the teaching of literature is the humanization of the student. Now let me ask you Pulvius, and you, Vulpius, whether in espousing your respective principles of selection you have not disregarded this answer.

Quintus: Hey! You think maybe they forgot it like I did.

Elanchius: Empiricus, does it appear to you that they have kept our answer in mind?

Empiricus: I see no logical relationship between the principles of selection they have proposed and our answer.

Elanchius: But if our question is truly antecedent, should not the principle of selection be determined in the light of its answer?

Empiricus: It must.

Elanchius: Then, if the ultimate reason for teaching literature is the humanization of the student, *only those books should
be chosen which have, at the very least, the latent power
to humanize*—for of course no others can be expected to do so.
The object of our quest, then, must be those works of literature
which, because they proffer the living, vivid acquaintance with
the adventures of the human spirit, can stretch the humanity
that lies in a man and needle it into its fullest growth.*

Libentia: Your words are memorable, Elanchius!

Empiricus: And persuasive.

Quintus: Maybe if we'd got around to putting it that way
at first, we wouldn't have missed the boat so bad. Hey! Looks to
me like Vulpius' books won't fill the bill! Guess we've got to
pick out some different ones.

Libentia: And we must also decide which students need to
read them.

Elanchius: We have, then, two large topics before us. But it
is now noon and we shall have to part for a time. Since we are to
consider not only which books are to be read but also which
students are to read them, let us next meet in a public place
where people of all sorts pass by.

Quintus: How about meeting in front of my shop this afternoon? Got a bench there looking right out on the market place.

Elanchius: Excellent, Quintus. Till later then.

---

* Elanchius' words here parallel almost exactly those of President
Nathan Pusey of Harvard University, as quoted in *Time* (March 1, 1954),
p. 62.

The Answer Regarded

Persons of the Dialogue

LIBENTIA MAGISTRA

PULVIUS GRAMMATICUS   VULPIUS MATERIES

J. QUINTUS   EMPIRICUS MARTIALIS

ELANCHIUS

Scene: Before the shop of Quintus

Quintus: Well, here we are. Glad to have you visit my little place.

Empiricus: You are modest, Quintus. It is a large establishment, and the square on which it fronts is fairly bustling.

Quintus: Best spot in town, no doubt about it.

Elanchius: And the environment is appropriate for our conversation this afternoon. We cannot forget here that the ultimate object of our concern is humanity.

Vulpius: Yes, we can observe individual activities in real-life situations. Pulvius, how do you like being out of your ivory tower.

Pulvius: One can see farther from a tower than some people imagine, Vulpius.

Libentia: Come, come, gentlemen. We must look at our subject this afternoon from both the tower and the market place.

Elanchius: Well said, Libentia. And now that we are settled on Quintus' bench, let us begin to consider that subject. We concluded this morning that our principle in selecting books must be derived from the answer to our antecedent question. Finally, we stated this proposition: *If the ultimate reason for teaching literature is the humanization of the student, only*

84

those books should be chosen which have, at the very least, the latent power to humanize him.

Vulpius: As a curriculum expert I must immediately confront you with two realistic questions: First, how do you propose to determine which reading materials have this humanization potentiality you speak of? And second, what fraction of the total pupil personnel do you suppose will be able to read such materials?

Quintus: Hate to try to answer either of those myself.

Elanchius: They are difficult questions, Quintus, but perhaps not unanswerable ones. First, Vulpius has asked how we can determine which books have power to humanize. Obviously, unless we can answer this question our principle of selection is useless.

Empiricus: I am on unfamiliar ground here, but I do know that some books, by general consent, are called "great." Are these the ones that have power to humanize?

Elanchius: Your question opens the problem at its center. If we could summarily answer "yes," our immediate task would be done! But we must answer two other questions before we can answer yours: First, what is it that makes a book great? Second, what is it that gives a book its humanizing power? Perhaps then we can discover whether a book's greatness and its humanizing power are to be equated.

Pulvius: Do you not exaggerate our difficulty, Elanchius? Time has answered the main question. Great books are those which have survived.

Vulpius: Do you assume that your outmoded reading materials have "survived," just because you read them yourself, Pulvius? Reading material values are more realistically measured by present-day responses of normative readers.

Elanchius: Perhaps we can agree in part with each of you. But in doing so have we even touched upon the qualities which make books great? Perhaps we can begin by asking what books are written about.

Pulvius: Why, they are written about anything and everything.

Vulpius: Definitely. Some reading materials relate to peoples, some to animals, some to foreign lands, some to occupations—any numbers of aspects.

Elanchius: True, they have great diversity in subject matter. And now let us consider whether they have a quality in common.

Pulvius: Literary documents all have one thing in common certainly—an author, whose point of view is necessarily restricted to what man can know.

Elanchius: And what can man know?

Pulvius: Why, anything that he can perceive through his senses.

Elanchius: Is that all?

Pulvius: Well, man can know through his intellect as it acts upon sense perceptions.

Empiricus: It is held that man also has knowledge which is intuitive, but this is perhaps impossible to demonstrate empirically.

Elanchius: True. But, however he learns it, what is it that man can know?

Libentia: Well, he can know what is going on around him and within himself.

Pulvius: Libentia's statement would be equally true in the past tense. Man can know what has gone on in the world in distant ages and in the minds of men of other times.

Elanchius: Then man's knowledge—whatever its source—is chiefly of *man*, his actions and thoughts.

Empiricus: The scientist would say that an important segment of man's knowledge is of the physical universe. But ultimately this knowledge is largely that of man's attempts to deal with the physical universe, and therefore much of it, too, is of man himself.

Elanchius: I am pleased to hear you make that qualification, Empiricus. Not all of your colleagues would do so. But now let me ask my next question: Are men equal in their knowledge of mankind?

Vulpius: Definitely not. Why, the mushrooming of the tests and measurements field demonstrates that individual differences are widespread, including differences as to general knowledge.

Elanchius: Doubtless we would all agree that men differ greatly in the range and depth of their knowledge. Must we not say the same of those who write books? Do all authors exhibit the same range and depth of knowledge of mankind?

Pulvius: No, indeed! Authors are quite unequal in this respect.

Elanchius: And would you say that those who possess the greatest knowledge are the greatest authors?

Pulvius: Well, I should say that although some of the great authors undoubtedly had an almost unbelievably comprehensive knowledge, it is not only the knowledge but their *use* of it that determines the level of their greatness.

Quintus: Say, I've read a few books myself. Not so many, of course, after I got out of school. Ones I liked best, the author really knew what he was up to. Lots of times I'd say, "Boy, this fellow really knows what makes people tick."

Elanchius: Thank you, Quintus. Can we not call this quality "insight"?

Pulvius: And that authors differ in the profundity of their insight there can be no doubt. But when I mentioned "use," I meant to imply something different—that certain authors have greater skill than others in giving their knowledge or insight formal expression in language.

Elanchius: And without this skill—may we not call it art-istry—could an author write a work which we would call litera-ture? Should we not then say that an *author* is to be called "great" if he has unusual insight—the understanding of the innermost and peculiarly human elements in man—and if his representation of these in language is characterized by its artistry?

Pulvius: Those are the distinguishing marks of the greatest authors, Elanchius.

Elanchius: Then is it not the books written by authors who possess the extraordinary powers we have just named which will be most likely to deserve the name of great books?

Empiricus: Agreed. But do all books by these authors have the desired qualities?

Pulvius: An apt reservation, Empiricus. Literary history is filled with instances of second-rate books by some of our greatest authors. *Bonus dormitat poeta.*

Elanchius: Therefore the teacher must choose with great care—not only among all books that have been written, but even among those written by the greatest authors. But now let us see where we stand. We have said that great books are written by authors possessed of extraordinary powers of understanding and expression. Shall we say, then, that *a great book is one which gives artistic expression to profound human insight?*

Quintus: Can't see anything wrong with that.

Elanchius: Now let us turn to the other question we must answer before we can answer Empiricus': What it that gives a book its humanizing power?

Quintus: Well, I'd say the author of a book that's got that kind of power has really got to know plenty about people.

Elanchius: Did we not say the same thing about the authors of great books—that they must have profound human insight?

Quintus: Yeh, that's what I mean. Stands to reason.

Elanchius: Then books which have humanizing power will express profound human insight?

Quintus: Said that about great books, too.

Elanchius: We said more, Quintus—that they must give artistic expression to this insight.

Quintus: Yeh. But does that fit in here too? Always heard a book had to be artistic to be a great book. But does it have to be artistic to be a humanizing book?

Elanchius: Indeed it must, Quintus.

Quintus: All right, if you say so. But why?

Pulvius: Ha!

Elanchius: Why, Quintus, *because it is by its art that a book gives pleasure.*

Quintus: Pleasure, eh? Guess that's so. But what's pleasure got to do with humanizing anybody? Lots of things give pleasure.

Pulvius: Ha!

Elanchius: But the pleasure provided by art is of a unique kind, Quintus.

Pulvius: Ha!

Quintus: Pulvius, what's the matter with you? Why do you keep saying "ha"?

Pulvius: *"Delightful scenes, whether in nature, painting, or poetry, have a kindly influence on the body as well as the mind."**

Quintus: What?

Pulvius: *"Poets in their phrases combine charm and high applicability to life."*

Quintus: What?

Pulvius: *"For he doth not only show the way, but giveth so sweet a prospect into the way, as will entice any man to enter it."*

Quintus: What?

Pulvius: *"What so much good doth that teaching bring forth . . . as that it moveth one to do that which it doth teach? For out of natural conceit the philosophers drew it; but to be moved to do that which we know, or—"*

Elanchius: I believe, Quintus, that—

Pulvius: *"Nothing can attain its full strength without the assistance of Art."*

Elanchius: Thank you, Pulvius. I believe, Quintus, that—

Pulvius: *"Are we not, I say, to hold that art (being a harmony of that language which is implanted by nature in man and which appeals not to the hearing only but to the soul itself) by these selfsame means allures us and invariably disposes us to stateliness and dignity and elevation and every motion which it contains within itself, gaining absolute mastery over our minds? But it is folly to dispute concerning matters which are generally admitted, since experience is proof sufficient."*—There, Elanchius, I have done!

Elanchius: Thank you, Pulvius.

Quintus: Yeh, but what's he done?

Elanchius: Why Quintus, Pulvius has been answering your

---

* The reader may be struck by the similarity between the words of Pulvius' authorities and those of Addison in *The Spectator*, No. 411, and hereafter, respectively, of Horace in *Ars Poetica*, Sidney in *An Apologie for Poetrie* (*bis*), Quintilian in *Institutio Oratoria*, Book Nine, Longinus in *On the Sublime*, Chapter XXXIX, and Thomas à Kempis in *De Imitatione Christi*, Book One.

question, "Why does a humanizing book have to be artistic?" It has long been known to men who have thought deeply about this matter that *art, through the unique kind of pleasure it provides, can move us to seek the virtues it recommends.* So you see, Quintus, that whereas a book that conveys its author's profound understanding of human matters, but lacks art, can teach us much, for example, of courtesy, or liberality, or courage, a book that expresses this understanding *artistically* can make us want to *be* courteous, or liberal, or courageous. And that, Quintus, is why a humanizing book must be artistic. For to humanize the reader is not merely to equip him with understanding, however profound, of human attributes, but to incorporate these in his being.

Pulvius: Bravo, Elanchius! *"I had rather feel compunction than understand the definition thereof."*

Empiricus: I now perceive, Elanchius, that my earlier question has been answered affirmatively. I asked whether "great" books and "humanizing" books are to be equated. We have found that "great" books are those that give artistic expression to profound human insight; and just now you and Pulvius have shown that "humanizing" books are inevitably the same. Even so, the problem of determining which *are* the great books— that is, the humanizing books—remains unsolved. And beyond that, for the teacher, remains the problem of determining which books are greatest and therefore most humanizing. Frankly, it is a problem which I would feel incompetent to solve, even if I were better versed in literature than I am. If the right books are to be chosen, obviously it must be solved. But who is to solve it? Do you, Libentia, as a teacher, feel capable of choosing, from among innumerable books, the few that are greatest and therefore have greatest humanizing potentiality?

Libentia: I could never make the attempt without a great deal of help.

Empiricus: Do you, Pulvius, feel that you could do so?

Pulvius: As a literary scholar, I describe books in terms of their respective ages, authors, and genres. It is not my primary responsibility to make the kind of decision about books that you speak of, Empiricus. Moreover, any one man who did so would be presumptuous unless he had the perspective of the deities.

Empiricus: Both you and Libentia have evidently learned humility from your studies, Pulvius—which, incidentally, is itself some proof of the power of literature to humanize. In disclaiming the ability to determine by yourselves which books are great, you imply that this ability resides elsewhere.

Elanchius: We must identify it, Empiricus. But Vulpius, you have long been silent. As a professional student of the curriculum, would you feel confident in undertaking the task which both Libentia and Pulvius, in their humility, have admitted their inability to perform?

Vulpius: I definitely can supply—

Pulvius: We have already seen your three lists, Vulpius!

Elanchius: In any event, the remarks of Libentia and Pulvius make clear that we have reached a crucial point. Your reaction, Empiricus, to their disclaiming the ability to select the greatest books was very like my own. I agree that it is not the province of any single person to identify unaided the greatest documents of literature. Yet somehow, we know, these books must be selected. To whom shall we turn? Libentia, did you have in mind some particular source of help?

Libentia: The very one, I suspect, that Pulvius has in mind—those intelligent readers whose critical faculties have been educated by long and intimate association with books.

Pulvius: Exactly!—the literary critics.

Elanchius: But not any one critic?

Libentia: Indeed not. I would not wish any one reader, however perceptive, to select the books that I must use. Though his judgment might be better than mine, it would still be inadequate.

Elanchius: Would you accept the decision of a majority of contemporary critics?

Libentia: Their judgment would be better than that of one, but still I would not accept it. Nor would Pulvius, I think.

Pulvius: Indeed not!

Elanchius: There seems to be an understanding between you two! Let me then turn to Pulvius. Why would you not accept the judgment of even a majority of contemporary critics?

Pulvius: Why, because the judgment of any one generation may sometimes be nearly as warped as that of a single critic. The history of literary criticism shows repeatedly that no generation is an infallible judge of either contemporary or earlier literary works. I could cite many instances, both of gross overestimate and of gross underestimate, of utter neglect and of misplaced esteem.

Empiricus: By asserting that whole generations of astute readers can be wrong, you postulate the existence of a more reliable standard.

Pulvius: Yes. It is the judgment of many ages and many critics. The more ages and the more critics, the greater the certainty that the judgment is right. In short, time is the ultimate judge, as I said earlier.

Elanchius: But has not your former statement been qualified by what has since been said? You asserted simply that survival is the proof of greatness. But certain books survive for generations, not because they possess the qualities we have ascribed to greatness—indeed, by which we have defined it—but for other reasons. Scholars find many literary works of former times interesting as specimens of the thought and taste of their respective periods and countries; yet many of these supply *only* such interest.

Pulvius: But scholars must be concerned with all books! Why, a hundred years hence they will have to examine even those on Vulpius' lists—as evidence of the taste of our time!

Elanchius: True. But our question is, what books has time— that is, time as represented by generations of perceptive readers— proved capable of speaking with such force and universal pertinence that in any age one finds himself personally addressed and may be deeply affected?

Pulvius: I agree. But I must reassert that to the serious literary scholar all books are important.

Elanchius: Well, then. Empiricus, does our conclusion seem reasonable to you?

Empiricus: It does indeed, and it gives us what we have been seeking—a sound principle of selection.

Elanchius: Libentia, will it direct you to the books that will best serve your purpose?

Libentia: I see no other way. If I had the perspective of the deities that Pulvius referred to earlier, I could no doubt choose unaided. But no one person—whether teacher, professional consultant, or even curriculum supervisor!—should think that his judgment is infallible. And, since the time given the teacher to present literature to the student is brief and therefore precious, the principle by which books are selected must be as nearly infallible as possible.

Quintus: Hey, wait a minute! What's the matter with Vulpius? He's getting sort of purple. Something stuck in your throat?

Elanchius: Perhaps we have been thoughtless in failing to let him speak before now. That is my fault, Vulpius. But I thought it best to let the conversation reach a fairly definite conclusion. Now you can make your comment on the whole matter at once.

Pulvius: Now we're in for it!

Vulpius: Visionaries! Non-professionals! Your thinking would set the curriculum planning developments achieved by we experts back more than fifty years. It is incredible that after all our researches individuals should still hold the outmoded notions and mere commonsense opinions advanced this afternoon. Not a one of you have cited any statistics as to individual capacities, interests, needs, differences, nor provided realistic data as to the social, economic, vocational, and environmental factors of realistic curriculum structuring.

Quintus: Back to normal now, all right.

Elanchius: All things considered, Vulpius, your outburst is quite understandable. But now let us go back in an effort to find precisely where, in your opinion, we have erred in our reasoning.

Vulpius: Shortly after we arrived here this afternoon, Elanchius, you iterated what you called "our" principle of selection of reading materials for the school in this fashion: "only those books should be chosen which have, at the very least, the latent power to humanize."

Elanchius: That is correct.

Vulpius: I said at the time that I must pose two questions as a curriculum specialist—first, how you propose to determine which reading materials have this so-called humanization potentiality, and second, what fraction of the total pupil personnel you supposed could read them. You answered the first by equating "humanizing reading materials" and "great reading materials." But then you still had to confront the problem of determining which materials *are* great. This crucial task, you asserted, was one for your so-called critics—who are neither up-to-date nor credentialized. Let me remind you that we are selecting reading materials for the modern school. Now can you realistically hold that your literary critics are as well qualified as curriculum specialists?

Empiricus: Yet if only the judgment of the discriminating of many generations can surely identify the greatest books, and if, as we agreed much earlier, the highest purpose that literature can serve for students is met only by works of genuine literary force, how can you reject our conclusion that only the judgment of these readers is adequate to the task of selecting works for the schools—whether the schools are "modern" or otherwise?

Vulpius: Fantastic! Unrealistic! I reject this visionary thinking!

Empiricus: But how can you reject this conclusion?

Quintus: Don't see how you can myself, Vulpius.

Vulpius: Mere commonsense conclusions are worthless as compared to the findings of research specialists. Is your so-called critic a reading specialist? Is he an expert on learning processes, adolescent responses, readability quotients, or any of the other specialized fields whose findings must be utilized in modern school language arts program developments? Has he ever served as a curriculum construction resource consultant? Why, most of your critics were dead before any of these findings were—were found.

Empiricus: But, Vulpius, however useful in its place may be the research you mention, is it not irrelevant as criticism of the reasoning by which, just now, we have reached this conclusion?

Vulpius: Evidently you fail to grasp my thought. Your

conclusion contradicts all that has been discovered and compiled by we in the profession in the past fifty years. It is therefore invalid. Furthermore, it is unrealistic. How can you conclude that your long dead critics should be the ones to determine the reading course content in our modern schools when there are specialists who have made this their life study? What do they know about such scientific aids to reader growth as graded reading materials and reading ladder achievement charts?

Empiricus: Still, you have not found a weak link in our chain of reasoning. Elanchius, should we therefore review the logic by which we reached the conclusion that Vulpius now rejects?

Pulvius: I doubt that a review will free Vulpius' mind from its own strait-jacket. But go ahead.

Elanchius: Do, Empiricus. Since you are accustomed to dealing with logical sequences, it is appropriate that you yourself retrace our steps.

Quintus: Go to it, Empiricus. Some of that arguing we did back there sort of left me in the dust. You're just the one to clear it all up.

Empiricus: Why, thank you, Quintus. You will recall that earlier we distinguished between the kind of education whose ultimate end is the humanization of the student and the kind whose effect is specialization. We agreed that the study of literature belongs in the former.

Quintus: Yeh! We got to have shoemakers and artisans and teachers and everything else, but the school's got to educate first what they've all got in common as human beings. That's where the books come in, because they can get at that job.

Empiricus: Right, Quintus. Our first conclusion, then, was that the highest function of the study of literature is to contribute to the humanization of students. From this conclusion our reasoning led us inevitably to a second: that only those books should be selected for study which contain a potentiality for humanizing their readers. We were then confronted by the necessity of identifying such books, and our third conclusion was that the "humanizing books" are the "great books." Our task then, logically, was to identify the "great" books, and our fourth conclusion followed: that the only infallible guide is that provided by the most discriminating readers over a long period of time. Our fifth and final conclusion, therefore, was that a teacher of literature should select for study books that have been thus reviewed by time and whose greatness has been unfailingly asserted. It was at this point, Vulpius, that you took exception, rejecting the conclusion that literary critics are more able choosers of books for the curriculum than are specialists in the curriculum.

Quintus: You sure laid it all out, Empiricus! Got it all straight in my head now.

Elanchius: Empiricus has summarized our reasoning with admirable precision. Can you, Vulpius, with equal precision, point out the flaw in this sequence which has caused you to reject our conclusion?

Vulpius: The whole line of thinking is entirely unrealistic. No matter how good it may sound, it is not workable. And if it cannot be utilized, it cannot achieve the desired outcome.

Empiricus: But, Vulpius, you still are not pointing out any one precise flaw in the argument. Would you prefer to summarize your objections to the arguments as a whole?

Vulpius: Definitely. First, your proposal is made without empirical evidence as to the reading levels of the modern school pupil population. Reading materials selected by your literary critics are, by and large, too *difficult* for adolescent readers. Second, all the reading materials you would tend to utilize are *old,* and therefore they cannot possibly communicate to the interests of modern youth, but using student interests as a criteria is an important trend in modern educational thinking. Third, such traditional materials are *not adapted* to the needs of present-day youth.

Elanchius: You have mentioned three generalized objections, Vulpius; you charge us with ignoring the abilities, interests, and needs of present-day students. You will recall that earlier this afternoon we spoke of the appropriateness of this place for our present conversation since here all sorts of persons are to be observed. Now, Vulpius, the substance of your criticism is that despite the bustling reminder there on the market place we have been quite oblivious in our reasoning to what you have called the realities of individual students—or, what I should prefer to call the essential nature of man.

Vulpius: Definitely. For all the utilization you have made of the realities here before us, we might as well have assembled in Pulvius' ivory tower.

Libentia: Elanchius, I have listened attentively to Vulpius' charges, for they sum up the argument which is most frequently brought against the study of literature in the classroom. Indeed, this very argument has been presented so persuasively that many teachers have substituted for literature what Vulpius aptly calls "reading materials" and "work-type readings." Since this argument has led so many teachers—even those who once believed in the values of literature—to revise their whole attitude toward their fundamental responsibility, it is clearly a critical one.

Elanchius: It is indeed, Libentia. And, indeed, if we cannot meet Vulpius' objections, there is a serious deficiency in our argument. But you will note that the shadows in the market place have lengthened while we have been speaking. Shall we not then suspend our conversation until we can examine more fully the basis of his argument?

Quintus: Good idea, Elanchius. Got to go inside here and shut up shop for the night, anyhow.

Pulvius: Before dinner I find an inopportune time to begin chewing over Vulpius' regurgitations.

Empiricus: I agree, Elanchius, that postponement of our discussion seems appropriate.

Elanchius: Since the moon will be full tonight, many whom Vulpius has charged us with ignoring will be strolling about the market place. Let us therefore return here shortly, and perhaps we can make a fresh start on the problem.

PART III

WHO SHOULD BE TAUGHT LITERATURE?

All These

Persons of the Dialogue

LIBENTIA MAGISTRA

PULVIUS GRAMMATICUS   VULPIUS MATERIES

THE FAMILY VEXAPARIUS

J. QUINTUS   EMPIRICUS MARTIALIS

ELANCHIUS

Scene: The same

Quintus: Well, all here but Libentia and Empiricus. Look at that moonlight on the market place! Great sight, hey?

Pulvius: The young people strolling hand in hand and laughing happily together remind me of the idyllic scenes drawn by our poets. If this urban square were only a forest or field, this could be a pastoral.

Vulpius: Nonsense! You are witnessing the realities of human existence, not the imaginary fictions of your so-called classics. The individuals you see there experiencing leisure-time activities have real blood in them.

Quintus: Ho, ho! You fellows sure don't see eye to eye, do you?

Elanchius: I see two shadows detaching themselves from the throng. Are they not our missing pair of friends? Yes, they are coming toward us. Greetings, Libentia and Empiricus.

Libentia: You are all here before us!

Empiricus: We had a pleasant walk—and this place, I see, is charming by moonlight.

Elanchius: It does seem a different place at night. During

101

the day we saw people buying, selling, running errands. Now in the evening we see them as indistinct forms, walking and talking, drinking in the beauties of the night, and enjoying the company of one another. The scene is changed, and the interests of the evening have replaced those of the day. But after all, are these figures, seemingly changed by the moonlight, essentially different? A man is a man at all times, regardless of what he is doing, and not less so at one time and more at another. The qualities that make him a human being, though not always equally manifest, are present in him always, whatever his occupation at the moment. The same qualities are also in his neighbor, however different the two men may appear.

Libentia: Ah! You have brought us back to our subject! What you have said of those people in the moonlight may also be said of children—and I am thinking now especially of my students. Through literature I want to reach and affect the quality that makes them not *different* but *alike*—their common humanity. That is why I will go on teaching literature in spite of all the difficulties—and in spite of the counselors who keep telling me that "it can't be done!"

Elanchius: Let us then turn to the subject at once. You objected, Vulpius, that our principle of selection is unrealistic because, as you said, the books thereby chosen will not suit the reading levels, interests, and needs of the students. Instead of books of the kind indicated by our principle of selection, you would of course use such titles as those in your lists.

Vulpius: Definitely!

Empiricus: You will recall, Vulpius, that we have named the power to humanize as the highest attribute of the books to be chosen by our principle. Therefore, when you urge books other than these, you must mean either that the books on your lists possess humanizing power as great as those chosen by our principle, or that you reject our often repeated conclusion that the highest function of the study of literature is the humanization of the reader. Will you tell us which is the case?

Elanchius: You have put it well, Empiricus. In order to know whether our discussion of the objections raised by Vulpius can be fruitful, we should know his answer to this question.

Quintus: Yeh! Only fair you tell us, Vulpius.

Vulpius: The answer is definitely not *which* is the case. Some of the materials on my lists may have your humanizing power, although we have not as yet devised formulae for measuring this ingredient. On the other hand, the functions which reading must perform are multiple, and humanizing the individual, supposing it to be an empirically valid objective, could be at best only one of them.

Pulvius: Then your answer is yes and no!

Empiricus: And, Vulpius, if any books on your lists have power to humanize, they were included not because of it but for some other reason?

Vulpius: Definitely. That factor would be only incidental. The selection principle utilized in compiling my lists was based on statistically verified data as to individual learner interests, needs, and reading levels. Since curriculum specialists approach curriculum planning realistically, they find that these data are the only empirically valid factors in selecting reading materials for classroom utilization.

Elanchius: You have made it quite clear by now that humanizing power is not, with you, a matter of primary importance in selecting books.

Pulvius: In fact, Vulpius simply does not care whether the books taught to students have any literary merit at all so long as they satisfy his infernal trinity of needs and what-not.

Vulpius: Let us face facts. Your "great books" are too difficult for average youths, and moreover are not adjusted to their needs and interests. Only scientifically adapted reading materials must be utilized.

Pulvius: And the authors of such books are your specialists!

Vulpius: Obviously, since they have surveyed reading levels, interests, and needs of modern school-age youths. No one else can have the necessary knowledge of these factors.

Pulvius: But do these—er—persons also have the necessary knowledge of humanity?

Libentia: And the creative power to *move* humanity?

Empiricus: These are basic questions, Vulpius!

Vulpius: But we must be empirical, Empiricus! Neither the

so-called humanizing power nor the greatness of reading material is as yet—and perhaps never will be—susceptible of precise measurement. Therefore, the only empirically measurable difference between your "great books" and the books on my list is that the former are not as well adapted to the needs, interests, and reading levels of young learners.

Pulvius: By all the eyeless deities!

Empiricus: But you must remember, Vulpius, that the scientist never concludes that what lies beyond his reach as a scientist is therefore non-existent.

Pulvius: There are more things in heaven and earth, Vulpius, than are dreamt of in *your* "science."

Elanchius: Well, then. Earlier Vulpius raised three specific objections to our principle of selection. He has referred to them again briefly in the past few minutes. Let us now ask him to speak more fully, for we must be sure we thoroughly understand them if we are to seek ways of answering them.

Quintus: Good idea!

Vulpius: My first objection is that your "great books" are not adapted to the reading levels of individual learners.

Quintus: You mean they're too hard for the kids to read?

Vulpius: Definitely, Quintus.

Elanchius: And why do you say great books are too difficult, Vulpius?

Vulpius: Principally because their authors were not familiar with the reading-level concept. Therefore, they failed to adapt such characteristics as vocabulary and sentence patterns to the realities of adolescent abilities.

Elanchius: Do you imply that all great books are equally difficult?

Vulpius: So long as you speak exclusively of your "great books," the answer, in general, tends to be affirmative. I suppose that there are individual differences among them as to their range of readability, but none—including the least difficult—are adapted to the reading rate and reading comprehension level of modern youths.

Pulvius: Bah! You have succumbed to a mere superstition—that books are necessarily difficult because they are great.

Elanchius: But would you say, Pulvius, that great books do not confront the reader with difficulties?

Pulvius: No, indeed. They confront even the literary scholar with difficulties. These difficulties do not discourage the scholar, nor should they discourage the student reader. But Vulpius would not even allow him *access* to great books, simply because they are difficult.

Elanchius: Let me ask you the same question that I asked Vulpius. Do you believe that all great books are equally difficult?

Pulvius: Certainly not. Vulpius evidently believes that a book's difficulty is proportional to its greatness. Thus, the world's greatest book would *ipso facto* have to be the world's most difficult book. But this idea does not accord with fact—as those acquainted with great books are aware. The reverse is nearer the truth, for many of the world's greatest books are among the most lucid. Indeed, the lucidity of great books is one of the proofs of their greatness. On the other hand, an inferior book may be difficult simply because it is badly written. Listening to you, Vulpius, one would think that you had never read a great book!

Vulpius: And listening to you, Pulvius, the "greatest" books are the easiest. But let's at least try to be realistic. The reading materials you propose to use are not suited to the normative demands of the school reading program.

Pulvius: By all means, let us be realistic! Great books are not equally difficult. Indeed, among them there is a considerable range. Therefore, any teacher genuinely interested in giving her students the best books available will find some that are suitable. She will never need to look elsewhere.

Quintus: That's right. Give 'em the best there is they can handle. That's that!

Vulpius: I have another objection, Pulvius. By depending upon the critics' opinions, it is clear that your principle of selection would result in a program of antiquated readings. Such readings, because of their age, tend to present especial difficulties for modern youths. Hence, what you propose to do by delimiting the reading curriculum to your "classics" tends to have a detrimental effect education-wise.

Elanchius: You hold, then, that older books are necessarily more difficult than newer ones?

Vulpius: By and large, the answer to your question tends to be in the affirmative. Furthermore, the older the material the more difficult it tends to be.

Pulvius: Ah ha! You have been taken in by more than one popular superstition, Vulpius. A moment ago you equated difficulty with greatness; now you are equating difficulty with age. But the briefest scrutiny of this idea destroys its truth as a generalization. You and your colleagues argue that since recent books are written by authors who speak from pressures and experiences familiar to present-day readers, their books are more easily comprehended than are those written by authors who died hundreds or thousands of years ago. But here also the reverse is often nearer the truth. What makes a book readily comprehensible to its readers is not its element of newness. On the contrary, its newness may make it difficult! The fact is that books are made understandable by the employment of ideas that have become familiar and by the use of forms that do not distract the reader by their novelty.

Elanchius: You accused Vulpius of equating difficulty with age. Are you now equating it with newness?

Pulvius: To some degree, Elanchius. The new, being unfamiliar, is therefore likely to be more difficult than that which is already known. Vulpius may even have some tests and measures to verify that assertion! However, literary history can supply us with all the evidence we need. There one finds many instances of authors considered difficult by their contemporaries. We can now see why they were so regarded: they were ahead of their time—as authors commonly are, Vulpius—and hence were speaking of ideas and in ways with which their contemporaries were not familiar; or the allusiveness of their style distracted the reader because of his very nearness to the contemporary scene. Works difficult for the first reason were likely to discourage all but the most intrepid reader. Works difficult for the second reason were so because they tempted the reader to search for elements of timeliness and thus distracted him from the timeless and universal qualities that made the works great. But now note what followed—as, Vulpius, literary history clearly records. Works of the former kind, as they lost their aura of novelty, came to be regarded by later generations of readers as having a familiar aspect that rendered them less formidable. Likewise, works of the second kind, their contemporary and merely superficial aspects having been diminished by the passage of time, no longer confronted the reader with that distracting allusiveness which had earlier made them difficult.

Empiricus: I am reminded of a comparable instance in the scientific field. A theory of the structure of the universe propounded not so long ago was not immediately acceptable because it seemed to contradict appearances. One could say that although this theory was at first difficult either to understand or to accept, now it appeals even to the general public unskilled in scientific knowledge. Truly, it is commonly the new, not the old, that is difficult—either to comprehend or to value.

Elanchius: We have been considering for some time the problem raised by Vulpius' charge that great books are too difficult for Libentia's students. Let us now—since two other charges yet remain—take stock of the progress we have made. We have pointed out the fallacy in two popular assumptions— that great books are necessarily more difficult than inferior ones, and that older great books are more difficult than new ones. Pulvius, drawing upon his extensive knowledge of the world's literature, has further assured us that *there is a sufficient range of difficulty among great books to provide choices appropriate to all reading levels*. It is my understanding that Pulvius has not, however, wished to argue that great books are easy to read. Indeed, you will recall his insistence that even scholars may find them difficult to understand fully. Now, Pulvius, may we ask you to clarify your position? In opposing the views of Vulpius, you have seemed to argue that great books are not difficult. Yet you asserted, almost in the same breath, that they *are* difficult. Will you resolve this apparent contradiction for us?

Pulvius: Gladly, Elanchius. As you suggest, the contradiction is only apparent. Vulpius objected to great books as *too* difficult.

It is this emphasis that I reject. Books are not great just because they are difficult or difficult just because they are great, and they are certainly not all as difficult as Vulpius supposes them to be. In any event, most of them are not *too* difficult.

Elanchius: One difference between you evidently lies in the meaning of the word "too." Vulpius, what do you mean by "too" when you say that great books are *too* difficult?

Vulpius: That they are beyond the reading levels of the individual learners.

Elanchius: And you, Pulvius?

Pulvius: A book is "too" difficult when the difficulty it poses is greater than the value that can be derived from it.

Elanchius: Does it follow from your argument, Pulvius, that certain books, however difficult, may contain value so great that almost any amount of effort necessary to understand them is justified?

Pulvius: I could name a hundred such books.

Elanchius: And does the converse follow also—that certain books exist which, however slight the effort necessary to understand them, are still not worth reading?

Pulvius: Vulpius has shown us three lists of such books!

Vulpius: But adolescent learners can read these materials, and with speed and comprehension. That is a realistic fact.

Empiricus: No one present, Vulpius, has cast doubt on what you have called the "readability" of the books on your lists. However, our present question is *not whether they are readable, but whether they are worth reading*.

Vulpius: But you keep insisting that your "great" books are worth reading in spite of their difficulty. Why all this unrealistic insistence?

Pulvius: First of all let me repeat, Vulpius—I do not deny that a great book may be difficult. If it is difficult, it is so because a book to be great must confront the complexities of human life—not superficially or casually, but deliberately and honestly. Easy answers to the eternal human questions, which great books invariably ponder, are shabby and inadequate, if, indeed, not positively immoral. Such answers are oversimplifications and hence distortions of truth. Surely it is better to present to a reader a book which is honest, though thereby necessarily somewhat difficult, than a book which is dishonest, however easy.

Quintus: I'll buy that anytime! But, say, just where have we got to, anyhow?

Empiricus: Why, Quintus, the logic of our discussion has been as follows: *humanization is the pre-eminent end of that kind of education of which the study of literature forms a part; the books that have the power to humanize their readers are great books; therefore, great books, whether difficult or not, alone are appropriate for the reading program.*

Quintus: I'll buy that too!

Elanchius: And now a further question, Vulpius. Do you consider the ease with which your books can be read to be in itself a good?

Vulpius: As I have repeatedly pointed out, specialists in reading materials spare no effort in grading these materials to the reading levels of the individual learners.

Elanchius: Then you do consider easiness in books to be a good?

Vulpius: When reading materials are not properly adapted to the individual's known reading level, he is likely to become frustrated and may even become a non-reader.

Empiricus: It appears that you must try a different approach, Elanchius, since this one fails to elicit a definite statement, either affirmative or negative.

Elanchius: Then, Vulpius, since you hesitate to assert that easiness is in itself a good, let me ask whether you consider difficulty to be in itself an evil.

Vulpius: Obviously, problems which exercise a challenging force on young minds tend to be desirable. However, recent findings have tended to show conclusively that problems which are too difficult alienate the modern adolescent learner.

Elanchius: Then if you were choosing between two books of equal merit, of which one was so easy that it afforded no obstacle to a reader and the other was written in such a manner that it frequently stretched his mind to its limit, you would prefer the former?

Vulpius: We who have explored the learning process field

recognize that an elastic substance which is stretched too much loses its elasticity. The mind of a young learner when thus continuously activated tends to react like such a substance.

Empiricus: It is true, Vulpius, that constant overstretching has this effect upon an elastic substance, which eventually will lose its power to return to its original dimension. It is for this property that an elastic substance is valued. But is this the property we should value in the developing mind of a young person? We should not desire the growing mind to resume its former dimension, but to continue forever expanding.

Elanchius: Ah, Empiricus! I asked Vulpius whether difficulty in reading was to be considered an evil. But you suggest that the antithesis is true.

Quintus: Antithesis? Don't quite get you, Elanchius.

Elanchius: I was merely asking, Quintus, whether difficulty may in itself be a good.

Quintus: You mean the hard way is better than the easy way.

Elanchius: Look there, Quintus. Do you see that man crossing the market place?

Quintus: The big fellow, stepping along this way? Yeh. Know him, in fact. Fine young athlete—one of the best!

Elanchius: Would you say that he developed those muscles by taking the easy way, or the hard way?

Quintus: Why, heard just the other day that Discobolus— that's his name—spends a couple of hours every day just chinning himself.

Libentia: I can believe it, for his arms fairly bulge with muscle.

Elanchius: Indeed his arms look powerful, Libentia. But would they ever have attained their unusual development without rigorous training? Clearly, since he desired to have strong arms, the hard way was better than the easy way.

Quintus: Get you, Elanchius. If Discobolus wants to develop his muscles, he's got to work at it. Pretty hard work, too. So hard work was good for him.

Libentia: And, Quintus, if a student develops his mind by reading difficult books, the hard work required is likewise "good" for him. The difficulty of great books, to which Vulpius objected, may not then really be a reason why they should not be given to students to read, but rather an additional reason why they *should* be given to them!

Elanchius: Precisely. Still, let us not permit our praise of this "good" to obscure our greater purpose. We would not place a certain book before a student merely because it was difficult. The exercising of the mind is a function of literature and as such is a good. But it is nevertheless secondary. None of us, I believe, would place the exercising of the mind, as an end, above what we have determined to be the highest end—the humanizing effect of literature.

Vulpius: But you are unrealistic, all of you. You have not cited a single statistic to support your contentions. Your "great books" are definitely not adapted to contemporary adolescent reading levels.

Elanchius: All of us agree, Vulpius, that ways must be found to overcome the difficulties if great books are to do what they, perhaps better than anything else the world has to offer, can do for their readers. If we genuinely believe in the potentiality of literature, we must find the way—not merely to overcome these difficulties, but to use them to advantage.

Libentia: I know of some teachers who have abandoned literature as a study for all but the more gifted children. Finding it difficult to teach to the others, they have blamed literature for their lack of success. They should have charged it to the inadequacy of their own understanding and approach. I have already confessed my own sense of inadequacy. I hope, therefore, that before we end our conversations we shall consider how the difficulties may be overcome—and for *all* my students.

Elanchius: We shall help you find the way, Libentia, because it must be found! But first we must consider Vulpius' remaining objections. Your second, as I recall, Vulpius, is that great books do not appeal to the interests of students.

Vulpius: Definitely. A large quantity of professional research tends to demonstrate the validity of this. Your great books were written, obviously, by authors unaware of the scientific evidence as to modern youth interests. When the materials selected for reading pre-date the learner, the curriculum is likely to be constructed without regard to the bi-polar continuum concept and not to pattern properly for current usefulness. Reading material selection must consider immediate, special, and individually differing interests of the individual youths who are to experience the reading materials selected and to whom, therefore, the selection process must be adjusted.

Empiricus: You lay great stress on differences, Vulpius.

Vulpius: Definitely. Professional research demonstrates that there are many differences between individuals, and therefore these differences are the most important factors to consider.

Empiricus: And how do interests differ among students?

Vulpius: They differ in different ways, a large number of which have been carefully compiled. There are differences in the interests of boys and girls, those as between one community and another and among social classes and economic groups, and of course those as to levels of maturity and kinds of interests.

Empiricus: Is it impossible to generalize about interests, Vulpius, other than to say that people differ in them?

Vulpius: The most important factor to be utilized in sound curriculum planning is the fact that the interests of individual learners pattern differently. However, school curriculum construction specialists have succeeded in determining general broad interest areas functioning at different levels. For example, children from eleven to fourteen tend to have interests centering around sports, animals, and one another, especially as to their peer-groups, hobbies, real-life stories, adventure, and mystery. I cannot say too often that boy-learners differ from girl-learners, and this fundamental difference is basic both in curriculum development and extracurricular activities. On the other hand, youths of fourteen to eighteen are interested in different ways of life, advances in science, problems, striving for personal acceptance, improving and utilizing their individual tastes, achieving manners and personalities approved by society, and developing new and different interests.

Empiricus: An imposing list of differences, Vulpius! And it is on the basis of such differences that books are to be chosen?

Vulpius: Definitely. The teacher thus realistically confronts students' real interests, and is therefore able to utilize interesting materials for each individual according to his particular differences both as to his reading level and as to his interests. At the same time she will be achieving the rich opportunities for vital pupil-teacher relations by the shared exploring of the learner's particular interests. A worthwhile classroom situation thereby results.

Pulvius: But does any genuine education result? No wonder I failed to recognize a single title on your list of books chosen according to student interests!

Quintus: You're forgetting something, Pulvius. Vulpius has two more lists. Remember?

Pulvius: No matter. I recognized nothing on them, either.

Elanchius: You and your colleagues have produced a remarkably extensive description of the variety of interests about human beings, Vulpius. And it is clear that you assign great importance to the diversity of students' interests. But will you tell us just why you assign so much importance to it?

Vulpius: As I have pointed out in other connections, it is essentially necessary that those who train the rising generation of today's youth must take a realistic approach to the real nature of the teaching situation as it actually exists. Students are different. This is a verifiable datum. Hence, if we are to make a realistic tabulation of their interests, we must acknowledge the existence of differences in individuals as to interests. Could anything be clearer?

Empiricus: Perhaps, Vulpius.

Elanchius: If I understand you, Vulpius, you are saying that individual interests are important as a basis for selecting books because these interests exist. And do you believe that all interests of students are equally important? Or are some more important than others?

Vulpius: Why, it is possibly true that from an authoritarian point of view some interests may be considered more important than others; for example, that an interest in making personal adjustments to social situations is more important than an interest in developing hobbies as leisure-time activities. But we must not forget that the basis of education rests upon the ultimate necessity of providing for the individual youth as to his differentiating characteristics. Hence, since certain interests are of major importance to the individual child, the teacher must recognize this sincere sense of their importance and not tend to impose upon the individual his own preconceived concepts as to the relative importance of other interests.

Elanchius: Then you do believe that one interest is as important as another. And do the interests of students remain constant, Vulpius?

Vulpius: Definitely not. The whole area of changing and developing student interests is now being thoroughly researched, and many data are now available to demonstrate adolescent interest mutation and growth.

Empiricus: And is an attempt made to choose books for reading so that they suit students' changing interests?

Vulpius: The most important professional finding for the teacher to utilize as to this aspect of the education process is that reading programs must be adjusted to immediate, felt interests of individual youths.

Pulvius: Then it makes no difference to you whether a book selected is *good*, so long as it feeds the momentary interest of the student?

Vulpius: But, Pulvius, if certain materials directly appeal to the interests of adolescents, they are not just "good," they are the best materials for them.

Pulvius: By all the long-suffering deities!

Empiricus: You have said, Vulpius, that that book is best for a child which appeals to his immediate interest. If, then, the teacher discovers that a child at a given moment is interested in bee-keeping, she should place in his hands a book on that subject?

Vulpius: Definitely.

Empiricus: And this would be the best possible book for that child?

Vulpius: At that time, obviously.

Empiricus: And the best book for a child interested in developing his personality would be a book on that subject?

Quintus: Got a nephew who'll be in Libentia's class next year. Want to get him interested in shoe-making. Like to have him help me in my shop some day. But all he is interested in is twiddling his thumbs. Do you have a book on thumb-twiddling for him, Libentia?

Libentia: I am afraid I haven't Quintus.

Pulvius: Well, don't worry. Vulpius' reading experts can write one before school opens—with its readability measured too!

Vulpius: You are unfair in selecting a trivial interest, Quintus.

Pulvius: Ha!

Empiricus: How can you say that any interest is trivial, Vulpius? You have implied that all interests of children are equally important. If, as you are now saying, some are trivial, then it follows that others are of greater importance. And among these must be some of the greatest importance. If you object that some interests are too trivial for the teacher to nourish, does it not follow that those which stand at the opposite extreme are the ones most desirable for her to nourish?

Pulvius: Well said.

Elanchius: When you speak of important interests, Empiricus, do you have any particular ones in mind?

Empiricus: Perhaps you will not all agree with my notion of what is important, but I believe that those interests are greatest which hold the minds, not of particular individuals at particular moments only, but, in one form or another, of all men at all times.

Elanchius: And does it follow that the interests of greatest importance are the ones which the teacher ought most to nourish?

Empiricus: It does. Because the time given the teacher to affect the student is limited, she has none to waste on trivial interests, as Vulpius himself has implied—or even on those of secondary importance.

Elanchius: Then it follows that she should choose books which appeal to the most important interests?

Empiricus: Precisely.

Elanchius: Well, then. A moment ago you spoke of important interests as those which appeal to all men at all times. Will you specify some of these for us?

Empiricus: Above all, man is interested in understanding his own nature—his origin, his being, his purpose and destiny. He is also interested in the nature of his universe. And he is deeply interested in the questions of right and wrong, of good and evil, of appearance and reality.

Elanchius: Surely none of us would dispute your assertion, Empiricus, that these are matters of deep concern to mankind. Then the books most proper for a teacher to choose are those which hold up these matters to the light?

Empiricus: That would follow.

Elanchius: And the best books to choose will be those which examine them with honesty?

Empiricus: Indeed.

Elanchius: And since these books are to be read by young students, is honesty enough?

Empiricus: I should say that they should also be as pleasing as possible.

Elanchius: And when you come upon such books, what do you call them?

Empiricus: Why, I would call them great books, Elanchius.

Pulvius: Excellent, gentlemen! The wheel has come full circle. We have reached once more the only proper—indeed, the inevitable answer.

Vulpius: You've moved in a circle, all right, and got your "great books" back in again. But you have ignored the realities of individual differences as to student interests. Moreover, your assertion, Empiricus, that such things as man's own nature, problems of good and evil, and et cetera are the most important interests is contradicted by the findings of researchers who have explored the real interests of adolescent youths by utilizing the latest techniques of factorial analysis.

Elanchius: Let us take your newest charges in order, Vulpius. You say we have ignored the fact that the interests of students vary. But have we really done so? Is it not rather that you and Empiricus have been talking about interests of two quite different orders?

Vulpius: Definitely. Mine are realistic and his are visionary.

Elanchius: Those were scarcely the orders I had in mind, Vulpius. The interests Empiricus has mentioned are no less real. The interests which you have listed are immediate and subject to change, as you have stated; those named by Empiricus are permanent and changeless. Yours arise from personal predilection; his, from the nature which, as human beings, all of us inevitably share. The effect of yours is to differentiate person from person; the effect of his is to bind men together in their common humanity.

Vulpius: Are you inferring that such interests as I have named are unimportant and should not be utilized by the teacher?

Elanchius: I do not deny the importance of either that order of interests with which you are primarily concerned or that which Empiricus has distinguished. Our question should be, whether these orders are equally appropriate matters of concern *to the teacher of literature.*

Libentia: I have struggled with just that question, Elanchius. But how is it to be answered?

Elanchius: Libentia, do you recall that we distinguished, not long ago, three kinds of education?

Libentia: Yes. We spoke of education for doing, for knowing, and for being.

Elanchius: And where did we place the study of literature?

Libentia: Why, in the third kind. And it was therefore that we found great books to be the most proper objects for study, since they have most power to educate man's common humanity.

Empiricus: Then you have found the answer to Elanchius' question, whether the two orders of interests are both proper concerns of the teacher of literature.

Libentia: Why, since her purpose is to affect the reader's essential humanity, she must be most concerned with those interests which are permanent and are common to all men.

Pulvius: Bravo! The wheel has come full circle again! We have already said that the books which treat those interests honestly and pleasingly are great books. So obviously, Libentia, if it is your proper responsibility to nourish the common and permanent interests of men, you are led inevitably to choose great books.

Vulpius: But you have completely ignored my second charge. I repeat that you are unrealistic if you think that these are the real interests of adolescent youth! You talk about high-sounding matters, but can you demonstrate that youths are really interested in them?

Elanchius: It will not be easy to do so here and now, but perhaps a kind of demonstration is possible. Quintus, do you know any of those couples passing before us on the market place?

Quintus: Let me see. Ought to know plenty of 'em. Yeh, that couple over there—the ones with the little kid. Customers of mine.

Elanchius: Will you ask them to come here for a moment?

Quintus: Get 'em right away.

Pulvius: Elanchius, what are you up to now, sending Quintus hustling off after those people?

Elanchius: Perhaps nothing will come of it, but then it is just possible my purpose will appear. Ah! here they are.

Quintus: Folks, meet the Vexaparius family. Told 'em you wanted to talk to 'em for a little bit.

Elanchius: Friends, good evening. And you, my very young friend there, what is your name?

Vexaparia: Go on, Tarbus Minimius, speak to the nice gentleman!

Quintus: Doesn't seem to want to talk at all.

Vexaparia: He's a shy one with strangers all right. But at home he chatters all day long.

Libentia: Little chatterbox, are you, Tarbus Minimius? And what do you talk about?

Quintus: Cat's still got his tongue.

Vexaparia: Why, he chatters about everything under the sun! And questions! He asks more questions in a day than I could answer in a week—even if I knew the answers.

Elanchius: So you ask your mother questions, do you? All of us here, madam, are interested in children and their questions. In fact, that is why we asked you to join us just now. Would you mind telling us what some of the questions are?

Vexaparia: Oh, at first, when he was younger, he wanted to know the names of things. Later he wanted to know everything there was to know about them. But now mainly what he asks is just why? why? why? all day long—about everything he sees and can think of. Why does a fly have wings? Why do people go off to work in the morning? Why is the moon round? Why does he belong to our family and not to our neighbors? There is no end to his questions.

Elanchius: I can well believe you, madam. Can you recall any question that you found particularly difficult to answer?

Vexaparia: Oh, that's the kind he asks most often! Let me think a moment.

Vexaparius: How about the one he asked you yesterday, when you were working in the garden?

Vexaparia: In the garden? Oh, yes. He was trying to help me weed the garden, and a nettle pricked his finger. After I had destroyed the nettle and soothed him, he asked me, "Mother, why are there nettles in the world?"

Quintus: That's a stopper, all right!

Libentia: Your son seems to have found something interesting out there in the darkness, Vexaparia. He is staring intently in the direction of those trees. Ah! He is listening to that nightingale's song.

Vexaparia: We must say good night now. Come along, Tarbus Minimius. It's past your bedtime.

Quintus: Still hasn't ever said a word, has he?

Tarbus Minimius: Mother, does that bird always sing that same song?*

Vexaparius: Come along, son. Good evening, friends.

Elanchius: Good evening, and thank you.

Pulvius: Well, Vulpius, how did you like the demonstration?

---

* " . . . the self-same song. . . ."–Keats

Vulpius: Why, this child's questions demonstrate nothing significant. You must remember that we were speaking of adolescent youth interests. That little individual was of pre-school age—not more than five.

Elanchius: Is it possible, Vulpius, that you have not—but no matter!

Libentia: I understand you, Elanchius.

Pulvius: What, Vulpius! Are you now saying that the five-year-old is more interested in the great human questions than are older children?

Vulpius: Why, older children find other interests, which are more important to them and more immediate. These tend to replace mere childish wonder, particularly as they approach puberty. Then the whole new world of adolescence begins to open out, and they tend to be chiefly concerned with orienting themselves to their new interests.

Pulvius: What! Do you dismiss as mere wonder such interests as this child's questions evinced? I should think one ought rather to regard them as the beginnings of intellectual curiosity. It is thus that the higher nature of man reveals itself.

Empiricus: I agree with you, Pulvius. It seems a great pity that curiosity of this order should suffer attrition. I am distressed by your assertion, Vulpius, that it does so.

Elanchius: I can see, Empiricus, why you, as one whose studies depend so vitally upon intellectual curiosity, are so deeply concerned. Let us therefore try to get to the bottom of the matter.

Empiricus: You said, Vulpius, that the interests you earlier enumerated replace the questions which seemed so naturally to come to this child. Do you mean, when you say replace, that the earlier interests disappear and therefore are no longer matters of real concern to the older child? If so, let us ask what this means. Have the former interests withered and died? Or do they remain, but become obscured by the welter of immediate interests you have named? Or are these interests, which *seem* new, no more than the external manifestations of greater questions that continue to underlie them?

Vulpius: I can only reassert again that the teacher must take the child where she finds him. The realities of the classroom situation must be the dominant factor. And the reality is that, whatever may have brought about the shift in interests, the earlier ones are gone.

Empiricus: And do you think it desirable that they have been allowed to go?

Vulpius: Desirable or not, they are gone. We in the profession are not visionaries but realists. We are not concerned with what ought or ought not to be, but with what is.

Elanchius: Can you be positive that the earlier interests are not merely obscured?

Vulpius: Definitely. Normative and ideographic interest inventories as to pupil personnel so demonstrate.

Elanchius: Quintus, will you observe that tree, off to the left?

Quintus: Looking right straight at it.

Elanchius: And with what is it covered?

Quintus: Why, leaves, of course. Anybody can see that.

Elanchius: And can you perceive nothing but leaves?

Quintus: All there is to see.

Elanchius: Then you can see no trunk?

Quintus: No.

Elanchius: And would you say, therefore, that this tree *has* no trunk?

Quintus: Course not! No one but a fool'd say that.

Pulvius: Ha, ha! But Vulpius said that!

Quintus: He did? Didn't hear him.

Empiricus: In a sense he did. Vulpius, you have said that the best educational practices are based on studies of adolescent interests—by which, it is clear, you mean new and immediate interests. Now, if the teacher is concerned with these, is she not assuming—to use Elanchius' analogy—that a tree has no trunk?

Pulvius: All your researchers have been doing, Vulpius, is counting the leaves on the tree.

Libentia: It is clear, Elanchius, that as a teacher of literature I must not be misled by externals—that I must reach the underlying interests of my students.

Elanchius: Indeed you must, Libentia. Even when these are not apparent, we cannot assume that they do not exist.

Pulvius: And, Libentia, the nature of such underlying interests is precisely in accord with the nature of great books.

Empiricus: We have been speaking of students' interests for some time. And no matter from which direction we approached the problem, our answer has inevitably—and rightly I should say—been the same, that the worthiest interests can best be nourished by the study of great books.

Quintus: Noticed that too, Empiricus.

Vulpius: Naturally. That is because not one of you are realistic.

Elanchius: Well, Vulpius. Let us see if we can deal with your third objection in a way that will be more pleasing to you. Will you restate it for us?

Vulpius: Frankly, I don't expect you to be any more realistic in dealing with it than you were in speaking of student reading levels and interests. My objection is simply this, that your "great books" are definitely not suited to the needs of present-day readers.

Elanchius: And when you speak of their needs, do you mean something quite different from students' interests?

Vulpius: Definitely. There is a large body of need studies and I have already said that there is a large body of interest studies I referred to earlier. This demonstrates that there has been a successful differentiation between needs and interests. Moreover, you will recall that the book lists based on needs and interests, respectively, which I showed you earlier, contain titles which do not overlap but specifically suit the nature of the two categories.

Elanchius: Well, then. Will you enumerate the needs of students which you believe the study of literature serves?

Vulpius: First it must be kept in mind that needs are different, for students themselves are different, and these differences obviously extend to their individual needs.

Empiricus: How do these needs differ? Does the research you mentioned provide a basis for classifying them?

Vulpius: Indeed it does. Individual needs differ as to age, sex, ability, and individual interests. Group needs differ as to family, community, ethnic, socio-economic, national, and religious affiliations of pupil personnel. Such need differences are demonstrated through sociometric tabulation forms.

Empiricus: You have evidently been diligent in classifying needs. But is the teacher of literature to build her program upon these differences?

Vulpius: Definitely. The realistic teacher motivates successful learning responses by recognizing student felt needs.

Empiricus: And what are these needs?

Vulpius: There are first of all the general education needs, such as the need to learn and to grow; the need to achieve skills in group action processes; the need to maintain democratic relations in family and other group situations; the need to participate in leisure-time activities; the need to explore high interest-content materials; the need to work out personal adjustments within peer-groups; the need to utilize effective behavior patterns; the need to—

Pulvius: I feel a great need to—to—

Quintus: What's the matter, Pulvius? You seem to be gagging.

Pulvius: Let it pass, Quintus.

Empiricus: You have called these the general educational needs, Vulpius. Are there other kinds?

Vulpius: There are, of course, the specific reading needs of individuals, including both felt and developmental needs. There have been more than two hundred careful studies of these. The consensus of findings recognizes such needs as the need to identify, to attain a sense of belongingness and security, of loving and being loved, the need to achieve, the need to participate in sharing experiences through reading, the need to desire to learn to read, the need to think and feel as a reader, the need to experience work-type materials, the need to achieve desirable responses to group processes through reading experiences.

Empiricus: And are there others?

Vulpius: These are merely some of the felt needs. There are also the developmental needs. These have been classified by factorial analysis of growth phases. They include the need for vocabulary building, the need to develop word recognition, the need to develop functional reading abilities, the need for ophthalmic improvements in the reading skills, the need to develop self-diagnostic evaluation patterns for appraising personal progress in reading. And besides these—

Pulvius: By all the impatient deities!

Empiricus: I believe you have listed enough to indicate both their nature and your industry in anatomizing the subject of needs. And now will you explain how these needs were determined?

Vulpius: Why, empirically, Empiricus. By longitudinal studies, basically, designed to elicit from individual learners an expression of their needs.

Empiricus: You have answered my questions unstintingly, Vulpius. And now, will you restate the relationship of what you have been saying about needs to the problem of selecting books for children to read?

Vulpius: Reading materials should be selected which are adapted to these empirically tabulated needs.

Pulvius: To all of them?

Vulpius: As I said, I have named only a minimal list of the most obvious needs.

Libentia: But can you mean that each book the teacher chooses must be adapted to all of these needs, or is there to be a separate book to meet each need?

Pulvius: And a separate book to meet each separate need of each individual child, don't forget, Libentia!

Empiricus: As a scientist, Vulpius, I would appreciate some illustrations of how particular books and particular needs are matched.

Quintus: Yeh! Ought to be interesting.

Vulpius: Let's first take the case of an older boy having symptoms of loneliness who needs the satisfaction of achieving personal group status. That youth could be given such materials as Peevish's "Short Doublets," Cronius' "Purple Months," Gallus' "Spear of Canina," or Janus' "North Knife."*

Quintus: Know any of these books, Pulvius?

---

* Because the authors and titles of the originals are no longer known, others have been substituted which may be more readily recognized.

Pulvius: Not one.

Vulpius: Or, if you have a pre-adolescent female student whose home environment has caused her to develop abnormally aggressive tendencies due to her socio-economic superiority over her peer-group, you would tend to select books that would aid her to contact in a realistic manner the trials of underprivileged groups. Such a book is Westias' "The Tuffets." Or the basic insecurity of a child of parents who are geographically unstable due to their occupation as migratory artisans might find therapeutic release through such reading material as Janus' "Green Tule."

Libentia: If the teacher finds the exact book to fit such specific needs, Vulpius, will the reading experience correct the child's fault?

Vulpius: Not necessarily. But the teacher can utilize additional experiences of other kinds to achieve the desired outcomes.

Pulvius: Although these may not be books?

Vulpius: Of course.

Empiricus: In such instances might books become only an incidental part of the experience?

Vulpius: Definitely. And for the slow learner perhaps disregarded altogether in favor of a more vital activity.

Pulvius: What do you do if, even in your remarkable list of books, you find none which precisely fits the needs of a particular student?

Vulpius: Fortunately, such a deficiency has been anticipated. Where it is determined that no book exists to exactly fulfill a felt need, specialists in adolescent reading have written suitable materials. I have myself written six or seven.

Pulvius: Angels and ministers of grace defend us!

Elanchius: There are undoubtedly questions which some of us would like to ask Vulpius about the implications of his remarks on students' needs.

Quintus: Seems to me several things need to be cleared up. Anyway, I didn't understand all he said. But you know how to ask the right questions, Elanchius. Why don't you do it?

Elanchius: Well, then. Let me begin by asking three questions. It is evident, Vulpius, that you think it most desirable to provide books which meet the particular needs of the individual child. Does it follow that you would find it undesirable to use the same books with all the students in one of Libentia's classes, for example?

Vulpius: Definitely. Ideally, since no two children are identical, no two would read the same book. Of course, there are many practical difficulties, but the teacher must approach this ideal as nearly as she can.

Pulvius: Her difficulties would no doubt be eased had she several sets of identical twins among her students!

Elanchius: Again, from what you have said about needs, Vulpius, I assume that you would not advocate using the same book or group of books with students of different communities. Am I correct?

Vulpius: Definitely. Just as no two children are identical, no two communities are identical, for each has its own special interests and socio-economic patterns. The progressive teacher will reflect these differences in her reading program.

Elanchius: We must consider this point at greater length, I believe. But before we do so, let me ask my third question. Does it also follow that you find it undesirable and unnecessary to provide the same book or group of books to the corresponding classes of students in different years, or decades, or generations?

Vulpius: Definitely. The realistic teacher will adjust the reading materials to the changing needs of successive years, and the reading program will thus be progressive and move along with the students.

Pulvius: Progressive! Progress requires a sequence of well-considered steps leading from a known point to an end that can be at least partly determined. But what you have described, Vulpius, is not progress but sheer chaos, for it pursues the merely casual and spasmodic.

Vulpius: Oh, come out of your tower, Pulvius. Surely you do not mean to infer that times have not tended to change?

Pulvius: Of course times change. No one denies that. But you are being absurd by insisting that because times change the reading list must be changed!

Quintus: Well, you fellows are at it again.

Elanchius: Empiricus, you are much concerned with the changing times. Will you give us your opinion?

Empiricus: It is apparent that Vulpius values, above all, individual differences and change. No one, of course, denies that there are differences among students, among communities, and among successive decades or generations. But having admitted their existence, have we said anything which is relevant to our purpose? As Vulpius has said, children differ in age, sex, and capacity. We all know that our community here, which is surrounded by extensive vineyards, is quite different in its economic make-up from the olive-growing neighborhood across the river. We also know that those people walking there about the market place have immediate needs which are somewhat different from those which their parents and grandparents felt. These are the differences which, I suppose, Vulpius regards as the "realities" of life.

Elanchius: Thank you. And now, why do you ask whether such matters are relevant to our purpose?

Empiricus: I suggest that Vulpius is speaking of an order of affairs that is irrelevant to the study of literature. We have frequently asserted that the highest function of literature is to humanize the reader. Do we educate his essential humanity by concentrating so single-mindedly upon his differences from his neighbor, or upon those which distinguish him from his ancestors? The books which Vulpius would give the students emphasize these differences—as they perforce must do, for they are adapted specifically to individual—and hence different—needs. But is this quality not a mark of their shortcoming? Should not the books upon which the student spends his time be those which do precisely the opposite—which speak to him not as a unique individual unlike all others, not as a member of a certain geographic region and of a certain temporal unit, but as a human being who shares with all others regardless of time and place those essential qualities which make him a human being? As I have said, I am not a literary man; but the conclusion that I have tried to state is the only one that follows logically from what we have said.

Elanchius: You have drawn the issue clearly, Empiricus. You have reasserted that literature is a part of that education whose purpose is the enhancement of the student's essential humanity—the one quality which he shares with all others. Vulpius, on the other hand, places literature in that kind of education which has as its purpose the training of the unique individual occupying a particular geographical position at a definite moment in time. Have not all the disagreements voiced here ultimately arisen from this basic disagreement about the function of literature?

Vulpius: My thinking is that the disagreement goes even further, for we seem to be talking about different aspects of the problem. You and Empiricus have made high claims for literature, and Pulvius has frequently seconded you by citing his "great books." This all may sound charming, but it fails to contact the realities at many points. In the last analysis, no education program, in reading or any other subject, will tend to succeed unless it confronts the realities of differentiation among students, among differing communities and groups, and at different times.

Empiricus: You have made this charge often, Vulpius, each time asserting that education not predicated upon individual difference is "unrealistic." Since this is apparently your severest condemnation, it seems only fair to ask you precisely what you mean by "unrealistic." For example, what do you mean when you say that the teacher must be realistic in meeting the needs of her students?

Vulpius: Why, obviously, that program of reading materials is realistic that fulfills such needs as I have listed.

Elanchius: Is his answer acceptable to you, Empiricus?

Empiricus: By no means. For his list of needs omits the one that is most important and that the study of literature can most appropriately serve—the need of humanization. Therefore, it follows that only a program which is designed to serve *this* need can be said to be "realistic."

Pulvius: Bravo, Empiricus! What it comes to, Vulpius, is this. Your misguided trust in the importance of superficial differences in students' interests and needs has led you to select what you aptly call "reading materials" of such abominable character that they cannot conceivably contain an atom of literary value.

Elanchius: Or humanizing force.

Pulvius: Precisely. "The Tuffets"—bah!

Quintus: What do you say now, Vulpius?

Vulpius: Say what you will about interests and needs. At best your "great books" meet only one of the least vital needs of only one segment of the total school population—the need of the select few who continue their education and therefore need to be prepared for the ivory tower kind of study you insist on, Pulvius. But even if it met all the needs of these few, for all the others it is inadequate, impractical, and undesirable—and this is not an age in which we can afford to ignore the masses. Any realistic program must remember all these.

Elanchius: Indeed, Vulpius, *especially* these.

Libentia: Especially these! You have hit upon my gravest problem as a teacher, Elanchius. To which students *must* I teach literature? Especially those who will go on to Pulvius, or especially those who will not?

Elanchius: Your question is a profound one, which I believe we cannot hope to answer this evening. The market place is now almost deserted and the moon is hidden by the tree in which little Tarbus Minimius heard the nightingale sing. Let us adjourn, then, until tomorrow.

Empiricus: And, since we are to be concerned with Libentia's question, should we not meet once more where many people congregate?

Quintus: Say! I've got it. Tomorrow's the first day of the big games. Let's meet at the stadium right by the entrance. There'll be lots of people there.

Elanchius: Good, Quintus. If it is agreeable to everyone, let us meet where Quintus suggests. And now shall we say good night?

Empiricus: The cobbled street is treacherous by moonlight, Libentia. Let me take your arm.

And Especially These

Persons of the Dialogue

LIBENTIA MAGISTRA

PULVIUS GRAMMATICUS   VULPIUS MATERIES

J. QUINTUS   EMPIRICUS MARTIALIS

ELANCHIUS

Scene: The entrance to the stadium

Empiricus: Stand back a little from the gateway, Libentia. The crowd rushing in to the games will trample you!

Libentia: Thank you, Empiricus. They *are* impatient.

Empiricus: Pulvius! Here we are by the bench.

Pulvius: Ah! Good morning, Libentia and gentlemen. I am delighted to have found the right place at last. I had no idea where to look for the stadium, but the crowds, I see, have led me to it.

Vulpius: Congratulations, Pulvius.

Quintus: Ho, ho! You fellows already sniping at each other again.

Libentia: Evidently the night's rest merely interrupted their disagreement of yesterday evening, Quintus. And that disagreement reminded me of my student days. Pulvius and Vulpius were then the main forces in preparing me to teach, but because they pulled in opposite directions I was only confused. If a compromise could be found in their points of view, I would be happy indeed!

Elanchius: The thread of their disagreement has run through all our conversations. Since you have mentioned it, perhaps we should at once attempt to find a basis for compromise. And no topic we have discussed lends itself so well to the purpose as that on which we ended yesterday. Empiricus, you have repeatedly shown that you are a discriminating observer. You can help us now by restating the terms of last evening's disagreement.

Quintus: Go ahead, Empiricus. Line 'em up for us.

Empiricus: Very well. Pulvius objected vigorously that Vulpius, in his selection of books, placed emphasis only upon individual reading levels, interests, and needs and paid no attention to literary quality. This kind of reading, he insisted, meant inadequate preparation for those students who later come up to his classes. Have I represented you fairly, Pulvius?

Pulvius: Exactly.

Empiricus: To this objection Vulpius replied that at best a program of reading such as Pulvius demanded would meet the needs of only the small group who would later become his own students, and that for all the rest it would be inadequate, impractical, and undesirable. Have I summarized your argument fairly, Vulpius?

Vulpius: An accurate digest of my thinking.

Elanchius: Excellent, Empiricus. And now that the opposing points of view are before us, let us find whether they can be reconciled.

Quintus: Easy enough. Let Pulvius' stuff be used on the students that'll go on to his classes and Vulpius' on the big bunch that'll quit and go to work.

Vulpius: Quintus, you have identified a programming plan that is already widely utilized. Libentia will support this assertion, for great progress has been made in her school toward total utilization of what is termed homogeneous grouping by we in the profession.

Empiricus: An interesting term, Vulpius. Will you tell us precisely what is meant by it?

Vulpius: Gladly. Homogeneous grouping is a realistic concept based upon recognition of the need to provide optimal classroom learning situations and worthwhile pupil-teacher environments for *all* youths. Individual differences as to needs and capacities are utilized as the differentiating factors in determining desirable groupings. Thus, those whose future objectives will involve scholarly-type readings are allowed to experience those kinds of materials. On the other hand, by far the greater percentage of the pupil personnel, whose education will be terminated and who will soon enter into real-life situations, are given work-type materials to equip them to meet the practical needs of these situations.

Empiricus: Then homogeneous grouping is a practice of segregating students according to their future plans?

Vulpius: First let me remind you that grouping is now considered the proper term. Of course, what I have said by no means exhausts the subject. Homogeneous grouping embraces many concepts besides vocational aims and objectives. To instance an example, classes are often pre-structured into several groups— three is considered minimal—in order to as fully as possible accommodate individual differences as to, for example, reading speed and comprehension, leadership abilities, and interest differences.

Empiricus: Then homogeneous grouping aims to bring students together who have comparable abilities, needs, or interests. Clearly, this is a highly complex and delicate undertaking, considering the complexity of human beings.

Vulpius: There are numerous difficulties, to be sure, but none that cannot be overcome by sufficient data. Our researchers are always accumulating more.

Empiricus: Are your methods precise enough to make it unlikely that a student will be misplaced?

Vulpius: Our methods have achieved high reliability. Occasionally an individual may be misplaced, but a sufficient degree of group arrangement flexibility enables adjustments to be made when they are considered worthwhile.

Quintus: But see here, Vulpius. Looks like some of those groups might be more—uh, uh—

Libentia: More elite than others, Quintus?

Quintus: Yeh. Don't some parents get sore when their kids get put with a bunch that's not as good as others?

Vulpius: This reaction is the reason why some professional thinking tends to doubt that grouping should be utilized. However, the pupil personnel soon find that they can achieve success in their homogeneous groups, where they can win peer acceptance and approval and are removed from competitive situations involving more gifted individuals.

Empiricus: Then except for occasional parental disapproval, you are aware of no objection significant enough to warrant abandoning the practice?

Vulpius: None that cannot be effectively minimized in the hands of experts who are professionally concerned to prove its practicability.

Elanchius: Vulpius has now defined homogeneous grouping, explained how it operates, and asserted that it is practical. Before we ask Pulvius whether he accepts this practice as a basis of compromise, are there other questions which we should put to Vulpius?

Quintus: Well, I want to make sure I'm straight on it. Let's suppose one of Pulvius' sons goes to Libentia's school. Now anybody'd know Pulvius' boy'll want to go on and be a scholar, or something. Vulpius, just how'd you go about grouping young Pulvius?

Vulpius: Why, evaluative instruments administered by counseling and guidance experts will be utilized to determine whether he has the capabilities for academic-type work. He will then be placed in a peer group having similar interests and abilities. This group will utilize academic-type materials.

Quintus: Suppose on the other hand that one of my boys is in Libentia's school—is, in fact. He knows he's got to go to work in the shop soon as he gets out of school. What'll your system do with him?

Vulpius: Why, it can do much more for him than it can for Pulvius' son, because his program is *entirely* in the hands of our experts, who are free to devise what they determine is most adapted to his interests and needs. Your son, Quintus, will have all the advantages of a curriculum developed by professionals.

Empiricus: Then, presumably, his reading will consist of the books that your specialists have chosen?

Vulpius: Definitely. Freeing the non-academic learner group from the demands imposed by academicians has enabled our reading specialists to utilize scientifically compiled reading-material lists exclusively.

Pulvius: Those miserable lists again!

Empiricus: Why, Pulvius, I thought perhaps we were reaching an agreement between you and Vulpius. Yet you seem displeased. Are you, then, unwilling to accept this arrangement?

Pulvius: To speak bluntly, I am willing to accept *any* plan so long as the students who come to me have a prior acquaintance with literary documents! As for all the others, whom I trust never to see in my classes, I could wish a better diet than Vulpius will serve—but I shall not insist that my view prevail. If Vulpius and his "experts" think their synthetic trash is best for all these, let them have it!

Empiricus: Then, in fact, you do accept Vulpius' plan of grouping students?

Pulvius: I do.

Empiricus: And, Vulpius, since you have described the plan with obvious enthusiasm, I assume that you have no reservations about it?

Vulpius: Research findings make it impossible to concede that Pulvius' reading material selections are best adapted even for the students who will go on to him. However, we in the profession know that at present the schools must yield to some academic dictation, irregardless of how unrealistic it is. Moreover, since we thus gain unchallenged control of the bulk of the total school population, leaving our specialists free to develop realistic programs for these youths, we feel that this is the most we can hope for at present.

Empiricus: I take this to mean that you hold no serious reservations?

Vulpius: Definitely not.

Empiricus: Then a workable compromise between you has been found in homogeneous grouping. Though I have questions concerning the wisdom of this compromise, I recognize Pulvius as a distinguished literary scholar and Vulpius as a spokesman for his profession. It would seem inappropriate for an outsider to intrude his private doubts into an agreement of experts. I shall therefore refrain from asking my questions.

Quintus: Hey, Empiricus, I'll have to hand it to you! You got these fellows to see eye to eye and made everybody happy. Pulvius' bunch will get what Pulvius wants them to have, and the big bunch will get what Vulpius says they need. This'll really fix things up good, hey, Libentia?

Libentia: I suppose, Quintus. But—

Quintus: Glad Pulvius and Vulpius got together, aren't you?

Libentia: I have always hoped they would.

Quintus: Fine! Fine! Everything's patched up, then. Didn't think we'd get done so quick. Tell you what—let's celebrate by taking the rest of the day off. All go in here and watch the games.

Elanchius: Wait a little, Quintus!

Quintus: What's that? Hey, Elanchius! Been so long since you said anything I'd forgot you were here. Got something on your mind? Got Pulvius and Vulpius together, didn't we?

Elanchius: True, and doubtless their compromise is a workable one—for indeed, their discussion has been almost exclusively concerned with the workability of Vulpius' proposal for classifying students. But before we accept this solution as final, should we not ask something other than whether it is workable?

Quintus: Don't see what. If it works, it works.

Libentia: I'm sure you don't really mean that, Quintus. Clearly, we must also ask whether it is desirable.

Quintus: Looks like it's desirable if it just gets Pulvius and Vulpius together. But all right—how do we go about showing that it's desirable?

Elanchius: It may be, Quintus, that we shall *not* demonstrate that homogeneous grouping of the kind agreed on by Pulvius and Vulpius is desirable. We may even conclude that it is quite undesirable!

Vulpius: It would not surprise me if your thinking did terminate in some such ridiculous opinion, which you will maintain in spite of empirical evidence.

Quintus: Well, if we've got to find out whether this grouping business ought to be done or not, let's get at it. What do we do, Elanchius?

Elanchius: Must we not begin by asking how desirability is to be determined in this case?

Libentia: That means that we need some basis for judgment.

Elanchius: And have we established one?

Empiricus: Since we are to judge the desirability of a system of grouping students in a program of reading, clearly we must consider what we have concluded to be the first purpose of the study of literature.

Elanchius: Then our question is not merely the general one, "Is homogeneous grouping of students desirable?" but the specific one, "Will such grouping further the highest purpose of the study of literature?"

Quintus: That ought to get us somewhere.

Libentia: It should, Quintus. Elanchius' phrasing reminds us again that *decisions about the manner in which literature is read and about the students who are to read it must be made in the light of the most important reason for reading it!*

Quintus: Ho! Back to that antecedent question business again!

Elanchius: You remember the term, Quintus. Do you also remember our answer?

Quintus: Be stupid if I forgot it already. Said it was to humanize 'em.

Pulvius: Bravo, Quintus!

Quintus: All right, but what's the next answer? Will this homogeneous business help books to humanize 'em, or won't it?

Elanchius: When you say "'em," Quintus, which group of students do you mean—Pulvius' or Vulpius'?

Quintus: Tell you the truth, I never—hey, I think I see what you mean.

Elanchius: Well, then. But wait. Libentia, perhaps you can help us here. Have I not seen you nod to some of the young people passing by us to the games?

Libentia: Why, I have seen nearly all of my students this morning! Ah, there goes another one now—shouldering his way past the old couple at the entrance.

Elanchius: Is his present conduct characteristic of him?

Libentia: I am sorry to say that it is. He seems an insensitive, rough, rude boy. He is not one of my most intelligent students, but it is not intelligence that he most lacks.

Elanchius: Do you know anything about his life outside of school?

Libentia: A little. I have visited his home and met his family.

Elanchius: What was your impression?

Libentia: Mainly I noted the absence of books—and for that matter, of anything suggesting cultural interests. I certainly do not mean that there were signs of poverty. His father is an artisan, and the family appeared to possess not only all the necessities but most of the comforts and even many luxuries. At least they looked like luxuries to me! But beyond material things I sensed a great lack. In fact, I felt a kind of emptiness in their lives in spite of their abundant possessions.

Elanchius: You have drawn a vivid picture of a kind of home that all of us recognize. You must have many children in your school whose backgrounds are comparable.

Libentia: Most are like this, I think. Oh, their homes differ widely in many respects, but there is often this common lack, which I feel but cannot fully describe.

Vulpius: Let me commend your general analysis of the actual home environments from which the bulk of the school population comes. What you have said about this individual youth corroborates professional evidence. Obviously, for a typical early adolescent like this, such reading materials as Pulvius would impose on the schools have no suitability or interest appeal whatsoever. Programs of homogeneous grouping recognize that these youths must be provided with reading materials suited to their interests, needs, and levels.

Elanchius: Should we accept your conclusion, Vulpius, before we have considered other students in Libentia's school, some of whom—as you have assured us earlier—differ from this one? Can you identify such a one, Libentia, whose background is known to you?

Pulvius: One moment, Elanchius! I believe that I glimpse my own son in the crowd. Whatever could he be doing here? Can it be that he, too, is going to these games?

Elanchius: Why not call him over, Pulvius? Let us all meet him. And no moment could be more opportune!

Pulvius: Puervius, lad! Over here! I want you to meet some friends of mine.

Puervius: Yes, Father.

Pulvius: Libentia, this is my son Puervius. You will see much of him this fall, when he will be enrolled in one of your classes. Puervius, here are the gentlemen with whom I have been conversing.

Puervius: How do you do.

Elanchius: Are you going to the games, Puervius?

Puervius: Indeed I am, thank you. And I believe they are about to begin.

Elanchius: Then, do not let us detain you.

Puervius: Thank you. I am happy to have met everyone.

Pulvius: Good-bye, son. I shall see you at home this evening.

Quintus: Nice kid you got there, Pulvius.

Empiricus: It seems, Elanchius, that the question you asked of Libentia has been answered in part by the timely arrival of Pulvius' son, whose conduct, like his background, differs so markedly from that of the student whom Libentia pointed out to us.

Quintus: Yeh. Guess you've got plenty of books at your house—hey, Pulvius?

Elanchius: Books certainly, Quintus, and, what is more, a way of life that the presence of books implies.

Libentia: I have several children whose backgrounds are like that of Puervius. None of them, I think, would better exemplify the contrast with which we are concerned.

Vulpius: It is obvious that Pulvius' son should be grouped with youths whose interests and abilities tend to correlate with his. For such a group the reading materials that Pulvius insists upon are utilizable. The background of this youth has pre-conditioned him to experience satisfactions through academic-type readings. Homogeneous grouping enables the structuring of programs adapted to this group.

Elanchius: Evidently, Vulpius, in the contrast between these two boys you find confirmation of your faith in the practice of grouping. But before we conclude this discussion I should like to make absolutely sure that all of us understand your position exactly. Your comments on the rough student who passed by a few moments ago left no reason to question that you would place him with others who would not read literature as we have defined it, but rather such "reading materials" as those on your lists. Will you tell us whether this is in fact your conviction?

Vulpius: Definitely. Only through such grouping can realistic provision be made as to his interests, needs, and abilities.

Elanchius: And on the other hand, you have stated that Pulvius' boy should be placed with others who *would* study literature.

Vulpius: Definitely. These youths are preconditioned by home-life factors to experience such materials.

Elanchius: Thank you, Vulpius, for making these explicit statements. Now that you have done so, let me proceed to—but no, for I see that Empiricus wishes to speak. And from your expression, Empiricus, I judge that you are impatient.

Empiricus: Let me say first, Elanchius, that I have followed your questioning of Vulpius most attentively, and perhaps I have caught its drift. Perhaps I guess why you took pains to have Vulpius' view stated so unequivocally.

Elanchius: It may well be, Empiricus. Will you go on?

Quintus: You fellows look like you've got something up your sleeves. What are you up to?

Empiricus: One moment, Quintus. Vulpius, you are aware that during two periods of my life I have been a soldier. While you were speaking with Elanchius, I was reminded of a problem that once arose, for it was analogous to that involving the two boys whom we have been discussing.

Quintus: Say, this could be exciting!

Pulvius: "The battles, sieges, fortunes I have pass'd . . ."

Quintus: What's that, Pulvius?

Pulvius: Nothing at all, Quintus. Let us hear Empiricus.

Libentia: Shh, Quintus.

Empiricus: During a certain campaign in which our city was engaged, I was compelled to make a decision about which

I should like to ask you, Vulpius. I am sure that all of us will be interested to learn whether, in the same circumstances, you would have made the same one.

Vulpius: Of course you realize that I am not a military man, Empiricus. However, I shall be happy to participate in the experiment if you will provide me with data.

Empiricus: The situation was this. Our forces were disposed in two widely separated outposts at considerable distance from the city itself, upon which both were dependent for supplies. One outpost was situated in extraordinarily rough and hazardous terrain, which made access to it extremely difficult. Moreover, it had been under almost incessant attack for a long period. Indeed, it bore the brunt of the enemy's fury, and the safety not only of the other outpost but ultimately of the very city depended upon its holding firm. The second outpost was easier of access from the city, for there were excellent roads and it was not at the moment under attack; indeed, the likelihood of attack was relatively slight so long as the first outpost held. On the other hand, as I said, should the first fall, the second would soon cease to be tenable.

Quintus: I get you, Empiricus. What happened?

Libentia: Shh.

Empiricus: Why, really nothing at all, Quintus! But eventually there arose the necessity of making a critical decision. Since I was then in charge of a vital part of the operation, the responsibility was mine. It was a question of supplying the outposts with military equipment and provisions from our stores here in the city. We knew that the supplies on hand at the first outpost had fallen to a dangerously low level—in fact, were virtually depleted. On the other hand, since the troops at the second outpost were engaged only in patrol activity, the supplies there were not critically short. It was at this point that an expedition was readied to rush fresh supplies from the city. It was my personal responsibility to determine the destination of these materials. Now, Vulpius, have I described the general situation clearly enough for you to grasp the problem?

Vulpius: Definitely, if all of the factors in the situation have been stated.

Empiricus: Then, will you tell us to which of the two outposts I should have dispatched the expedition with the supplies?

Quintus: You kidding, Empiricus? I was all set for a tough question. That's no problem! Anybody'd—

Empiricus: But let us hear Vulpius' answer.

Vulpius: I am surprised also, Quintus. The answer is absurdly obvious—unless Empiricus has omitted some data or has a trick in mind.

Quintus: How about it, Empiricus—you pulling our leg?

Empiricus: No, gentlemen, nor have I intended to hold back any relevant facts.

Vulpius: Then you should have sent the supplies to the first outpost, of course.

Empiricus: Why?

Vulpius: Obviously it *needed* them most.

Empiricus: But for the second outpost?

Vulpius: Your description indicated that it hardly needed any supplies.

Empiricus: But, Vulpius, have you not forgotten the vast difference in accessibility of the two outposts?

Vulpius: Definitely not. You asserted that the second outpost was readily accessible, whereas the first was situated in rough and hazardous terrain which made access extremely difficult.

Empiricus: Indeed, many said that it was impossible! Then do you still insist that the supplies should have been dispatched to it in spite of the difficulty and the danger?

Vulpius: Definitely. Where the need was so urgent, no difficulty should be allowed to stand in the way.

Empiricus: But, Vulpius, in this case the difficulty was as extreme as you can possibly imagine.

Vulpius: Then obviously means must somehow be found of overcoming it!

Quintus: Come on, Empiricus, tell us what you did. Didn't cut off the supplies from those poor fellows, did you?

Empiricus: Indeed not, Quintus. Nor would I have done so against even greater odds! I did exactly as Vulpius has insisted that I should have done.

Quintus: And did the stuff get through?

Empiricus: Not all. But enough did. Our city still stands!

Libentia: A moving story, Empiricus—and apt!

Quintus: Good yarn all right. But I don't get it. You have some special point?

Elanchius: You may be sure he had, Quintus. Can you make out what it is?

Quintus: Must have something to do with what we've been talking about. Let's see—what was it? Oh yeh—grouping students.

Elanchius: Right. And we were speaking of two particular boys.

Quintus: Yeh, Pulvius' son and Libentia's student—the one that bulled his way through here.

Elanchius: And do you remember in which groups Vulpius insisted they should be placed?

Quintus: Course I do. He was plenty emphatic about it. Said Pulvius' son should go with the group that reads literature and the other fellow with the bunch that reads reading materials.

Pulvius: Ha, ha!

Elanchius: And, Quintus, are you satisfied with this disposition of these boys?

Quintus: Looks clear enough. Hey! You mean Empiricus' story should have changed my mind or something?

Elanchius: Empiricus' story suggested, did it not, that a need can be so urgent that no effort necessary to satisfy it is too great?

Quintus: That's just what Vulpius said.

Elanchius: Well, then. Let us reconsider the case of our two boys. Do you remember, Quintus, *why* Vulpius wished to place the first boy not with the few who study literature, but with those who are given the "reading materials" on his lists?

Quintus: Why, he said books like Pulvius wants wouldn't fit a boy like that one.

Elanchius: And why would they not?

Quintus: Too tough, for one thing. Besides, books like that don't have anything to do with the way he lives. Libentia said he didn't have a book in his house. Wasn't brought up that way.

Elanchius: Now let us think of the other boy for a moment.

Do you remember why Vulpius considered it proper to place Pulvius' son with those who study literature?

Quintus: Well, he said Pulvius' son's background would make him right at home with the books. He's a natural for 'em. Anyway, since he's going to keep going to school, he'll have to know 'em.

Elanchius: Excellent! And now, once more, will you be kind enough to repeat what we have concluded to be the greatest single reason for teaching literature to students?

Quintus: That again! Well, we said it was to humanize 'em.

Elanchius: Now, does that purpose help us decide the case of these two boys?

Quintus: Must be some connection, or you wouldn't bring it up.

Libentia: Which of these homes, Quintus, do you think would be more likely to exercise a humanizing influence on the boy?

Quintus: Well, guess you'd say Pulvius' boy's got those influences all around him. Ought to, with all those books. But according to what you said, the other boy's got none at all. But, hey! Wait a minute! Something's wrong here.

Elanchius: Wrong?

Quintus: Looks like Vulpius' notion of which way to group these boys is just exactly backwards!

Elanchius: Why do you say that?

Quintus: Because it's this rough kid and not Pulvius' son that *needs* humanizing the most!

Elanchius: And therefore, Quintus?

Quintus: He's the one that should read the books that can get to him—humanize him!

Elanchius: And that means great books, since these are the ones with power to humanize?

Quintus: Got to be. Funny the way that worked out, hey? No doubt about it, though. Not a bit.

Vulpius: Oh yes there is, Quintus! You have achieved just the outcome I predicted, Elanchius. Your mere commonsense thinking has resulted in a conclusion that is unsupported by any professional research findings. To utilize Pulvius' so-called classics in this youth's group is unrealistic. Let me give you additional data. This youth of Libentia's by no means represents an extreme example of that type of youth. Today's pupil personnel includes many individuals who have developed much more unacceptable social behavior patterns.

Quintus: Mean those young hoodlums I keep hearing about?

Vulpius: Some of these youths would rap you over the head if they caught you in an alley, Quintus. Look! There's one of them slinking along in the crowd now. He has been pointed out to me before by our counseling and guidance experts as a member of a troublesome gang of youths who beat up other youths and become involved in many other anti-social activities. There are many youths like him, and their number shows a rapid increase in the school population.

Elanchius: Thank you, Vulpius. But in mentioning these facts have you destroyed our argument—or have you in fact *proved* it?

Quintus: Looks to me like he's really proved it. Plain enough these boys need stuff that'll work 'em over from the inside out.

Elanchius: Well said, Quintus. We all know that, as Vulpius has just declared emphatically, there are in school youths who have a spark of savagery in them. One of the aims of civilization is to smother that spark. The school is a principal agency for that purpose—and we have been saying that literature offers the school one of its best means.*

Vulpius: But your thinking is utterly fantastic in proposing that it can be done. Teach your unadapted materials to these youths! Do you really think for a minute that you can teach your classics to a youth like that one slouching there in the leather jacket? Why, the difficulties are insurmountable!

---

* Elanchius' words here parallel exactly those of J. B. Priestley in his observations on one kind of brutalizing force in modern life: "It will be as well if the citizens of tomorrow do not take it for granted that people they dislike should be beaten, pounded, minced. The red-pulp view of life should be discouraged . . . this cruel violence . . . is by no means an essential part of us. No doubt there is in us the germ of it, a spark of savagery, especially in youth. One of the aims of civilization is to smother that spark." *New Statesman and Nation*, 48, (July 24, 1954), 95.

Empiricus: Ah! Can you have forgotten so soon, Vulpius, your own decision on the question of dispatching supplies to the outposts I described?

Quintus: *I* didn't forget it! You said, Vulpius, that where the need is so urgent, *no* difficulty must be allowed to stand in the way. Those are just about your exact words.

Vulpius: But that was different. Professional research findings prove conclusively that the difficulties of utilizing so-called literary classics for most youths are too great to be attempted.

Empiricus: And do you suppose, Vulpius, that the difficulties encountered by my expedition in reaching the endangered outpost were negligible? Men died in carrying out that mission.

Quintus: Yeh, Vulpius. And you yourself said they *had* to get the supplies to that outpost, no matter what!

Libentia: And I must get literature to my students, no matter what! Thank you all, gentlemen. You have made me see that *the humanizing effect of literature is most needed by the very students whom it will be most difficult to reach!* Indeed, the very obviousness of the difficulty is itself the signal of the need! And certainly the students' own sense of their need is an untrustworthy guide.* It is plain that my task as a teacher is to release literature's potentiality for humanizing so that this effect will penetrate *all* my students. It will be easiest, of course, to reach those like Pulvius' son. It will be harder to reach most of the others, and hardest of all to reach those whose need is desperate. But these—*especially these*—are the ones I *must* reach.

Elanchius: Yes, Libentia—all, but especially these. Therefore, if you were forced to separate your students and for some reason were forbidden to teach literature to both groups—those who will go on up to Pulvius and those who will not—*then by all*

---

* Cf. Joel H. Hildebrand, president of the American Chemical Society, in his presidential address, September 12, 1955: "A person whose life might be enriched by developing an appreciation of the fine arts or of the elegance of mathematical reasoning, or who might be a better citizen for some acquaintance with history, can hardly be expected to become aware of these things unless they are brought to his attention. His situation may be clearer . . . if it be recalled that in any gathering the person who most needs a bath is not the one most aware of his need."

means give it to those whom Pulvius will never see, for their need is greater!

Vulpius: But the difficulties! The difficulties!—

Elanchius: —must be overcome, Vulpius. And therefore we should next consider the *means*. But now the crowds have entered the stadium, and the games are underway. Quintus, you earlier expressed a desire to see them, and we have detained you overlong. Shall we part for a time, and each go his chosen way?

Libentia: May we meet again this evening?

Elanchius: If all agree.

Pulvius: I shall be delighted to have you at my house. We can have complete privacy in my study.

Quintus: Yeh. Like to see inside that ivory tower they say you live in.

Vulpius: Definitely. You may observe there some specimens of the dry bones he chews on, too, Quintus.

Elanchius: Come, come, gentlemen!

PART IV

HOW SHOULD LITERATURE BE TAUGHT?

The Arrangements Debated

Persons of the Dialogue

LIBENTIA MAGISTRA

PULVIUS GRAMMATICUS   VULPIUS MATERIES

J. QUINTUS   EMPIRICUS MARTIALIS

ELANCHIUS

Scene: The library of Pulvius

Pulvius: Welcome to my study, Libentia and gentlemen.

Elanchius: Greetings, Pulvius. You were kind to invite us here.

Pulvius: It is my pleasure, Elanchius. Ah, Quintus! Did you enjoy the games?

Quintus: Great sport! Mighty fine bunch of athletes. Ought to have seem 'em yourself, Pulvius.

Pulvius: It was necessary to forego that pleasure, Quintus, in order to complete a little monograph I have been working on. I have spent the interim here among my books.

Quintus: Books! Boy, you've got 'em! Shelves clear to the ceiling on all four sides!

Vulpius: And no windows.

Quintus: Say, how can you ever find the book you want, out of such a lot of 'em?

Elanchius: Excellent, Quintus! Your question leads directly to our next problem.

Quintus: Don't think I get you, Elanchius.

Elanchius: Then perhaps we should let the matter lie until Pulvius answers your question.

Pulvius: I notice that Libentia and Empiricus are inspecting my bookshelves. Perhaps they will answer it, Quintus, for I sus-

149

pect that by now they have found the key to the arrangement of my books.

Libentia: I believe we have, Pulvius. Empiricus, you can explain the system to Quintus better than I.

Empiricus: That is hardly so, Libentia. But I shall try to describe it, subject to your correction and Pulvius'.

Quintus: This going to be complicated?

Empiricus: In a sense, yes, Quintus. Now, first observe that the shelves cover all four walls.

Quintus: Sure do.

Empiricus: And, Quintus, the walls play a part in Pulvius' system. Let us first consider the books on the wall we are facing. Here Pulvius has placed only books written by authors of our country, with a shelf or two left over for miscellaneous papers and boxes. And now note the books on these next two walls. Libentia and I have found that all of them were written by authors of our great neighboring country across the sea.

Quintus: Takes two walls for 'em, hey?

Pulvius: Yes, Quintus. For literary genius has there found especially fertile soil.

Empiricus: And now, on the remaining wall, Pulvius has placed representative literary works of other countries.

Quintus: Not such a complicated system, after all.

Empiricus: But we have not finished, Quintus.

Quintus: What? Not any more walls!

Empiricus: No, but let us examine the first wall again, more closely. Note that the books in the upper section to my left were written earlier than those in the middle, and that those in the third section below are most recent of all.

Quintus: Yeh. So if Pulvius wants to lay hands on the oldest book anybody wrote in this country he reaches up as far as he can to the left, and if he wants the newest one, he reaches clear down to the right in the last section.

Empiricus: That is roughly but not precisely true, Quintus. For Pulvius has used a further kind of classification, which we have not yet mentioned.

Quintus: Guess I was right at first. Getting more complicated all the time.

Empiricus: Yes, somewhat, Quintus. For, you see, Pulvius has arranged his books by literary type within each chronological period, so that all of the odes, for example, belonging to a certain age, are placed together.

Libentia: And while you have been describing this arrangement to Quintus, I have discovered also that individual works within the groups representing types and periods are themselves placed in chronological order. Moreover, within these groups the books are arranged alphabetically by author. And finally, an author's works of the same type are arranged in the order in which he wrote them!

Quintus: Boy! Pulvius's got to know a lot about a book before he can ever find it.

Empiricus: Indeed he must, Quintus. He must first of all know the country of its origin. Then he must know respectively, the historical period in which it was written, its literary type, the identity of its author, and its chronological relation to the author's other works.

Quintus: Wow! How come you use such a complicated system, Pulvius?

Pulvius: Why, Quintus, you asked me earlier how I was able to find a particular book. This arrangement enables me to do so.

Quintus: But, say! Suppose you forgot some of that business about it. Book'd be lost for keeps.

Vulpius: A not unworthwhile outcome!

Elanchius: Now, Quintus, let me tell you why I said earlier that your question about the arrangement of Pulvius' books was appropriate. Since we began to talk together, we have reached several conclusions. We have agreed—most of us—on the highest function to be served by the study of literature, on the kind of books which can perform this function, and finally on the students whose need for the humanizing force of literature is urgent. You will recall that we ended our talk this morning with the conclusion that the need of some students is, in fact, so compelling that we must find the means to reach them, however formidable the obstacles.

Quintus: That's where we quit before I went to the games.

Elanchius: Well, then. What problem should we first consider in seeking how to overcome these obstacles?

Libentia: Although we have decided on the principle by which books are to be selected, we have said nothing of the *order* in which they are to be presented so as to have their fullest effect—or whether *any* deliberate order is desirable. Is not this our first problem?

Quintus: So that's why Elanchius said my question about Pulvius' arrangement was a good one.

Elanchius: You are alert, Quintus. Now, Libentia, you have actually posed two questions. Which should we attempt first?

Libentia: Why, clearly, we should be illogical if we decided which arrangement is best before we decided whether any at all is desirable!

Elanchius: Let us then decide whether the teacher should adopt any deliberate arrangement of the literary works that she will present to her class.

Empiricus: I would ask at once whether it would really be possible for her to avoid some kind of order, even if she tried.

Quintus: Doesn't look like it to me. Any time you take one thing after another, you've got some kind of an order.

Empiricus: And what would you call that order, Quintus?

Quintus: Can't say as I know. It's not one that was worked out—but it's something.

Empiricus: Then may we not call it the order of chance—or the *random* order?

Quintus: Yeh, that's it. Don't think anybody could stand to go along that way though—not for long.

Elanchius: An acute observation, Quintus—and I suspect that it has grown out of your own experience.

Quintus: Now you mention it, guess it did.

Elanchius: And would you think this is a common human experience, Quintus?

Quintus: You mean other people have it, too? Wouldn't surprise me.

Elanchius: May we surmise that it is in the nature of the human mind to be dissatisfied with the merely random?

Empiricus: And not only to be dissatisfied with it, but to seek constantly some principle of order which will give meaning to what is otherwise meaningless.

Elanchius: We must all agree. It is man's way to seek to bring chaos to some conscious order. Libentia, you are nodding assent?

Libentia: I was remembering something that happened last year, Elanchius. Not knowing what else to do, I had decided to present to my students a number of literary pieces without any particular order. But my experiment lasted only a few days, because I found myself wanting to put works together somehow. Besides, I found my students inclined to do the same thing without any direction from me.

Elanchius: Most teachers have doubtless had that experience, Libentia. Well, then. Since our own minds will force some kind of conscious order on us in any event, should we not seek the particular kind that will best serve the study of literature?

Quintus: Yeh, that's Libentia's second question. Let's get at it.

Elanchius: Then let us begin by trying to list all the possible ways of arranging books for presentation to students.

Quintus: That ought to get us going. Suppose there are many of 'em?

Elanchius: We shall find how many, Quintus.

Quintus: Well, how about starting with all those ways Pulvius arranges books on his shelves? What do you call 'em, Pulvius?

Pulvius: The enveloping order might be called *geographical* since the works are first grouped according to the countries of their origin. Within that order I have used the *chronological,* and within that the *typological.* These are the principal orders— except for the *alphabetical,* of course.

Quintus: Mighty big words, Pulvius! Guess I get the idea, though, from what we said before.

Elanchius: And you may remember also that Pulvius uses these four orders in combination. Now, who thinks of a fifth possibility?

Libentia: Well, the teacher could arrange books according to the seasons of the year, notable holiday periods, great events, and so on. A name for that is the *occasional* order.

Empiricus: And, for a sixth way, she could reverse the chronological order, and present books from the most recent to the oldest!

Quintus: Well, how about putting them together by what they're about—I mean like war, sports, animals—things like that.

Libentia: That is often called the *topical* order, Quintus.

Pulvius: I have heard of teachers who *select* books according to the color of their jackets. Why not arrange them that way also, read the greens first, then the blues, then the reds, and so on!

Elanchius: A brilliant suggestion, Pulvius! Are there others?

Libentia: Why, there are countless such as Pulvius has facetiously suggested—by their size, number of pages, shape, longest to shortest, shortest to longest—and sometimes I think any of these ways would make as much sense as some that are actually used!

Elanchius: Wait, Libentia! Do not pass judgment yet! Vulpius, surely you have an order to nominate. You have been silent a long while.

Quintus: Say, he has, hasn't he? What's the matter, Vulpius? This ivory tower of Pulvius' shut you up?

Vulpius: My lack of participation is an outcome of my recognition that you are quite unrealistic in searching for an arrangement pattern, since you persist in including only your so-called great books. Nothing that I could share with you would achieve favorable response due to these circumstances.

Elanchius: It is true, Vulpius, that we are seeking a way to arrange only those books that deserve the name of literature. However, can you suspend your disbelief in literature momentarily in order to suggest how books might be arranged for the classroom?

Vulpius: I repeat that it is definitely unrealistic to group reading materials which are not adapted to classroom utilization. But since you invite my participation, I must advise you that there are only three realistic ways of arranging readings for young learners, and those are according to their reading levels, interests, and needs.

Pulvius: By all the repetitious deities! Are we to hear of those lists again! This is how you said books should be *selected,* Vulpius.

Vulpius: You would be confronting the individual learner more realistically if you utilized those lists in your own classes, Pulvius. But to continue. Whatever readings are utilized should be arranged according to the data that have been determined by professional researchers as best implementing the anticipated outcomes. However, as your so-called great books are not adjusted to meet the *needs* and *interests* of present-day youths in the realistically visualized classroom situation, it is obviously impossible to even attempt to make worthwhile interest and need groupings.

Elanchius: Then, if these possibilities are eliminated, Vulpius, you are in fact suggesting only one order, which we may call the order of *difficulty?*

Vulpius: Obviously. Since your selections have no data-supported classroom validity as to either interests or needs, only difficulty ratings are left to classify them by. Or, as I should prefer to verbalize it, their arrangement must be patterned according to a standardized reading-ladder program based upon accurately measured readability quotients.

Elanchius: Perhaps we have not as yet named all the possible ways in which books might be arranged, and others may occur to us later. However, since Vulpius has made a direct proposal that books be arranged according to their difficulty, let us now turn our attention to that proposal. But before we ask whether literary works *should* be so arranged, must we not consider whether such an arrangement of them is in fact possible?

Empiricus: I recall Pulvius' statement that there is a wide range of difficulty among great books. Now are we to understand you as meaning, Vulpius, that if a teacher were to use, say, one hundred works during a four-year period, she should grade them from one to one hundred according to the difficulty of each?

Vulpius: Definitely. The professionally oriented teacher will correlate the available data, thus adjusting the readability quotients of the materials to coordinate with the reading speed and comprehension coefficients of individual learners.

Quintus: I don't get that, Vulpius.

Empiricus: I think Vulpius means, Quintus, that the teacher will give the easier books to the less able students and the more difficult ones to the more experienced readers. But this hardly answers my question, Vulpius.

Vulpius: Why, I had not concluded my statement when Quintus interrupted. What I was going to say further is that, although in numerous instances there will be found to be variations on either side of the normative progressional ladder—a development which obviously makes the consideration of individual differences of fundamental and basic importance—it will be determined that more difficult materials can be utilized as between the different grade levels, thus permitting, as our data show, that those materials capable of functional employment in the final year of school, for example, should be more difficult than those utilized for one of the earlier years.

Quintus: Guess you mean they'd read the easy books before they went on to the hard ones, hey?

Empiricus: I believe that this is what Vulpius said before.

Elanchius: But now, Vulpius, let us suppose that the teacher is not able to find a book of the precise degree of difficulty shown by your tests to be required by a particular child. Then what should she do?

Vulpius: In a program based on our scientifically compiled reading material lists, such a possibility would not occur, as these materials have been graded as to their readability. However, observing that for various reasons, including the pressures exerted by the traditional content people, some schools feel the need for including so-called classics in their reading program, we in the profession have made progress in adapting these materials to the reading norms of adolescent learners. Our specialists are making available a growing number of versions of these classic-type materials, adjusting them to individual reading skill differences and grade levels.

Quintus: Mean you fellows rewrite those books so they'll fit?

Vulpius: Oh, definitely.

Pulvius: It is not possible!

Elanchius: I can understand your dismay, Pulvius. Though

by having literary masterpieces rewritten we might indeed arrange them in careful gradations of difficulty, yet great works so rewritten that they can be thus graded will retain few recognizable marks of greatness! They are therefore irrelevant to our discussion—or our thought. Now, Pulvius, what of the works that *are* relevant? Can they be graded in difficulty with precise intervals between.

Pulvius: They cannot, Elanchius. Oh, it is true that the line of literary masterpieces extends downward to those that tiny children can understand, and upward to those that tempt the scholar out of thought. It is undeniable that some great books are far more difficult than others and that there is a wide range of difficulty among them in general. But many literary works fall together as of approximately equal difficulty. Thus, of the hypothetical one hundred books mentioned by Empiricus, the teacher might find that, when only their difficulty is considered, fifty belong on the same level. Hence, she would still find it necessary to choose *an additional principle* by which to determine the order of presenting these fifty.

Libentia: It seems to me that there is yet another objection to the proposal Vulpius has made. By arranging books in this order one inevitably gives prominence to the degree of difficulty— as though the most important end of a program of reading were to progress through books of increasing difficulty.

Vulpius: But it is obviously the teacher's role to guide reading development on an ascending scale of difficulty, utilizing materials graded to achieve optimal results as to both comprehension and reading rate. Only by utilizing this concept can a worthwhile reading program arrangement be—arranged.

Pulvius: Why, Vulpius, your arrangement would make a *virtue* of difficulty—and what an absurd progression, since one way to make a book difficult is to write it badly!

Elanchius: Perhaps I need not ask this question. But are we indeed to conclude, Vulpius, that progress in the development of reading skills through the use of increasingly difficult texts, is, for you, a *purpose* as well as a means?

Vulpius: It is definitely the principal aim of the modern developmental reading program.

Elanchius: I must remind you that this purpose is remote from that which we earlier concluded to be the most important reason for the study of literature. Nevertheless, you are to be complimented, Vulpius, upon one thing—

Vulpius: So?

Elanchius: Upon your consistency. It is clear that your arrangement has been determined by, and perfectly accords with, your conception of the purpose of reading.

Quintus: Don't quite follow you, Elanchius.

Elanchius: I mean, Quintus, simply that Vulpius has chosen the arrangement that is most appropriate to his purpose.

Quintus: Don't see why you want to compliment him for that, though. You said he picked the *wrong* purpose to start with.

Elanchius: So it seems to me, Quintus. Nevertheless, he is to be complimented because his arrangement and his purpose go together.

Quintus: Well, what would happen if they didn't?

Elanchius: So powerful is the effect of arrangement, Quintus, that it can warp a purpose with which it is in conflict. Hence it is necessary not only to define the purpose *first*, but, as well, *to choose that arrangement which will support the predetermined purpose*. If the teacher had in mind one purpose, but arranged the books to fit another, she might actually change her original purpose fundamentally—so that it became something she did not like at all. Therefore, our choice of the best arrangement must be governed by our agreement that the highest function of literature is the humanization of the reader. Otherwise we need not have troubled to define that function!

Quintus: Had so much trouble with it, we don't want to let it go to waste by forgetting it.

Elanchius: No one who is concerned with the teaching of literature must ever forget it, Quintus.

Quintus: Well, the way Vulpius wants won't do. So let's get on with the job. We had a lot of other ways of arranging books. Which one'll fill the bill?

Elanchius: We have, as you say, several possibilities to consider. But, although we have rejected Vulpius' arrangement according to difficulty as an appropriate order, is there anything more to be said about it?

Quintus: Don't see what. Threw it out, didn't we?

Libentia: As a system of arrangement, yes. Nevertheless, we should not ignore it altogether. As Pulvius has pointed out, great books are not all equally difficult. The teacher should not, of course, place the *most* difficult books before her youngest and least experienced pupils and the *least* difficult before the oldest and most experienced ones. But only an absurd teacher would do so!

Empiricus: You are quite right. The difficulty of books is a matter of practical concern for the teacher, but it does not in itself constitute a system of arrangement.

Libentia: And progress in skill must not be identified with the *purpose* of reading! It is just such confusion that has led some of my colleagues to substitute for literary works readings that can be only a graded series of lessons in how to read, without regard to the quality of *what* is read.

Quintus: Yeh. No use learning how to read if you don't care what, so long as it's harder. Can we get on with the job now, Elanchius?

Elanchius: We can, Quintus. Now, which of the possibilities suggested a while ago should we consider first?

Quintus: Let's tackle the tough ones—the ones Pulvius uses for his books here.

Empiricus: A good idea, Quintus. Pulvius' system is apparently complete and eminently suited to his purpose in arranging the books in his study. I for one wish to learn whether it is equally appropriate as an order for presenting them to students.

Libentia: Pulvius' system is by no means limited to the walls of scholars' studies, Empiricus. In many schools—indeed, I think I may say in most that give serious attention to literature—it serves as the order of presentation.

Empiricus: Of course Pulvius' arrangement includes three orders in combination—the geographical, the chronological, and the typological. Do the schools you speak of use anything so elaborate?

Libentia: Indeed they do, although the emphasis varies, so that sometimes geography is most important, sometimes chronology, and sometimes type.

Pulvius: And it is well that the schools use this arrangement, Libentia. For while they continue to do so, we can be fairly certain that they are giving the students books of genuine literary quality to read.

Elanchius: Evidently, Pulvius, you consider this arrangement appropriate not only for the scholar's library but also for the teacher's presentation. You stated earlier that your system of classification was useful because it enabled you to locate a particular book. I assume that it is not merely for this reason that you approve its use by the teacher.

Pulvius: Not at all, Elanchius. And remember that I have just added a reason, which I may say I regard as of first importance—namely, that so long as teachers use this arrangement they continue to use genuine literature in their classes.

Elanchius: If the arrangement has that result, Pulvius, it is assuredly a valuable one; but let us make sure that the price paid is not too high! However, have you further reasons to offer?

Pulvius: Why, the appropriateness of this system is unquestionable since each book is the product of a particular *time* and *place* and is written in some classifiable *form*. Every book is at least in part characterized by the circumstances of its origin and must therefore be read with these circumstances in mind. What is more reasonable than to bring together for study books that are alike in belonging to the same country, the same period, or the same genre?

Elanchius: That would seem reasonable, Pulvius, if their likeness in these ways deserves the emphasis it will inevitably receive by being made the principle of arrangement.

Libentia: That is just the point! You will remember, Pulvius, our agreement that the arrangement chosen for the presentation of books should accord with the primary reason for teaching books, since another arrangement will have the effect of thwarting this purpose by substituting another for it.

Pulvius: I am afraid that I do not understand you perfectly,

Libentia. The arrangement I have described is a convenient one, which makes the entire range of literature available for systematic study. Why should the primary reason for teaching literature be thwarted by following it?

Libentia: Suppose, for example, that you group books according to the countries of their origin and present them so to students. Are you not really using them for a purpose quite different from ours? When teachers describe their courses arranged in this fashion, it is all too plain that they are less concerned with literature for its humanizing power than for the *knowledge* that students can gain through it of the particular country—or, sometimes, of merely one section of that country.

Pulvius: Nevertheless, as I have said, a book is produced by a country, and, indeed, by a particular region. It bears characteristic marks of its place of origin, and these must be identified if the book is to be understood.

Libentia: But to be understood for what purpose, Pulvius? By grouping books according to the region which produced them, do you not give an emphasis that suggests to your students that they are to read for greater knowledge of this region? Whatever other purpose you may have in mind, the one implied in the arrangement will be illumination of the locality that produced this "regional" literature. You become thus a teacher of a social study, not of literature!

Elanchius: Evidently you and Pulvius have reached an impasse, Libentia. Instead of attempting to untie the knot at this point, let us proceed to the second kind of order used by Pulvius in his arrangement.

Quintus: Good idea. You and Pulvius are really stuck, Libentia.

Libentia: Then the order I should ask about next is the chronological. I am especially concerned about it, because I have observed that it is the predominant order in schools where literature holds a strong place.

Vulpius: Definitely, Libentia—since that was the pattern in which the teachers read when they were students in Pulvius' classes!

Pulvius: Just so, Vulpius, and for good reason. The chronological order provides the most satisfactory means of describing the characteristic marks of successive literary periods. In no other way can the teacher adequately represent the relationship of a book to its age, compare it with documents that were contemporary with it, contrast it with works which preceded and succeeded it. Indeed, if books were not presented in their historical order, how could one even begin to establish a sense of literary history? Only by means of the chronological order can the student be made to see clearly the successive stages in the development of genres, traditions, and literary movements.

Libentia: But that is just the point again, Pulvius! Certainly, if the highest end that the study of literature is to serve is knowledge of periods, relations of books to periods, and familiarity with transitions from period to period—if the highest end is this, the chronological order of study will be best. For we have agreed that the highest purpose and the principle of arrangement need to accord with each other. But we have said that *not* knowledge of literary history but humanization of the reader is the highest function of the study of literature.

Pulvius: But Libentia! Surely you, who were one of my most promising young scholars, remember well enough that a book is a product of its time, closely bound to the social, political, and economic, as well as literary, environment which obtained when it was written. Now, to understand such a book, we must study it in relation to its time.

Libentia: But again I must ask, to what purpose would you have the book understood, Pulvius?

Elanchius: It is evident, Libentia, that you and Pulvius have returned to the same impasse that you reached earlier.

Quintus: Stuck again, all right!

Empiricus: Perhaps, therefore, you should now try the third order—the typological.

Quintus: Well, here we go again!

Libentia: Then, Pulvius, let me again mention some of my observations as a teacher. I remember that one of my fellow teachers had arranged the entire reading program for her class by literary types. For several weeks her students worked at a group of lyric poems. She called that her "poetry unit." Then they read a large collection of myths, and so on throughout the year. At the end, every literary genre had been represented. She was well satisfied with the arrangement she had worked out and recommended that I try it. But I was not sure that I wanted to use it after she showed me samples of her tests and final examinations. Can you guess what kind of questions she asked?

Empiricus: Why, I would guess that she asked for the identifying characteristics of the several forms of literature, for the special techniques used by writers in the different genres, for the subjects and themes traditionally associated with particular forms, and so on.

Libentia: Exactly! And I found out that she always asked such questions.

Quintus: Don't follow you, Libentia. How'd you get off the subject? We're supposed to be talking about arranging books, not about examinations.

Libentia: Why, Quintus, these questions reflected the arrangement used by this teacher. Indeed, they were the obvious and even inevitable ones, given that kind of arrangement. But more importantly, they showed all too obviously what the actual *purpose* of her reading program was.

Pulvius: I am pained, Libentia, that you seem to have developed a disregard for the importance of form in literature. Surely you cannot imagine that a student has been taught a work if he is ignorant whether it is an elegy, a myth, or an ode. These and other genres have long traditions behind them, and many conventions peculiar to a given form must be made known to the young students. The facts of tradition and convention must be taught if the student is to gain the fullest possible knowledge of the documents he reads.

Libentia: But again I must ask, knowledge to what end, Pulvius? Is it the same end as that which we have named the most important?

Quintus: Well, here we are again—stuck!

Elanchius: "Stuck" is the word, Quintus, and at the same

point each time. Now let us find how to resolve the difficulty. But, first, is the precise nature of the difficulty clear to all of us?

Quintus: I see they always get stuck. But how come?

Empiricus: I have attended closely to the conversation, and I believe I can describe the nature of their difference.

Elanchius: By all means do so, Empiricus.

Empiricus: It is thus, as I see it: Libentia has denied the appropriateness, in turn, of the three kinds of order used in Pulvius' arrangement of books on the grounds that by inevitably interposing new and contrary purposes, they thwart the purpose which we have agreed to be the most proper for the study of literature. Pulvius, on the other hand, has maintained that knowledge, respectively, of place, time, and type is essential to the understanding of any work of literature and has therefore insisted that these orders are appropriate because they contribute directly to this kind of knowledge. However, during the conversation, one question was three times asked by Libentia and left unanswered. This was the question, "Understanding of the book to what end?" If Pulvius were to answer this question, I think they might be nearer a resolution of their difficulty.

Quintus: Let's hear it, Pulvius. Get us out of this hole.

Pulvius: Why, I do not at all mind answering. By understanding a book, I mean perceiving it with all its characteristic marks upon it.

Empiricus: You have made this point before, Pulvius. But have you answered the question? You have told us what you mean by understanding a book. But is this the same as telling us why it should be understood at all?

Pulvius: Why, then, I mean that the book must be understood in order that it may be perceived as a specimen, or example, of a particular region, a particular age, and a particular genre and so that it can be placed in its appropriate niche in literary history.

Vulpius: Come, Pulvius. Let us be realistic. First, you wish to impose unadapted materials on adolescent readers. Next, you want these materials read for non-interest-arousing purposes. The modern school population will not be interested in your "classics," whatever arrangement plan you utilize. But with such

an unprogressive program as you propose, you are expecting
them to have interest also in mere academic-type matters such
as differences between types and periods. We in the profession
who have examined the student interest field scientifically have
much available data demonstrating that only a minimal number
of individuals are attracted to such areas.

Quintus: Looks like Pulvius wants to do it the hard way,
all right.

Elanchius: Yes, Quintus, it is the hard way. And let us remember that our search for the most appropriate arrangement is
part of our larger search for means of *overcoming* the difficulties
that face students in the study of literature.

Quintus: Yeh. Sure don't want to make things tougher!

Elanchius: Since we continue to be troubled by conflicting
views, perhaps we should redefine our problem in a wider perspective. We are in search of the best possible way of arranging
books for presentation. What are the appropriate criteria to use
in our search? Quintus has indirectly reminded us of one when
he spoke of the "hard way." Perhaps we should phrase that
criterion thus: that the arrangement we choose certainly *must
not add to the difficulty* which inevitably attends the study of
literature, but should ideally help to minimize it.

Vulpius: Definitely. Hence the reading ladder structuring
of materials is a realistic concept.

Elanchius: And now is not this the second demand that we
should make of our arrangement: that it *must not divert the
humanizing force* which literature contains and which must
reach the student?

Quintus: That's right. If it can't help, at least it shouldn't
hinder.

Elanchius: Well said, Quintus. Then may I suggest this as a
third criterion: by being in accord with the main purpose in
teaching literature, the arrangement *should actively contribute
to the attainment of that purpose.*

Empiricus: The difference between your second and third
criteria is of course only a matter of degree. Perhaps we can say
that by the second we mean the arrangement chosen must at

least not *thwart* our purpose and by the third that it should at most *further* that purpose.

Quintus: Yeh. It should help, but if it can't at least it shouldn't hinder.

Elanchius: Now let us judge the arrangement that Pulvius has recommended by these criteria which we have just named.

Libentia: Good! Then perhaps we'll find our way around our impasse, Pulvius.

Pulvius: A consummation devoutly to be wished!

Elanchius: Well, then. Pulvius' arrangement is composed of three orders that are frequently used in combination. You will recall that in their conversation Libentia and Pulvius met the same obstacle in discussing each order in turn. Perhaps, therefore, our most efficient way will be to consider them together rather than singly.

Quintus: Kill three birds with one stone, hey?

Vulpius: Birds of a feather too!

Elanchius: Let us then examine the total arrangement by each of the three criteria in turn.

Quintus: Good idea.

Elanchius: Well, then. Does Pulvius' arrangement minimize or does it add to the essential difficulty that attends the study of literature? Vulpius, you have already argued that this arrangement would add to the difficulty. Do you wish to elaborate?

Vulpius: Gladly. Research demonstrates that adolescent learner interests do not include such academic topics as Pulvius is championing—such as differences between reading material types and characteristic features of remote historical periods. Moreover, it is also an objectively established fact that when the interest level of the learner is negative the difficulty factor involved in utilizing materials tends to increase proportionately. You understand, of course, that I cannot approve your opinion that you can teach your so-called classics to the mass of the present-day pupil population, whatever your *modus operandus*. Hence I can only advise you that the arrangement Pulvius advocates merely makes the teaching of your "classics" even more impossible.

Libentia: I hope I may never believe it impossible to teach literature! But my own experience and observation require me to agree with Vulpius otherwise just now. It would truly be very strange if students should find the mere periphery of literature—all the facts about it—more attractive than the literature itself!

Vulpius: And what learners do not find attractive is demonstrably more difficult for them.

Pulvius: What! Are the schools to present nothing to students except what entertains them without effort on their part?

Elanchius: Mere attractiveness, with nothing else to recommend it, Pulvius, is hardly to be valued. But Libentia's meaning was more than this, I am sure.

Libentia: Why, Pulvius himself has said that the reading of great books is unavoidably a hard task. My argument, which partially agrees with Vulpius', is that we must not make the reading of great books more difficult by surrounding them with a periphery which is far less attractive than the books themselves.

Elanchius: You see Pulvius' arrangement, then, as a rather uninviting wall placed between the student and the book. But Libentia, a moment ago you referred to your own experience and observation. Had you something particular in mind?

Libentia: Yes! You will remember that Vulpius spoke about the double impossibility of teaching literature when it is arranged in Pulvius' way. What I have noticed is that some of my colleagues who formerly taught literature in this way have since given up the teaching of literature entirely as an impossibility. They blamed literature itself when perhaps they should have blamed the arrangement!

Quintus: Threw out the baby with the bathwater, hey?

Elanchius: Even so, Quintus. And I fear that a very great many other teachers have made the same error.

Empiricus: I am reminded of a situation which I believe to be analogous to this. The scientist in his laboratory who is attempting to form a certain compound from ingredients that are known to him does not cast everything aside when his trials according to a certain order result in failure. Rather, he experi-

ments with other orders and proportions until he finds the solution.

Quintus: That's just like making shoes. You don't throw out
all your leather just because you're using a last that turns out
shoes with the wrong shape. What you do is get another last.

Elanchius: Well, then. Our agreement is that Pulvius' arrangement increases rather than decreases the difficulty of study-
ing literature. Obviously, then, it has failed to satisfy our first
criterion. Shall we now consider the second?

Quintus: Well, if it failed the first one, what's the use in
going on to the others?

Empiricus: Although we have found the arrangement we
have been discussing to be unsatisfactory in one respect, we
should not yet dismiss it. First of all, we cannot be sure at this
point whether or not we shall find another which will be better
in this respect. Second, we agreed a day or two ago that difficulty
itself is not necessarily undesirable—indeed, we concluded that
there must be at least some degree of difficulty if any genuine
learning is to take place. And, finally, we have not conclusively
tested the suitability of Pulvius' arrangement until we have found
whether or not it serves the purpose which we have named most
important for the study of literature. For you will remember that
we agreed to judge all of our principles, whether those of selection, arrangement, or presentation, in the light of that purpose.

Quintus: Right as usual, Empiricus.

Elanchius: Then if we are ready to proceed, our second demand was this: that the arrangement chosen must not thwart our
highest purpose, which is the humanization of the reader.

Quintus: Why don't you ask us some questions, Elanchius?
I like it when you go at it that way.

Pulvius: I could wish that my students welcomed questions
so eagerly!

Quintus: Don't they like yours, Pulvius? Maybe you ask the
wrong kind.

Pulvius: Ha!

Quintus: What's that?

Pulvius: I said, "Ha!"

Elanchius: I am sure, Quintus, that Pulvius is master of the

art of asking questions. Pulvius, would you consider it an imposition if we asked you to exemplify the questions you pose in your
classes? They may aid us here.

Pulvius: I would never consider an invitation to ask questions
an imposition. My questions, Quintus, since you have challenged
me in this fashion, are always answerable if the student has acquired the knowledge required to answer them. I do not value
vague impressions, and so I do not ask questions which invite
vague impressions. If you were in my class, Quintus, I might ask
you this question: "What are the distinguishing characteristics
of the pastoral elegy?" Or this: "What elements in the periods
during which the pastoral elegy flourished were particularly
congenial to it as a literary genre?" Or this: "What evidence of
the region of its origin can be adduced from the nature of the
pastoral elegy?"

Quintus: Whew! You say those questions are answerable,
Pulvius?

Elanchius: Pulvius said, Quintus, that his questions are
answerable if the student has the necessary knowledge. And
certainly we must agree that they are of the kind that may be
answered with definite statements. Now perhaps our conversation of the past few minutes will help in our larger purpose of
determining whether Pulvius' arrangement of literary works
blocks their humanizing force. Let me begin by asking a question. We have earlier, you will recall, characterized great books
as those which have most power to humanize. Now precisely
where shall we say that this power resides?

Libentia: Why, Elanchius, your question is far easier than
Pulvius'. It lies *in the books themselves!*

Elanchius: And our task is to release it so that it can penetrate and affect the reader?

Libentia: Certainly. If we do not do that, then whatever else
is done instead will be something less than the best that books
can do.

Elanchius: And if we are to enable the books, in which lies
the potentiality, to exert their full force upon the reader, must
we not bring the books and the reader as intimately together
as possible?

Libentia: Well, if any kind of wall stood between them it would blunt the force. And if the wall were thick and solid enough, it might stop the force completely.

Elanchius: Well, then. Would you say, Libentia, that Pulvius' arrangement provides an intimate relationship—or is it in the nature of a wall?

Libentia: All that I have observed, in my own classes and in the classes of my colleagues, suggests that this arrangement does indeed act as a wall—or, rather, not one wall, but three, whose thickness and toughness blunt and divert the humanizing force that can emerge from literature.

Quintus: I don't get all this talk about walls. I know if you shoot an arrow at a target, a wall in the way won't help you any! That like what you mean?

Empiricus: An apt figure, Quintus! If the arrow becomes lodged in an intervening wall, it cannot reach its target. Libentia conceives of the innate force of literature as being released from a work of art, somewhat as an arrow is shot from a bow. For her, the target is no less than the inner nature of the readers. But the force never reaches that target if it sticks fast in the wall—that is, the three-ply barrier of time, place, and type. Or let me see whether I can make the matter clear in a slightly different way. Some of you know that colleagues of mine, in our laboratories, have recently succeeded in creating a new substance of such mighty force that the tiniest particle of it must be locked within leaden boxes with walls several inches thick.

Quintus: Hey! Heard about that. What'd happen if that stuff got loose?

Empiricus: Why, Quintus, it would kill you.

Quintus: Boy! Better keep it locked up tight! Tighter the better!

Empiricus: Most of us hope to do so, Quintus. To contain such a force as this, impenetrable walls are quite proper, since it must at all cost be prevented from escaping—

Quintus: Hey! I get it! That stuff'd kill you if it got out, so it has to be kept *in*. But Libentia's stuff—I mean this force in books —wouldn't kill you. It'd help you. So walls are wrong. Don't want to keep it in. Want to be sure it gets out!

Pulvius: My acquaintance with poets qualifies me to appreciate the taste for figures in which you and Libentia have been indulging, Empiricus. But let us not be carried away by a figure. I remind you that although you have asserted that chronology, geographical origin, and generic characteristics constitute barriers which block your high-flying arrow, you have done no more than assert. What proofs have you that the kind of arrangement I advocate does in fact prevent the humanizing force of the literary document from reaching the student?

Elanchius: A few moments ago, Pulvius, you posed three questions which you said you might ask Quintus if he were a member of your class. Do these fairly represent your usual line of questioning?

Pulvius: Given more time, I should have given them a more definite phrasing. But their substance I should not change.

Elanchius: Then these three questions do in fact represent the kind that you regard as appropriate to ask?

Pulvius: They do.

Quintus: Mind repeating 'em, Pulvius? I forgot what they were.

Pulvius: My first was this: "What are the distinguishing characteristics of the pastoral elegy?" My second was "What elements in the periods during which the pastoral elegy flourished were particularly congenial to it as a literary genre?" My third was "What evidence of the region of its origin can be adduced from the nature of the pastoral elegy?"

Elanchius: Now let us reconsider them one by one. What would you say is the purpose of your first question, Pulvius?

Pulvius: Why, to determine whether the student has acquired the knowledge needed to answer it.

Elanchius: And what, precisely, is that knowledge?

Pulvius: Knowledge of poetic form—of the conventional marks, in this instance, of the pastoral elegy. But more broadly, this kind of question aims to discover whether the student can relate a particular poem to an entire literary development and establish its place in that framework.

Elanchius: And the emphasis of your teaching is such that your students can reasonably be expected to acquire such knowledge?

Pulvius: Indeed it is, Elanchius. Although typological knowledge is not my only emphasis, as the second and third questions I posed for Quintus show, yet the attention of my students is drawn to the facts of literary genre, and it is therefore appropriate to ask them such a question.

Empiricus: Earlier this evening we noted the necessity for consonance of purpose and arrangement. Elanchius, in fact, complimented Vulpius because the order which he insisted upon using in the reading program—that is, the order of difficulty—was in perfect accord with his conception of the purpose of the reading program—namely, to enable students to comprehend materials of gradually increasing difficulty. Should we not now, for a similar reason, compliment Pulvius? For clearly, since the typological is one of the three orders which he uses in presenting literary works, it is entirely consistent that he ask questions about the characteristics of the pastoral elegy.

Libentia: Let us go even farther in complimenting him. Since these questions inevitably reflect Pulvius' essential *purpose* in the study of literature, it follows that his arrangement by typology is in perfect accord with that, also!

Quintus: Hey! But it's the *wrong* purpose!

Elanchius: Yet if one's purpose in teaching literature is to acquaint one's students with the distinguishing features of the several genres—as is evinced by Pulvius' first question—it is appropriate to arrange the literary works for presentation in a typological order.

Quintus: Yeh.

Empiricus: Precisely. That is in complete harmony with all our reasoning, if I have understood these conversations of the past few days.

Elanchius: And if one's purpose in the study of literature is to acquaint one's students with the special characteristics of particular periods of literature and with the transitions from one to another—as is evinced by Pulvius' second question—it follows that one would appropriately arrange the documents for presentation in chronological order?

Libentia: Certainly—if that is what one wishes!

Elanchius: And if one's purpose in the study of literature is to acquaint one's student with the facts of geographical regions —as is evinced by Pulvius' third question—it follows that one would appropriately group these works for presentation according to their place of origin?

Libentia: Certainly—if that is what one wishes!

Elanchius: And if one's purpose in the study of literature is threefold—to acquaint one's students with the characteristics of genres, periods, and places of origin—it follows that one would appropriately use a threefold arrangement in presentation—the typological, the chronological, and the geographical?

Libentia: Certainly—if that is what one wishes!

Elanchius: But if that is not what one wishes, Libentia! Will it not then be inappropriate to adopt any of these orders?

Libentia: The effect of arrangement on purpose is so powerful—as we have shown more than once—that no matter how one has defined his purpose to begin with, it will shift in order to conform to his arrangement.

Empiricus: But from what Pulvius has told us, we may conclude that his true purpose has *not* shifted. It has determined both his arrangement and the nature of the questions he finds appropriate to ask his students about the works read. Therefore his questions cannot be offered as proofs that his arrangement has diverted his purpose.

Elanchius: You have rightly called our attention to the logical design of Pulvius' teaching, Empiricus, and with your usual clarity have reminded us that since Pulvius' questions cannot be offered as proofs, we must seek elsewhere. Empiricus, you, I am sure, will know what kind of situation can supply us with the proofs we need.

Empiricus: I believe that is a relatively easy matter. Let us assume that a teacher has a purpose quite unlike that of Pulvius. Let us take that which we earlier defined as the highest possible one. Now this teacher, let us say, *declares* that he is teaching literature for the humanizing effect it can have on his students. But he uses Pulvius' arrangement, proceeding chronologically, typologically, geographically, or in all three ways at once. Now suppose that at last this teacher finds himself asking his students questions like those which Pulvius posed for Quintus. The questions in such a case could validly be used as evidence that the arrangement used has twisted the original purpose.

Elanchius: Now, Libentia, does this hypothetical instance recall the experience of any teacher whom you and I have some acquaintance with?

Libentia: I blush to say that it describes my own! Last year in one of the classes given me I did set out with a purpose—not clearly defined, I admit—that was essentially the same as that which we have now agreed on. At least I was sure that I did not want my students merely to acquire knowledge of period, genre, region, and so on. But because I myself had studied literature arranged according to Pulvius' plan, I very naturally adopted that plan. I was shocked later in the term to discover that all of the questions I was asking my students were aimed to test their knowledge of the very matters that I had meant to be only incidental. My incidentals had become ends! I realized then that no matter what one's purpose was, it would be lost if the arrangement did not support it.

Elanchius: Experience taught you, then, Libentia, that the humanizing force of literature is impeded by the kinds of arrangement that Pulvius insists on using?

Libentia: My experience has taught me, Elanchius, that any humanizing force which reaches the student in a course arranged chronologically, typologically, or geographically will do so not *because* of the arrangement but *in spite of it!* The best force that literature can exert will have to fight its way through three nearly impenetrable walls.

Quintus: Whew! Said a mouthful there, Libentia.

Elanchius: Then we conclude that Pulvius' arrangement fails to satisfy our second demand—that the arrangement chosen must not thwart the highest purpose in the teaching of literature. You will also remember that it failed to satisfy our first demand, that the arrangement used must not add to the difficulty which inevitably attends the study of literature. Shall we then proceed to the last of our criteria for determining the proper arrangement of literary works?

Quintus: Remember that one. We said the arrangement ought to help out the purpose.

Elanchius: Excellent, Quintus. The arrangement not only must not hinder, but by being in accord with our main purpose, should actively contribute to its attainment. But is it not now apparent that we need not test Pulvius' arrangement by this criterion?

Empiricus: Obviously, a device which impedes a force cannot be said to further it!

Vulpius: Don't tell me that you academically oriented individuals have concluded that the pattern traditionally maintained by Pulvius is unrealistic after all! We in the profession have known it for years!

Pulvius: Tripe!

Quintus: What's that, Pulvius?

Pulvius: You, Vulpius, would throw out literature altogether if we let you—not just the arrangement! What was the folk-saying you uttered earlier, Quintus—something about bathwater?

Quintus: Yeh. Said you shouldn't pour the baby out with it.

Elanchius: Libentia and gentlemen, we have talked long and still have far to go. But midnight has settled upon us. Shall we adjourn? We have concluded that certain arrangements of literature do not support the primary purpose in teaching it, but we have not yet chosen an arrangement that does do so. Perhaps after a night's rest we may have better success. If you agree, I suggest that we continue our search by the light of tomorrow's dawn.

Quintus: Yeh, getting late, all right. Pretty well done in myself.

Elanchius: Then may I suggest that we meet at my house? I shall conduct you thence by a path to an inspiring peak that looks down upon much that is beautiful.

The Arrangement Chosen

Persons of the Dialogue

LIBENTIA MAGISTRA

PULVIUS GRAMMATICUS   VULPIUS MATERIES

J. QUINTUS   EMPIRICUS MARTIALIS

ELANCHIUS

Scene: A summit

Empiricus: Let me take your arm, Libentia. This last stretch is quite steep.

Libentia: Thank you, Empiricus. I see that Elanchius has already arrived at the top.

Empiricus: And Quintus too is almost there. I see Elanchius extending his hand to help him up the last few feet.

Libentia: I wonder how the other two are bearing up.

Empiricus: Just two more steps and we shall be there.

Elanchius: Let me take your hand, Libentia. There you are, safe on top.

Quintus: Boy, that was a tough grind. Wouldn't want to do that every day. Don't think those two down there would want to either. Think they'll make it?

Elanchius: They do appear to be having difficulty.

Quintus: Oho there, Pulvius! Come on, Vulpius! Don't take all day about it.

Pulvius: Don't forget, young fellow, that you had a head start.

Quintus: Young, he says! Passed fifty last month. Hey,

176

Vulpius, what excuse you got?

Vulpius: I tend to think I took a wrong turn at the start of the ascent.

Quintus: Yeh! And didn't I see you slip clear off the trail a couple of times?

Vulpius: Not slip, Quintus. I merely failed to see just where the trail was.

Empiricus: Let me have your hands, gentlemen. All together now, up!

Elanchius: I am sorry to have put you to such a hard climb.

Libentia: It was hard, Elanchius, but the view is just as you described it last evening—inspiring.

Pulvius: Whew! I must catch my breath.

Quintus: Vulpius looks a little dizzy up this high. Say, Vulpius, don't get too close to the edge there!

Vulpius: I'll look out for myself, Quintus. You had better take care of Pulvius. He appears to be experiencing difficulty in breathing this fresh air.

Elanchius: Libentia and gentlemen, let us seat ourselves here in the warmth of the morning sun.

Quintus: Be a good thing for you, Pulvius. Give you a little better color.

Pulvius: I have watched while Ra-Tem's fiery wheel sucked up night's dank dew more often than you might suppose, Quintus.

Quintus: Huh, what's that?

Pulvius: And I may add, now that I have recovered my wind, that I am thoroughly delighted with the prospect from this summit—the vales below, the sylvan slopes, the distant lake.

Empiricus: It is a splendid view, Pulvius. I confess I find myself wishing we had reached an equally delightful conclusion last evening!

Quintus: How's that, Empiricus?

Libentia: I believe that Empiricus is comparing our efforts yesterday to find the best way of arranging books in the reading program to our struggles this morning to reach this summit.

Elanchius: And, Empiricus is also reminding us that, although we have reached the top of this hill, we did not yesterday solve our problem.

Quintus: Solve it! I'll say we didn't. Plenty tough going all right, but where'd we get to?

Empiricus: We made some progress, Quintus. Although we did not find the best solution, still we rejected certain arrangements which we found out of harmony with the primary reason for teaching literature.

Pulvius: To speak bluntly, what he means, Quintus, is that yesterday some of us saw fit to scorn the only tried and proven ways of arranging the documents of literature! But the fact remains that books are written in chronological order, that they are affected by the conventions of literary type, and that they are the products of definite geographical regions!

Vulpius: There you—

Pulvius: Let me say further that if you attempt to teach a document of literature without heeding the incontrovertible fact that it was produced in a particular place and time and form, you will be ignoring the subjects of principal concern to all reputable literary schol—

Quintus: Hold on, there, Pulv—

Pulvius: And another thing, let me tell you—

Elanchius: Pardon me, Pulvius. Before you continue, let us consider what you have just said. Must we not question your assertion on two grounds? In the first place, though perhaps we might agree with you that for the purposes of the literary scholar the arrangement according to time, place, and type is quite appropriate, still, for the teacher who is to reach all her students—as we have agreed she must—and whose purpose is quite different, the same arrangement may be quite inappropriate. So you see, Pulvius, perhaps you have not represented us quite correctly on this point.

Quintus: That's right, Pulvius. You're wrong. Don't want to make 'em scholars, just good human beings. Now what's your second point, Elanchius?

Elanchius: Perhaps this one will lead Pulvius to regard our decision with fewer misgivings. Libentia, did you understand from what we said last evening that the teacher of literature was to *ignore* the facts of time, place, and type?

Libentia: Why, no, Elanchius. We said only that these

should not provide the basis of arrangement, for if they do so, they will also provide the purpose.

Pulvius: But does it not come to the same thing? Will not the teacher be likely to ignore them altogether if they are disregarded in the arrangement?

Libentia: I think not, Pulvius. The teacher will use many of the facts that literary scholars have made available—but as part of the *background*. She must not allow factual knowledge about literature to usurp the *foreground*.

Elanchius: You have made the point admirably, Libentia. And we must return to this matter. But now, with this assurance, Pulvius, will you permit us to resume our search for a suitable arrangement of literature?

Pulvius: I agree that we must get on. But I shall have more to say about this matter at a later time!

Elanchius: You will have opportunity, Pulvius. Well, then. Besides the arrangements proposed by Pulvius yesterday, there were others suggested—several of them nominated facetiously, but some intended for our serious consideration.

Quintus: Let's not waste time talking about the silly ones. Anybody can see it wouldn't make sense to put books together according to their color or size. Don't think it'd make much sense to group them by the alphabet, either.

Elanchius: Quintus, your calling such arrangements "silly" interests me. Will you explain why you think them so?

Quintus: Well, it just doesn't matter what color books are. If you put 'em together because they're all the same color, you've not used a very important reason for putting them together.

Elanchius: Ah! Then you believe that books should be grouped together according to something they have in common that *is* important?

Quintus: That's right.

Elanchius: Would you say that perhaps books ought to be grouped not merely according to some important thing they have in common, but according to their *most* important common element?

Quintus: Well, why not? No use taking second best.

Elanchius: And if we can agree that books should be grouped

according to the most important thing they share, would you say
that we have solved our problem?

Quintus: Not yet. Still have to figure out what the most
important thing is.

Elanchius: And will this always be the same thing—for all
persons and purposes?

Quintus: Don't think I get you, Elanchius.

Empiricus: Perhaps I can help a little here, Quintus. Now
suppose for a moment that you are an artist employed to decorate
the home of one of our citizens. You must make the furnishings
harmonize with one another and with the walls, ceilings, and
floors in each room. Suppose further that one room is to contain
a large number of books on open shelves. Now, if the books are
to contribute to the harmonious effect of the whole, they must
be arranged with some care. Isn't it possible that in such a
circumstance the various colors of these books would be of considerable importance?

Quintus: Yeh! Guess so.

Elanchius: Indeed, isn't it conceivable that to you as the one
responsible for achieving harmony the color might be the most
important thing about them?

Quintus: You and Empiricus sure have a way of putting
things. Guess you got me there. Think I see what you're driving
at too. But just because the color'd be important in that house
doesn't mean it'd matter any place else.

Empiricus: You also said that it would not make much sense
to group books alphabetically. Is not that so?

Quintus: That's right. Doesn't make any difference because
books happen to be written by people with names that all start
with X, or Y, or Z.

Empiricus: But let us suppose that you are a cataloguer of
books. You must arrange them so that you can find a particular
one in the shortest possible time and with the least information.
Would you say that, in these circumstances, it would not make
any sense to arrange them alphabetically?

Quintus: Guess you got me again, Empiricus.

Empiricus: Then to a cataloguer the most important thing a group of books have in common may be that their authors' names all begin with the same letter.

Quintus: Yeh! That's right.

Libentia: You have made the matter very clear, Empiricus.

Elanchius: Indeed he has, Libentia. He has demonstrated clearly why the most important common element is not an absolute, but a relative matter. For the artist and the cataloguer color and alphabetical designation are of crucial importance in the arrangement of books. Must we not conclude that "importance" cannot be determined without reference to purpose?

Quintus: Yeh! See that now.

Elanchius: Then, Quintus, must not our earlier statement be modified?

Quintus: Don't quite remember what that was, Elanchius.

Elanchius: We said that books used in the reading program should be grouped according to the most important thing they have in common. Now, in the light of your conversation with Empiricus, must we not restate the principle thus: that they should be grouped according to the most important thing they have in common that is relevant to the purpose for which they are to be used in the classroom?

Libentia: And, since we have defined that purpose as the humanization of the students, the final statement of the principle would be this: *Books should be grouped according to the most important thing they share that is relevant to the humanizing purpose.*

Elanchius: Excellent, Libentia!

Quintus: Well, I'd say right off that their color doesn't have anything to do with that.

Elanchius: Or the alphabetical arrangement?

Quintus: No. Putting books together because their authors' names started with "X" wouldn't help any.

Elanchius: And what about the proposals we discussed more seriously—the chronological, for example?

Quintus: The fact a bunch of books were all written about the same time doesn't have that kind of importance. If you want the way you group books to help 'em do their job of humanizing, seems to me that you got to find something that's *in* the books and not outside 'em.

Elanchius: And would you say the same about putting them together because they were all written in the same form?

Quintus: Doesn't look like that'd matter much here either. Form's not inside the books. They're inside it.

Elanchius: And what of grouping them according to the place in which they were written?

Quintus: What difference does that make, if we really mean what we said about humanizing?

Elanchius: Libentia, I believe, mentioned the "occasional" order—grouping books with respect to seasons, holidays, and the like. Does that plan meet the requirements of our principle.

Quintus: Don't think so. But maybe I don't know how that's supposed to work.

Libentia: Since I mentioned the possibility, Quintus, let me tell you what I think about it.

Quintus: Go ahead, Libentia. But seems to me anyway there aren't enough holidays and things like that to take care of all the reading you ought to have 'em do.

Libentia: True, Quintus. If the occasional order alone were used, much literature that we should like to teach because of its humanizing potential would necessarily be omitted.

Quintus: Say, that's right! Guess there's lots of good books that don't have anything to do with things like holidays.

Libentia: Yes, including many of the best ones.

Elanchius: But even so, is this the most serious objection to the occasional order?

Pulvius: Serious? I'll tell you what's serious! The students will be reading shoddy, second-rate, maudlin pieces which should never even be allowed to get into the classroom. Why, I've seen scores of sentimental droolings and patriotic flourishes that have been passed off as literature, but the world would be better off without such tepid pap. If you arrange your reading program to match seasonal events, you make it congenial to introduce this kind of reading—and worst of all, at the expense of genuine literature.

Vulpius: But don't assume that your own arrangement is

any better, Pulvius. I've seen some of your reading lists, and they are full of dry specimens utilized only to fill gaps in your precious chronology.

Pulvius: Ho, Vulpius! Are you still here? I thought you had fallen off the hill.

Libentia: Certainly there is some truth in your charge, Vulpius. Nevertheless, I agree with much that Pulvius has said. Why, I've even known a teacher who herself wrote "poems" for special occasions and actually required her students to recite them at a school program—even though they were amateurish and naive—dismal things in which a humanizing potential could not possibly lurk. I suppose she thought it better to have something appropriate for the occasion, even if she had to write it herself, than to keep her students readings works of genuine artistic force which, however, were not specifically tailored to fit the occasion. Excuse me!

Quintus: Really mean that, don't you, Libentia?

Elanchius: I understand how you feel, Libentia. But even so, may there not be a still greater objection to the occasional order than that it encourages the omission of literature and the inclusion of poorer material?

Empiricus: I think I understand you, Elanchius. I believe you are alluding to the lack of accord between the occasional order and the principle we have established.

Elanchius: Ah, Empiricus! Have we not said that works of literature should be grouped not according to some superficial thing but according to the most important thing they have in common which is relevant to our purpose? Clearly then, the occasional arrangement is inappropriate, for the *occasion* of a literary work is rarely more than a mere circumstance of its origin or application. It is, in any event, unlikely to be what the work is really about.

Quintus: Outside of it instead of inside! Right, Elanchius? Guess that takes care of that.

Pulvius: And I must say, well dispatched!

Vulpius: And I must say that your thinking is unrealistic, for it overlooks an important consideration. You have not stopped to investigate whether research says something worthwhile in this area. If you had, you would have found that utilization of motivational material is a realistic approach. Pupil interests, research has discovered, are more likely to identify with material correlated with special occasions, interest shifts of a seasonal type, and similar factors. You forget that the teacher must motivate.

Elanchius: We can agree, Vulpius, at least that motivation is always desirable, though certainly it lacks virtue merely in itself and ought therefore never to be considered an end in itself.

Pulvius: A fact obvious to any reasonable mind!

Elanchius: It seems clear that the occasional order must be used sparingly. Although perhaps by relating specific pieces of literature to particular occasions the teacher may sometimes enhance their force, she should not adopt it as a complete method of arrangement or allow it to interfere with her proper purpose.

Libentia: Gentlemen, when we first began talking about arrangement, we quickly agreed that *some* kind of arrangement is necessary; as Elanchius and Empiricus reminded us, the human mind demands order. But now, of the proposals that were made, only a single possibility remains, for we have rejected all the others.

Quintus: Say! That's right. What'll we do if that one won't do either?

Elanchius: True. Only one—the topical order—remains of those suggested. But we remarked at the time, you will recall, that all the possibilities had not been mentioned.

Quintus: Looks like we're in a kind of tough spot, though.

Elanchius: Obviously, the safest way is to accept the topical arrangement without subjecting it to scrutiny! But, if I may judge from the character of our conversations, we shall not now substitute expediency for impartial examination. Remember, Quintus, that we began these conversations because of Libentia's request for help. But if we do not proceed with honesty and impartiality, we shall have failed her. Let us therefore examine the topical arrangement with candor.

Quintus: Well, guess someone'll have to tell me right off just exactly what the topical arrangement is.

Empiricus: Why, Quintus, you yourself suggested the topical arrangement. Moreover, you gave us an example or two at the time.

Quintus: I did? How's that?

Empiricus: Why, you said that works of literature might be arranged according to what they are about.

Quintus: Remember now—said they might be about country life, war, things like that. That's topical, hey?

Libentia: I must confess that I share Quintus' uncertainty about the meaning of this and similar terms. When I have heard teachers discuss ways of arranging books, I have been struck by the apparent confusion of the names they attach to various practices. I heard one teacher say "topical" when I thought she really meant "occasional," for she then described the very kind of organization we have just rejected. I have also heard of organization according to what was called "subject." And still other terms are used, some of them apparently intended to identify the same thing.

Elanchius: Your remarks properly remind us that we must define our terms carefully. Well, then. Quintus has suggested that works might be arranged "according to what they are about." Now, without yet giving this kind of arrangement a name, let us see whether it is in accord with our principle that books be grouped according to the most important thing they have in common that is relevant to the purpose they are to serve. We have concluded that to have their color in common is not important; so also for having their occasion in common—and so on. Now, what do you think of Quintus' suggestion? Have books an important thing in common if it is "what they are about" that they share?

Empiricus: It would appear to me, not as a literary man but simply as an observer of the natures of things, that if what they are truly about is what they have in common, they share something very important indeed!

Elanchius: Would it seem to you likely that this might in fact be the most important thing that books can have in common?

Empiricus: I would say so.

Elanchius: And is it also likely that numerous books have "what they are about" in common?

Empiricus: Let Libentia reply to that.

Libentia: No, not Libentia, but Pulvius, for whose superior knowledge of books Libentia has the deepest respect!

Pulvius: You are gracious, Libentia. I assure you, Elanchius, that a great many books share this that Quintus called "what they are about."

Elanchius: Then it is possible thus to arrange works of literature?

Pulvius: Quite so.

Quintus: Looks like we're getting somewhere!

Elanchius: Now what shall we call this arrangement? Is it what has been referred to as "topical"?

Libentia: I know that "topical" is often used in this way. However, it is also used to mean other kinds of arrangement which I believe we are not now considering.

Elanchius: Will you tell us what other kinds you mean, Libentia?

Libentia: You remember that Quintus mentioned "war" and "city life" as examples of topics that books are about. I think that these may properly be called topics, but I wonder whether they are what the works *are* truly about. It seems to me that they supply only the general field or area upon which the author draws in creating his work. In one sense, perhaps, a book is "about" its topic. But in a deeper sense there is a rather superficial connection between book and topic—not unlike that which exists between book and occasion.

Elanchius: You are saying, then, that although "topical arrangement" is a valid term for one kind of organization, it does not describe what we are seeking since the "topic" of a book is not what, in the truest sense, the book is "about."

Quintus: What? Mean to say a book about war's *not* about war? Sounds queer to me.

Pulvius: Such a conclusion may indeed seem paradoxical, Quintus, but paradoxical or no, it is true. To name merely the topic of a book is not to denote truly what the book is about.

Elanchius: Now let us see where the logic of our argument has led us. We have said that the most important thing books have in common is what they are about, and that it is according to this that they should be arranged. But we have also said that the *topic* is *not* what a book is about. Must it not follow that we reject the topical arrangement?

Quintus: Afraid you'd say that. Now we've thrown 'em all out the window. What do we do now?

Elanchius: But we haven't thrown our principle out the window, Quintus.

Quintus: What good's that if we don't have anything that fits it?

Pulvius: Aha! Now perhaps we are ready to return to the time-tested arrangement according to period, form, and regional origin!

Vulpius: Don't be unrealistic, Pulvius! Your arrangement is obsolete.

Pulvius: Nevertheless, Vulpius, although our friends have condemned it, they have not found a better one.

Empiricus: True, Pulvius. We have not yet found a method of arrangement which we deem appropriate. But, as Elanchius has just reminded us, we have enunciated the principle by which a proper arrangement can be chosen. Is not our task, then, simply to identify and name the thing which a book is truly about? When we have done so, shall we not also have solved the problem of arrangement?

Quintus: That's right. But how do we get there?

Elanchius: Perhaps Libentia has given us a clue. She mentioned "subject" as one of several terms that are sometimes used interchangeably. Let us consider whether it is what we seek.

Quintus: All right. But what's the difference between that and topic? We said war's a topic. So what's a subject?

Elanchius: To answer your question, Quintus, let us think of some book whose topic is war.

Quintus: Bet I know one, Elanchius. Story about a war that went on for ten years and wound up with the town all burning up. That do?

Elanchius: Good. Do you remember it well, Quintus?

Quintus: Still see those fellows fighting, and one fellow getting away carrying his father on his back while everything was blazing. He had quite a time getting another city started, too.

Hey! Don't read that book much any more in the schools, do they?

Pulvius: You won't find it on Vulpius' lists, Quintus!

Vulpius: You are apparently speaking of some ancient book ill adjusted to our modern youths.

Pulvius: Ha! Such abysmal—

Libentia: Shh, Pulvius!

Elanchius: Well, then. If war is the topic of this book, what is its *subject*?

Quintus: Looks like that'd be war, too.

Elanchius: Pulvius, you are our greatest authority on literature. What do you say is the subject of this book?

Pulvius: Why, "subject," generically speaking, is the particular substance—call it subject-matter, if you wish—within the area or field which we have called "topic." It is out of subject-matter, or "subject," that the author constructs his book; thereby he gives it its particularity. In this book the *subject* is the siege of the particular city, involving the particular opposing forces, provoked by the particular cause, conducted under the particular circumstances, and having the particular consequence.

Empiricus: If I understand you, Pulvius, the subject is selected from within the wider topic. It is the topic particularized, as it were, so that what was abstract becomes concrete.

Quintus: Whew! And that's what this book's about?

Elanchius: Your question is the crucial one, Quintus. We are seeking to identify and name what we have so far referred to only as "what the book is truly about." If *subject*, as just defined, designates what a book is truly about, then our quest for the most suitable method of arrangement is ended. For, if we have indeed identified that which a book is truly about, we have necessarily identified the most important thing that books can have in common.

Empiricus: Something in your tone suggests that we have not yet found what we seek.

Elanchius: True, Empiricus. But Pulvius seems impatient to speak.

Pulvius: I must remind you that the book in question is not "about" a siege and its particular circumstances. The author himself tells us unmistakably what his book is about—the wrath of his hero and its consequences.* In the truest sense what this book is *about* is that which also gives it unity—what is properly called its *theme*.

Quintus: Hey! That's a new one! What's the difference between theme and subject?

Pulvius: Why, Quintus, the theme is that which the subject-matter bodies forth, so to speak. Indeed, we may say that the subject-matter is the body of a work, and the theme is its soul.

Quintus: Hey! That's good!

Libentia: If "theme" names what a book is about, what should this mean to me as a teacher? For example, how shall I place the book we have just been speaking of?

Empiricus: Since we have agreed that books should be grouped according to what they are truly about, and since this author has told us what his book is about, does it not follow that we must place this work only with such others as celebrate also the ruinous wrath of this particular hero?

Pulvius: If that were so, then this book would stand virtually alone, for we should find precious few to place with it!

Empiricus: Then could we place with it books about other heroes whose wrath is similarly ruinous?

Pulvius: That is possible, for certainly there are other books in which the wrath of a hero has dire consequences.

Empiricus: And would the logic of our argument lead us to group other books together because they deal with the ruinous *grief* of their heroes, or with their excessive *joy*, or *love*, and so on?

Pulvius: It would appear so.

Empiricus: This would seem to suggest that we group books according to the human feelings which they treat. Is this what we seek?

---

* From the descriptions given by Quintus and Pulvius, it will be apparent to the reader that the work under discussion can be neither the *Iliad* nor the *Aeneid*, but is presumably some pre-Homeric masterpiece, very possibly an epic, which embraced elements perhaps separated in later versions drawn upon by Homer and Virgil. The work, unfortunately, is not extant.

Elanchius: One moment, Empiricus. Pulvius, you used the term "theme" for that which we have been calling "what the book is about." Now would you say that if books were arranged in the way suggested by your conversation with Empiricus, they would be arranged according to their themes?

Pulvius: Only in a general way, I believe. Strictly speaking, the theme of a literary work is an individual, particular, even unique thing. Such human feelings and attributes as love, grief, wrath, and the like are in one sense merely abbreviated and convenient suggestions of themes, and in another sense are the general qualities to which authors may choose to give specific embodiment in their books.

Empiricus: Then you are saying that love, grief, wrath, and the like may be regarded as themes only in a general sense.

Pulvius: As long as you say, "in a general sense," I will agree that these can be called themes. For example, one poem may have as its particular theme, let us say, "Love is best," and another that love prevents a man from fulfilling his highest potential; but nevertheless, although the assertions made by the two poems are quite different, they share *that about which the assertions are made,* and can thus be said to share as their *general* theme, love.

Quintus: But, how's this different from "topic"? Said a while ago a book's not really about its topic. Now you say it's about its theme. But what's the difference between war, for example, and wrath or love and so on?

Libentia: You have asked an important question, Quintus. I think I see how it must be answered, but I should like to be clear about it before I begin to arrange specific works of literature for my classes.

Empiricus: Perhaps the problem here is one of classification. Are not war and country life, on the one hand, and wrath, love, and the like, on the other hand, of essentially different categories? One is concerned with the externals and the other with what I, not being versed in the critical terms of literature, would have to call the essential ingredients. That is, "topic" is the area or field which supplies the environment, surrounding both the subject-matter and the theme. But what Pulvius has called the general theme is not external but internal; it is rather a human trait, or quality, or attribute which informs the thoughts and actions of the characters. Or, if I may risk an epigram, the topic is "about" the book, but the book is "about" the theme.

Quintus: Hey! What I said all along—one's outside, other's inside.

Pulvius: Bravo!

Libentia: Bravo indeed, Pulvius. The distinction is clear, but can we agree on some examples? In my school there is an anthology in which a number of short pieces are grouped under the heading, "Occupations." Would you call this thematic, or topical grouping?

Pulvius: I should call that [——].*

Libentia: Pulvius!

Quintus: Sounds topical, if I know what we've been talking about.

Pulvius: A student of mine who at the time was taking a "professional" course required to qualify him for teaching showed me a book one day in which some trashy little "materials," as Vulpius calls them, were arranged under something headed "Family Relations." What might that be called, pray?

Quintus: Topical, too, I'd say.

Libentia: And what would you say of "Courage"? Is it a theme?

Quintus: Looks different than the others, anyhow.

Elanchius: Empiricus indulged in an epigram a moment ago. Another may help us here—that "topic" names that which a man exists within, but "theme" names that which exists within a man.

Quintus: Hey! Not bad, Elanchius. A fellow's *in* an occupation, but courage is in *him*.

Elanchius: If we are now clear on what we mean by "theme," presumably we should be able to name the full list of human

---

* The editors have had no choice but, because of its pungent flavor, to delete the word used by Pulvius. It is in such shockingly bad taste as to make its authenticity suspect. A gentlemanly scholar of Pulvius' taste and learning would clearly not have spoken it—least of all in Libentia's presence. Accordingly, the offensive term has been deleted; this is the only such deletion it has been necessary to make in the text.

qualities which, because they *are* human qualities, have served as the themes of literature.

Empiricus: That task should not be difficult for anyone well versed in literature. But now another question occurs to me: will all works recognized as literary prove to be classifiable according to one or another of these qualities?

Pulvius: It is true, Empiricus, that there is often much in a book which because it is on the surface and therefore obvious may blur the reader's conception of what the book is truly about—may in fact quite mislead him if he does not read perceptively. But in any genuine work of literature, if one probes deeply enough and with sufficient discernment, he will find that it indeed concerns some human quality or attribute. Hence I would say that all literature is classifiable according to one or another of these qualities.

Elanchius: Ah! Then it is possible to classify works so that those qualities which must be considered as central if literature is to humanize the reader will be kept central *even in the arrangement itself.*

Quintus: If I get you, Elanchius, you're saying books ought to be arranged by these themes. Now you showed me how themes are different from topics, but guess I still don't quite get why one's better than the other. You said things could be arranged by themes. But you could do it by topics, too. What's the advantage?

Elanchius: Do you recall, Quintus, that we established three criteria for determining whether or not a proposed arrangement is suitable?

Quintus: Yeh, remember that. The first one was that the arrangement oughtn't to make the job of teaching literature any harder. Suppose that means it ought to make it easier. Will these themes do it?

Libentia: Let me try to answer that, Quintus.

Quintus: Go ahead, Libentia.

Libentia: Then I'll begin by asking some help of Vulpius.

Pulvius: Vulpius!

Libentia: Have I not heard you say many times, Vulpius, that students will find least difficult that which they are most interested in?

Vulpius: Now your thinking is realistic, Libentia! Research says that individuals achieve more worthwhile outcomes if they are interested in what they are experiencing. It has been demonstrated statistically that there is a close correlation between reading comprehension and reading interest.

Libentia: We know that students do not naturally find interest in such matters as literary chronology and typology, and that therefore to arrange literature thus is to increase rather than decrease the difficulty of teaching it. But we did not consider whether a topical arrangement would help to diminish the difficulty. Are students naturally more interested in topics like "sports" or "occupations" or "family relations" than in such matters as "the ode" or "the silver age of literature"?

Vulpius: Definitely, Libentia! The three areas you have just instanced are, in fact, among those which the present-day school population show they are interested in. These areas are much less remote from individual interests than concepts such as "odes" and "silver ages." Hence, any youth tending to have normative interest patterns will naturally be more interested in them.

Pulvius: And you are thereby led into supposing that students should read such "masterpieces" as those on your lists, Vulpius!

Libentia: Then you would say, Vulpius, that the student is most interested in that which is least remote from him?

Vulpius: That is a basic principle governing the learning processes, established on the basis of carefully compiled empirical evidence.

Libentia: Then, if there are matters still less remote than those commonly used in topical arrangements, should we not conclude that they will hold the potentiality of even greater interest for students, and therefore will help to lessen the difficulty of reading?

Vulpius: Definitely. But our researchers have compiled no data tending to demonstrate that there is anything less remote.

Quintus: Maybe because they looked outside instead of inside, Vulpius.

Vulpius: Whatever you may say, the fact remains that, as our statistical research has shown, typical present-day youths are interested in such areas as sports, occupations, and family relations, and not in such abstractions as those you call themes.

Elanchius: Undoubtedly, many students are interested in books whose topics are, for example, sports and occupations. But may it not be the human qualities represented in such works, rather than the topics themselves, that are the real sources of interest?

Vulpius: Intangibles are not utilized in the thinking of we in the profession.

Pulvius: You should try them sometime, Vulpius. You should try them!

Elanchius: Much more might be said here. But now, Libentia was leading us toward an important conclusion. May we not say that, since the themes of books are expressive of essentially *human* qualities, arrangement according to them will necessarily prove least remote, and therefore will make the reading least difficult? For this arrangement invites the reader to be interested in that which in fact lies *within himself*. In contrast, even the best topical arrangement will prove to be more remote since it must concern matters which, however near, are nevertheless outside rather than within the reader.

Quintus: Just what I said! Outside instead of inside!

Elanchius: Well, then. It appears that an arrangement which is truly thematic will not increase the student's difficulty in reading, but should lessen it. If so, this arrangement clearly satisfies the demands of our first criterion. May we now turn to the second?

Quintus: Let's. Remember what it was, too. We said the way books are arranged oughtn't to get in the way of the job of humanizing the student.

Elanchius: Good, Quintus. You have succeeded in stating our second proposition more forcefully than we did before.

Empiricus: It is clear that in considering whether the thematic arrangement meets the demands of our first criterion, we have actually been considering also whether it satisfies the second.

Quintus: How's that, Empiricus?

Empiricus: We agreed, you recall, that the effect of an

arrangement according to literary chronology, for example, is
to place a wall between book and reader.

Quintus: Yeh, remember that wall all right. Thick one, we
said. The kind that'd stop an arrow, too.

Empiricus: But an arrangement that is truly thematic would
set no such wall between.

Quintus: Hey! Now I get it! You got human qualities in the
book and human qualities in the *student,* and this way you bring
'em together.

Libentia: Ah, Quintus! Since the arrangement is constructed
of the very stuff of literature itself, it is in effect not a wall but a
channel—through which the humanizing force of a great book
may flow.

Elanchius: And does it not then follow that the thematic
arrangement meets the demands of our final criterion also?

Quintus: Remember that one, too. It goes on from where
the second leaves off. The second one said the arrangement
oughtn't to hinder the job books ought to do. The third one said
it ought to help 'em do it.

Pulvius: I confess, Elanchius, that here your logic eludes me.
I am willing, for the present, at least, to concede that the thematic
arrangement will not obstruct the humanizing power of literature. But does it necessarily follow that it therefore augments
this force?

Elanchius: Your question is justified, Pulvius, for to disprove
a negative is not in itself to prove an affirmative. One part of our
argument is as yet only implicit. But perhaps we can make it
explicit. We have agreed that a truly thematic arrangement of
books is nearest the ideal because it juxtaposes what is essentially
human in literature and what is essentially human in the reader,
with no barrier between. So much is clear. But now our question
is this: whether, *when books are brought together in a thematic
arrangement, the humanizing force of the individual book may
thereby, in effect, be enhanced.*

Empiricus: That is to say that when books are placed together in this way something may accrue to the force of each
which was not present earlier?

Elanchius: Yes, Empiricus.

Quintus: Sounds good, but still don't see how it works.

Elanchius: Then let us seek a way to clarify the matter, Quintus. Tell me—have you ever had occasion to help push back onto the road a cart that had become stalled in the mire?

Quintus: Well, I've helped push out a cart or two in my time. Matter of fact, just last week one of my own got stuck on the way in to the shop, loaded with leather. And I mean it was really stuck.

Elanchius: What did you do, Quintus?

Quintus: Tried to push it out, of course.

Elanchius: And were you able to do so?

Quintus: Not a bit. Gave it all I had, too, but couldn't budge it.

Elanchius: And what then, Quintus?

Quintus: Got another fellow who was passing by, and he tried. Couldn't do it either. Big fellow, too. Awful big—like Discobolus. Thought he could do it alone. But he couldn't. So we both tried and still couldn't.

Elanchius: And what then?

Quintus: Then a couple of husky lads came along and we *all* got behind it and gave it a boost.

Elanchius: And what happened, Quintus?

Quintus: No trouble at all. Set her right back on the road.

Elanchius: But no one of you was able to do so by himself?

Quintus: I'll say not! Took the bunch of us.

Elanchius: Would you say, Quintus, that when you pushed with the other three you were able to push harder than when you pushed alone?

Quintus: Course not. Pushed as hard as I could when I tried it by myself.

Elanchius: But then your effort was quite unsuccessful?

Quintus: Never budged an inch.

Elanchius: But when you pushed with the others your effort was entirely successful?

Quintus: Cart was back on the road in no time.

Elanchius: Then, although in reality you pushed no harder when you pushed with the others, yet *in effect* your effort was greatly enhanced, since it met with success whereas before it had failed?

Quintus: Guess you're right. Didn't do any good at all to push alone, but plenty when I pushed with the rest of 'em.

Elanchius: And now, Quintus, do you see any connection between your experience with the cart and our conclusion that the humanizing force of each book is, *in effect*, enhanced when books are brought together thematically?

Quintus: Books? Say, I'd forgotten all about them. Got to thinking about that cart in the mud. Now you mention it, though, guess there's plenty of connection. Lots of books together will help each one do the job.

Elanchius: Well, then. We set out to find the arrangement of books which would best satisfy the exacting demands of the most relevant criteria. We have found it to be an arrangement in terms of the human themes of literature. And Quintus has summed up the matter with direct eloquence: "books put together this way will help each one do the job."

Quintus: Looks like that's done. What's next?

Empiricus: I agree, Quintus. We have found what we sought—the ideal arrangement.

Libentia: As a teacher, I find this a particularly happy and most welcome end to our immediate quest. From this conversation I have come to see more clearly what it is that I must do in bringing student and book together.

Elanchius: Quintus has asked, "What's next?" But before we proceed, perhaps some will want to question our conclusions. However, may I remark that the sun is now directly overhead and is very hot.

Quintus: Golly! I'll say it is. Forgot about it while we were talking. Hey! Take a look at the color of that bald spot on Pulvius' head!

Vulpius: If he experiences much more of this sun, it may tend to thaw out some concepts in there. Then he'll have to re-write all those lectures he foists on his young learners.

Pulvius: My head does feel a trifle warm. Is there some shade at hand?

Elanchius: Yes indeed, Pulvius. Do you see there, just below, that figure now approaching the little grove of olive trees at the nearer end of the lake?

Libentia: I see him. He appears to be carrying a heavy burden of some kind.

Elanchius: So he is, Libentia. And that burden is neither more nor less than our lunch. Shall we set out for the grove? There we can have shade and refreshment, and afterwards continue our conversation.

Pulvius: You are omniscient, Elanchius!

Empiricus: And a thoughtful host.

Quintus: I'll say! Let's get started down the trail. Boy, I'm hungry!

Empiricus: Lead the way, Quintus. Libentia, may I help you down this first steep incline?

Libentia: Please do.

Pulvius: Heigh-ho! and all after. You too, Vulpius. But mind you don't wander off the trail again going down, now!

The Arrangement Questioned

Persons of the Dialogue

LIBENTIA MAGISTRA

PULVIUS GRAMMATICUS   VULPIUS MATERIES

J. QUINTUS   EMPIRICUS MARTIALIS

ELANCHIUS

Scene: A lakeshore grove

Libentia: The refreshments were delicious, Elanchius.

Pulvius: Verily, a noble repast.

Elanchius: You are kind to say so, but I am sure that these beautiful surroundings have contributed much to our pleasure.

Libentia: I have been admiring the beauty of the scene, Elanchius. And even as we were speaking about how well we have all feasted, I was thinking of the natural harmony of our setting. The lake is being fed by those tiny rivulets running into it, and these lovely old olive trees are being fed by the fertile soil.

Elanchius: Ah! You are essaying the allegorical mode, Libentia.

Pulvius: Marry, how? Tropically?

Quintus: Say, what's this all about?

Empiricus: Why, Quintus, Libentia has likened our feasting to the natural processes occurring all about us. And while you are at it, Libentia, why not go even further?

Libentia: What have you in mind, Empiricus?

Empiricus: You might liken this sparkling lake to the great store of literature which is the possession of mankind.

199

Libentia: True, Empiricus, and this store is being eternally replenished by fresh streams of artistic inspiration, even as the lake is fed by its many rivulets!

Pulvius: Not to crack the wind of the poor figure running it thus, but what, Libentia, can you make of this stream that flows through the grove? It runs *out* of the lake, not into it. Your inveterate allegorist would fit that in somewhere.

Quintus: Hey! What's up? You have too much of Elanchius' wine?

Libentia: Perhaps, Quintus.

Empiricus: And what an elixir it is! But Pulvius asked you a question, Libentia.

Libentia: Well, since you press me, why not say that this stream watering the fields below corresponds to Pulvius' work and mine as teachers of literature? Even as it taps the inexhaustible lake, so we draw upon the reservoir of books to nourish the humanity of our students.

Vulpius: You are indulging in some rather high-flown rhetoric, Libentia.

Pulvius: High-flowing, you should have said, Vulpius. And perhaps it is high time it was dammed up.

Libentia: Oh, Pulvius!

Pulvius: I'm sorry. I couldn't resist the temptation!

Empiricus: Speaking of damming up the stream, Pulvius— haven't we been seeking, in our morning's conversation, a way to avoid just that?

Quintus: Say, will somebody tell me what this is all about?

Elanchius: Why, Quintus, if I have correctly interpreted our trio of wits, they have been discovering, as Pulvius might say, books in the running brooks, sermons in stones, and—

Quintus: Big help!

Elanchius: More seriously then, Quintus, they have reminded us of our search for a way of arranging books that will create no barrier between literature and the reader.

Quintus: But we settled all that this morning. We said the thematic way's best because it doesn't get in the way. Hey, I see what they were talking about now—just like a dam in this stream. We don't want any dam.

Elanchius: Exactly, Quintus.

Pulvius: Since it is out in the open again, I have some more to say on that head. In fact, I have three specific questions in mind.

Elanchius: I noted this morning that your countenance was sometimes troubled, Pulvius, and surely it is right that you express your doubts. But will it not be helpful if we first restate the conclusions that we have reached thus far?

Pulvius: By all means.

Elanchius: Empiricus, may we once again impose on you?

Empiricus: Let me begin by reminding you of the first important conclusion we reached—that no problem in the teaching of literature will be solved wisely unless it is solved in the light of the answer to what we called the "antecedent question"—namely, what is the highest function that the study of literature can serve?

Quintus: Remember that, all right!

Empiricus: We agreed that the highest function is the humanization of the reader. This we then called our "antecedent answer," since all subsequent decisions were to be referred to it.

Quintus: Wouldn't be right if they weren't.

Empiricus: The decisions which we made with respect to the selection of books and to the kinds of readers who had greatest need to be reached by their force were wholly in accord with this answer.

Quintus: Wouldn't be right if they weren't, either.

Empiricus: Having concluded that some kind of arrangement is not only desirable but indeed inevitable, we sought the most suitable arrangement for books in the reading program. After rejecting various possibilities as not in accord with our antecedent answer, we finally accepted the arrangement by themes, for, being a grouping according to the most relevant affinity among books, it best contributes to the high purpose which we have said the study of literature must serve.

Elanchius: Thank you, Empiricus. A precise recapitulation.

Quintus: Made things clear, that's for sure.

Elanchius: And now, Pulvius. There are matters about which you still have doubts.

Pulvius: "Doubts" is the proper word, Elanchius. I shall not call them objections, but I must confess that I have some misgivings about the efficacy of this arrangement.

Elanchius: By all means, let us hear them, Pulvius.

Pulvius: Then let me phrase them as direct questions. First, can I be certain that the teacher who adopts a thematic arrangement will include only documents of genuine literary quality? Or, will she succumb to temptation and fill out her thematic classifications with—

Vulpius: Those are called "units" by we in the profession, Pulvius.

Pulvius: Whatever you call them, will the teacher be tempted to pad them out with shoddy or inconsequential stuff just because it happens to fit the theme?

Elanchius: It is one thing to be tempted, Pulvius, another thing to fall! Certainly it is our assumption that the teacher will *not* be led by the thematic arrangement to deviate from the principle of selection upon which we have agreed. If she *were* induced to substitute works of the shabby kind you have described, not only would she have been grossly misled by the arrangement but she would also have abandoned her proper role as a teacher of literature! For, by choosing books that lack even the potential for humanization, she would have precluded the possibility of attaining her highest purpose. Rather than see her thus misled by the thematic arrangement, or the arrangement debased by her use of it, I for one would say, let her adopt the chronological or typological arrangement!

Quintus: Wow! You sure laid that right on the line, Elanchius.

Pulvius: Your unequivocal declaration allays my fears, Elanchius. I had scarcely thought that anything could strike such a heat in you!

Quintus: Yeh, those gray eyes of his fairly blazed! Hey! Never noticed they were gray before.

Elanchius: Believe me, Pulvius, I share your horror lest the arrangement we have chosen as most likely to aid in releasing the force of literature prove to be the very means of preventing

the attainment of that end! Let us trust the wise teacher to understand that the best possible kind of arrangement will be vain if
the works so arranged are in themselves empty! Let us trust her to
remember that *she must select first and arrange afterwards,
and never the reverse.*

Libentia: The wise teacher will not betray your trust.

Elanchius: Your avowal of faith in the teacher is heartening,
Libentia. All depends on her, at last! And now, with this assurance, Pulvius, are you ready to state your other misgivings?

Pulvius: Another is this: Does your rejection of the plans of
arrangement that I proposed mean that literary works will be
presented to students quite without regard to the times and
places of their origin and to the forms in which they are cast?
The incontrovertible fact is that some works are written, for
example, as odes, or dramas, or satires. And it is no less incontrovertible that all are the products of given times and places.
These are facts of too great moment to be ignored.

Elanchius: They are indeed. But just now you used the
phrase, "presented to students." We must soon examine, in the
light of conclusions reached in the past few days, the entire
matter of *presenting* literature in the classroom.

Quintus: You mean the business of how to get the books
into their heads? Was wondering when we'd get to that.

Elanchius: The time has almost come, Quintus. And since,
Pulvius, it is in the actual presentation of literature in the classroom that the matters you mention will be either introduced or—
as you fear—neglected, may we postpone our answer to your
second question?

Pulvius: I am agreeable. However, you will remember that
I have a third. May not the teacher, in arranging the literary
pieces according to their themes, become so preoccupied with
the categories of her arrangement as to make *them* the primary
matters of her teaching, relegating literature itself to secondary
place? Indeed, in this arrangement may not the artistic wholeness
of the individual masterpiece be quite neglected?

Quintus: See what you mean. You're afraid she'll teach
themes instead of *books*.

Libentia: I have some questions also, which seem to be directly related to this one. Should I mention them now, Elanchius?

Elanchius: Certainly, Libentia.

Libentia: First let me say that I share your misgivings, Pulvius. There is obviously danger that the thing you fear may come to pass. But besides, as a teacher who must try to put our principles into practice in the classroom, how am I to proceed?

Elanchius: Then your questions are of a practical nature, Libentia?

Libentia: Yes, they are, Elanchius. First of all, just where do I begin in setting up a thematic arrangement? Do I decide on a number of thematic categories, and then look for suitable works to fill them out? Or, do I begin by choosing the works and then build up the general classifications? Furthermore, how many such categories may I expect to find—a great many, each including relatively few literary works, or a very few, each including a great many works? And finally, can every work I want to use be fitted into a single category, or will some be so complex that they will either defy classification altogether or suffer distortion by being placed in a category?

Elanchius: Very proper questions, Libentia. And as you suggested, they are closely related to Pulvius' third question. Perhaps if we succeed in answering yours, we shall find that we have answered his also.

Pulvius: That may be, Elanchius.

Vulpius: Well, I can answer your questions, Libentia, and as for Pulvius', that should not trouble us for a moment. Research has provided many findings in this area. Obviously, Libentia, you must begin with the categories, so that you can develop a program of pupil-oriented readings. There is no doubt on this point, for researchers have scientifically determined what adolescent needs and interests are. You need not, then, hunt themes in the materials your youths will experience, as research has already determined what is the best way of classifying reading materials. This, as you see, also answers your second question. Since the research just mentioned is available for utilization, reading materials are readily classified and their number determined thereby. Indeed, this has already been done, and more than once, by our specialists. And as to your third question, any reading material that is too complex to fit into a pre-devised unit can either be rejected in favor of one that *will* fit, or it can be retained and those portions not adapted to the unit can be omit-ted. The important matter for the teacher is to structure units adapted to student interests and needs, and to select suitable materials for them, which is hardly a difficult problem when one considers how much has been written in recent years that is aimed directly at the adolescent learner.

Empiricus: It is evident, Vulpius, that you do not share Pulvius' fear that the teacher who presents books in a thematic arrangement may be led to teach the categories rather than the books themselves.

Vulpius: Definitely not! My thinking on the matter tends to make me regard it as a hope rather than a fear. And why not? Our professional researchers have determined the worthwhile categories into which reading materials may be grouped by com-piling adolescent interest and need inventories. It follows that the themes themselves are worthwhile to teach, and the materials to be read by the learners are merely the instrumentalities.

Pulvius: Having seen your lists of "reading materials," Vulpius, I do not wonder that you value the categories more than the works placed in them! I doubt that they include a single piece worth prizing for itself. What you forget is that, if books have no genuine force in themselves, they are not worth arranging. Inclusion in one of your "units" cannot make an inconsequential book important or an inferior one great.

Elanchius: Pulvius and Vulpius have just now expressed sharply contrasting points of view, which—

Quintus: Yeh! but where did it get us? Don't think Libentia's questions are answered yet at all!

Elanchius: Well, then. We have agreed that all questions must be answered by reference to our conclusion that the highest function of the study of literature is the humanization of the reader. Must we not therefore examine Libentia's questions in this light?

Quintus: Right.

Elanchius: Now, Quintus, where does the humanizing power

of literature reside? In the frame—thematic or other—which is used for the grouping of books? Or in the books themselves?

Quintus: That's easy. We've said all along it's in the books themselves. That's why we want to use books!

Elanchius: Then the frame itself has no such power?

Quintus: Of course not. That'd be like me telling my customers to wear the shelves I keep shoes on instead of the shoes I keep on 'em.

Pulvius: Ah!

Elanchius: Then, however essential it is that we choose the most suitable kind of arrangement, the arrangement itself is only secondary in importance?

Quintus: Sure! But, wait a minute! We've been beating our brains about arrangement for a couple of days. Now are you telling us we've been wasting our time?

Elanchius: Not at all, Quintus. We have agreed that arrangement is indispensable and inevitable. We have also agreed that a thematic arrangement is best. So our time has not been wasted. But we must not mistake the shell for the kernel—or as you put it, the shelf for the shoe. Well, then. If the power to humanize lies in the books, just where in them shall we say it lies?

Libentia: Why, I believe that Pulvius has told us a moment ago. You were alarmed lest something be neglected because of the thematic arrangement. What was the expression you used, Pulvius?

Pulvius: I mentioned the artistic wholeness of the work, Libentia. Is that what you have in mind?

Libentia: Artistic wholeness—that's it. Perhaps the wholeness of a work of art, or its—its *totality*, one might say, is the thing which has power to move the reader, and by moving him, to affect his humanity.

Empiricus: It appears to me, Libentia, that you are now suggesting the answers to your own questions. You first asked whether to begin the task of grouping works thematically by setting up a number of preconceived categories and then finding pieces to fit into them, or to begin by examining the themes of individual masterpieces and proceeding inductively to construct the categories. Now if it is the totality of the work of art which must, at any cost, be preserved intact when the work is set in an arrangement, does it not follow that you must proceed from the particular to the general?

Quintus: Not sure I follow you, Empiricus.

Libentia: What he means, Quintus, is that if I decide on the classifications first and then fit literary pieces into them, I shall be more likely to do violence to individual works than if I begin with the works and seek in them the thematic affinities by which to group them.

Quintus: Yeh, I see. You've got to take care of the books, and the classifications'll about take care of themselves. Do it the other way around, and you might put down a lot of headings that the books you ought to use won't really fit under—unless you slice 'em up some.

Elanchius: And to "slice them up," Quintus, would be to destroy that totality in which, as Libentia has reminded us, the humanizing force resides.

Quintus: I'd say that's settled, Libentia. You've got to start with the books, not the headings.

Elanchius: Let us turn to her second question—whether she may expect to have many categories with relatively few works in each, or few categories with many works in each. Empiricus, can you show us how Libentia's own remarks about a work's totality also provide the answer to this question?

Empiricus: Hardly, Elanchius. It is clear that there must be a sufficient number of categories to preserve the integrity of every work placed in them. If the categories are rigorously limited, it would seem likely that the works will be forced to accommodate themselves to the categories. But on the precise question which Libentia has raised I am afraid that I cannot speak with much assurance. Perhaps Pulvius will help us.

Pulvius: Perhaps. We have agreed that some kind of arrangement is inevitable and that literary documents should be grouped according to the most important thing they have in common. But in its totality, a literary work is unique; therefore, *as* a totality it cannot possibly be grouped with *any* other works. However, what we earlier called the *general themes* of literature are shared by a large number of documents. On the other hand, if more specialized themes are used, the number of pieces which will fit into each category will be much smaller.

Empiricus: Then an absolute answer cannot be given to Libentia's question? Let me try to state the case. If the classifications are broad, they will be few in number and less likely to distort the totality of individual works placed in them; but if they are *too* broad, they will scarcely serve as helpful frames at all. On the other hand, if the classifications are narrow, they will be more numerous and more effective as organizational frames; but if they are *too* narrow, they may destroy the totality of particular works.

Quintus: It about comes down to this, Libentia. They'll have to be just wide enough so you can put the whole book in without slicing it up. But you can't have too few of 'em either, or they'd have to be so wide they won't do you any good.

Empiricus: Exactly, Quintus. But now the thought occurs to me, Libentia, that you may need general categories, which will be relatively few, and subcategories, which may be fairly numerous. This combination may provide what you are seeking—a framework at once more helpful to the teacher and less injurious to the individual work than either would be if used alone.

Quintus: Sounds pretty good, but just how'll it work?

Empiricus: I could answer you in only the most general way, Quintus. But Libentia, no doubt, can draw upon her experience and her greater knowledge of literature to suggest how it might be done.

Libentia: Well, let me see if I can illustrate with one of the themes we mentioned earlier. We said that "love" is one of the general themes of literature. Obviously, a large number of works would fit into a category with such a broad designation as this—indeed, so many that further classification would be necessary to provide a really helpful arrangement. But a smaller number of works have in common the assertion, for example, that "love is best." Others assert that "the course of true love never did run smooth." Still others that love may be a—a millstone about the neck. These more specific statements of the general theme would, I believe, provide subgroups of the kind which Empiricus has suggested.

Quintus: Sounds reasonable. And could you do that with other things we mentioned, like wrath and courage and all the rest?

Pulvius: Quite easily, Quintus. Although writers have dealt with some themes less frequently than with others, there are scores of literary documents on any number of general themes —courage, loyalty, pride, honor, and so on—which are classifiable into subgroups.

Quintus: I get you, Pulvius. Well, that ought to take care of your second question, Libentia.

Elanchius: Then let us turn to her final one.

Quintus: Yeh! That's the one about the books that are so big that maybe you can't make 'em fit anywhere unless you slice 'em up.

Elanchius: Right, Quintus. We have agreed that the totality of a literary work is so important—I had almost said "sacred"—that *no* arrangement must be permitted to violate it. If certain works, whether because of their size or for some other reason, cannot be categorized without having violence done to them, does it not follow that we must avoid placing them in a category?

Empiricus: The inevitable conclusion, Elanchius.

Quintus: Well, but if you can't put 'em in anywhere, what are you going to do with 'em? Looks like you might have a lot left over!

Elanchius: Ah, Quintus! Let us ask first whether we shall have *any* left over.

Libentia: Surely, most of the works that the teacher will use are comparatively brief and uncomplicated. Finding the proper classification for these, although a delicate task, should not prove an impossible one. But there will be a limited number of works having much greater bulk, chiefly of the dramatic and narrative kinds. It is these which will be difficult—if indeed not impossible— to place.

Pulvius: You speak of works of great bulk. And will they be genuine works of art also?

Libentia: Certainly! After these conversations, I would not willingly use anything else!

Quintus: Nobody'd better try to make you either!

Pulvius: Then rest assured that although your task will be difficult, it will not be impossible.

Libentia: Your tone is encouraging, but I'm not sure I understand.

Pulvius: Tell me, Libentia, what qualities are shared by all true works of art, no matter how different their genre or content?

Libentia: Why, as we have said several times, the most important thing they share is the power to affect the humanity of the reader.

Pulvius: True! But what is the source of this power? From what qualities in the work does it derive?

Libentia: Well, a true work of art has genuine insight into human behavior and reveals the author's knowledge of human problems, and conflicts, and aspirations. I suppose you might call this wisdom.

Pulvius: Excellent, Libentia. But is this all?

Libentia: No. The great work also has beauty.

Pulvius: Good. You have named the two qualities indispensable to the literary work. But do you think of wisdom and beauty as having separate existence?

Libentia: On the contrary, Pulvius. In the finished work of art they are inseparably fused.

Pulvius: And what do we call that which fuses them?

Libentia: Why, it is art. I've already used the word when I called the masterpiece "a work of art."

Pulvius: That is precisely what a masterpiece is, Libentia— a work of art. The wisdom and beauty are fused by the magic of what is called art. And it is by virtue of its art that a masterpiece is able to affect the humanity of its readers. And now—what would you say is the most basic of the *formal* requirements of art?

Libentia: Why, unity—as I tell my students. True composition cannot exist at all without unity.

Quintus: Boy! Things are really getting complicated. How are you going to work this all out?

Pulvius: Patience, Quintus. The end is in sight. And now, Libentia, you have rightly said that the work of art has unity. But in what respects has it unity? What elements does the principle of unity pervade?

Libentia: Why, I should think it must extend to all elements— the action, the mood, the characters—

Pulvius: And the *theme*, Libentia?

Libentia: The theme, of course—that, especially!

Elanchius: Libentia, you asked whether works of greater bulk can be grouped by their themes without damage to their artistic wholeness. Have not you yourself answered this question in replying to Pulvius?

Libentia: Yes, Elanchius. Since a true work of art, no matter what its bulk, must possess unity of theme, among other attributes, clearly it will be possible to place it with other works which share that theme. Still, the task of finding the proper place for a long and complex work will not be easy. Many such works seem to possess several themes, rather than a single one.

Pulvius: Ah, Libentia! It is precisely for this reason that the teacher herself must be a critic—a skilled and perceptive student of literature. If she is not, she may mistake a subordinate theme for one that is central, or she may not see that the subordinate theme supports the central one. She may even find half a dozen themes in a work to be of equal importance and divide the work six ways!

Quintus: But what'll Libentia do, Pulvius, if she reads one of these big books and in spite of everything it *still* looks like it has half a dozen different things it's about?

Pulvius: Then, Quintus, Libentia should suspect that it is no work of art and cast it aside!

Quintus: Just what I thought you'd say. If the pieces don't even add up, it can't be much of a book. So throw it out, Libentia!

Elanchius: Exactly, Quintus. And now, Libentia, it appears that we have arrived at the answer to your third question. Are you satisfied with our conclusion?

Libentia: Well satisfied, Elanchius.

Elanchius: Let us then return to Pulvius' question which immediately preceded and, in fact, precipitated yours. I suggested that, if we could answer Libentia's three questions, we might, in doing so, answer Pulvius' as well. Have we done so?

Quintus: Don't know, Elanchius. Fact is, Pulvius' question has sort of slipped my mind.

Empiricus: If my memory serves, Pulvius asked whether the teacher who has arranged books by themes may not become so preoccupied with the categories as to make *them* primary and the literary works themselves secondary.

Elanchius: You have recalled it precisely, Empiricus. Well, Pulvius, are you still distressed by this possibility?

Pulvius: We would delude ourselves indeed if we supposed no such possibility to exist. The danger is both real and obvious. And I confess that I should be most fearful but for the kind of reassurance that Libentia herself has given us. In the concern which she expressed for the totality of the work I find reason to believe that she will not permit the mere frames to usurp the place of the works themselves.

Libentia: To do so would be to abdicate my role as a teacher of literature. And that I refuse to do!

Elanchius: May we not trust that there are many teachers who will show the same integrity?

Quintus: Yeh, how about it, Libentia? Have we got many teachers like that?

Libentia: Far more than you might suspect, Quintus. Indeed, I believe almost all are devoted to their work.

Quintus: Glad to hear it. But if that's so, how come they don't do the kind of a job we've been talking about?

Libentia: Perhaps they would, Quintus, if they were not so often misled.

Vulpius: Misled, Libentia! What do you mean? Who is misleading them?

Pulvius: Ha! I would answer that, Vulpius, if I weren't a gentleman!

Quintus: Ho! Think I'm beginning to smell a rat.

Elanchius: Libentia and gentlemen, we have been talking for some time. It is midafternoon, and only now are we ready to take up the important matter that was first broached shortly after lunch.

Quintus: What's that, Elanchius? Can't seem to remember.

Elanchius: Clearly, Quintus, our task is not done when we have determined how literary works are to be arranged. We have yet to speak of their presentation in the classroom. If we fail to consider that, we shall not have given Libentia all the help she seeks.

Quintus: Yeh! That's right. No use arranging books if you don't know how to get 'em into the students' heads.

Pulvius: Since, Elanchius, we are now to consider the actual presentation of works, I remind you that we earlier postponed discussion of a question of mine, saying that we would deal with it under this head.

Elanchius: I remember the question, Pulvius, and the grave concern you expressed—which I share. We must examine the matter carefully. Will you restate the question, so that we shall all have it before us and can determine whether it would be more appropriately considered now or later?

Pulvius: My question was this: Will the presentation of literature in a thematic arrangement occasion the complete neglect of such matters as chronology and typology?

Quintus: Still afraid all that stuff you teach'll get left out, Pulvius?

Pulvius: At least as I present literature, I can be certain that all the facts will be adequately represented. But I am unconvinced that they will even be mentioned when the thematic arrangement is used.

Elanchius: Before we argue the point, let us decide whether now is the proper time to do so. We are confronted by the large matter which we have called the presentation of literature in the classroom. Clearly, our examination of it should be orderly. Empiricus, you have several times demonstrated your great ability to perform this kind of task. As it appears to you, how may we best attack this problem? What are the main steps and in what order shall we take them?

Quintus: Yeh! Lay it out for us, Empiricus.

Empiricus: As I have said many times, I am not a specialist in literature and must therefore speak only in the most general terms, and will need much help—especially yours, Libentia.

Libentia: I shall be happy to give you any help I can, Empiricus.

Empiricus: Thank you. Since it is within the literary work itself that the humanizing force resides, a supremely important step in the humanizing process is the *reading* of the work—its immediate and actual presentation in the classroom. Shall we call this the "presentation proper"?

Quintus: Guess you mean the real business of getting the book in the student's head.

Empiricus: Exactly. However, I should suppose that prior to the presentation proper, or actual reading of the book, the teacher will find advantageous some sort of preparation—some form of introduction to the given work. Shall we call this the "approach"?

Quintus: You mean just how you get ready?

Empiricus: Exactly. Finally, I should suppose that some kind of activity should follow the actual reading. I am not sure just what form this would take, but I think of such things as discussion and writing.

Quintus: You mean whether they make anything out of what they got?

Empiricus: Exactly, Quintus.

Elanchius: Thank you, Empiricus. Indeed, you have, as Quintus put it, "laid out" the matter for us.

Empiricus: But I have spoken only in general terms. Libentia, you will have to carry on from here.

Libentia: As you spoke, Empiricus, it seemed to me that a specific question might be posed for each of the three steps. One pertains to the *approach*: Just how shall the teacher determine the nature and amount of the background to be introduced and the best means of introducing it? Of the *presentation proper* one could ask: Just how shall she decide the best way to "get the books into the students' heads"? And finally, for *accompanying and following activities,* there is the question: Just how shall she determine the nature and scope of the activities to be used?

Quintus: Never saw anyone so full of questions.

Elanchius: It is one of her virtues, Quintus. And you will note that her questions are appropriate and penetrating. She did not ask, for example, "What background should the teacher introduce?" but rather "How shall the teacher *determine* the nature and scope of the background to be introduced?" You are to be congratulated, Libentia, for seeking not merely some ready answers but principles by which the best possible answers can be determined.

Pulvius: Would that all the teachers' mentors might do likewise!

Empiricus: Indeed, Pulvius, ready answers are all too often unprincipled!

Pulvius: Yes, and unprincipled mentors are all too often ready!

Elanchius: In addition to Libentia's questions, we still have before us the question raised by Pulvius concerning chronology and typology.

Pulvius: My question is clearly only one part of the total problem posed by Libentia's three questions.

Elanchius: Then we must first be concerned with the nature and amount of the background to be introduced and the means of introducing it. We must restate Libentia's first question to make evident its relation to our conclusion about the highest function of the study of literature.

Libentia: How will this do: *What kind of background will best help the literary work to reach the student with its humanizing force?*

Elanchius: And when you say "what kind of background," do you have certain elements in mind as possibly appropriate?

Libentia: Why, I suppose I am thinking of such elements as Pulvius has mentioned—the facts of time, place of origin, biography, and so on.

Elanchius: All these, clearly, pertain to the genesis of the given work. Do you think of anything more that might be introduced?

Libentia: Well, I had not intended to limit the background to facts about the work's origin. Since authors frequently write about times and places other than their own, information about these might be provided.

Elanchius: You have added to the possibilities. And are there still others?

Libentia: I think of none, but perhaps Pulvius can help us.

Pulvius: Yes, there are several others which are possible. The history of the reputation of the work might be considered, and also there are the textual and bibliographical data. Further, one might look into the history of the work's influence—on other writers of the author's own time and on those who came later. A very important matter is the form of the work, its structure and literary technique—in short, all the qualities which help to establish it in a framework of literary convention. And there are others. But to be brief, the valid approaches include your bibliographical, your textual, your historical, your biographical, your typological, your ideological, your critical-analytical, your critical-judicial, your critical-linguistical, your critical-historical-judicial.

Quintus: Whew!

Elanchius: And do you think of any other possibilities at all, Pulvius?

Pulvius: There are a few others, but they are eccentric and probably not worth mentioning.

Vulpius: Eccentric, he says!

Elanchius: Then, practically speaking, everything upon which the teacher might draw as background has been mentioned either by you or by Libentia?

Pulvius: Yes, I think so, Elanchius.

Quintus: Good thing, too! I'll bet if the teacher ever got through one-tenth of the stuff Pulvius has been talking about, she never would get to the book she was going to teach!

Elanchius: You have a point there, Quintus. But tell us, Pulvius, have you listed these as possibilities, or do you mean that Libentia should make use of all of them in her teaching?

Pulvius: Well, they are all available, Elanchius. But I shall not dictate to Libentia.

Libentia: I should think it would be unwise, if indeed not impossible, to make use of all the available information. But the teacher can draw whatever facts she wishes from the wide range offered by Pulvius.

Elanchius: You have used the expression, "draw from," Libentia. Will you draw at random? Or do you have in mind some principle? Will you choose facts because they are *interesting?* Or because they are *timely?* Or because they are conveniently at hand? Or might you choose some simply because they represent general knowledge that you believe the students should have?

Libentia: You are jesting, Elanchius!

Vulpius: How do you infer that, Libentia?

Libentia: Because I know that Elanchius would consider my approach intolerable if I brought into my class quantities of ill-assorted matter, taken at random or merely because it was at hand! Or picked out because it was interesting, however irrelevant to my purpose! Or seized on because, being somehow related to the news of the day, it might be shown to have "timeliness"!

Vulpius: You astonish me, Libentia. Professional research has much to say about motivational techniques and their correlation with subject-matter achievements. This research demonstrates that motivational materials should be utilized that appeal to present-day adolescent learners because they are timely, provide useful information, and have a high interest quotient.

Quintus: Don't follow you, Vulpius.

Vulpius: Then let me deal with specifics. You have been discussing the approach to reading materials. Research is now highly developed in the area of motivational materials and their effective classroom utilization. Instead of traditional lectures, Pulvius, delivered to inattentive learners not optimally premotivated toward worthwhile dynamic work-type class-activity participation, our experts have developed worthwhile teacher techniques to insure classroom effectiveness. For example, there are available illustrational materials depicting the life of the authors read, the regional background, and situational data. These can be mounted as attractive wall-type displays by special democratically appointed committees, who, in assuming this responsibility function dynamically in worthwhile growth-oriented situations. If you would ever descend from your ivory tower long enough to visit our modern classrooms, Pulvius, you would be aware of our present-day motivation techniques. You might, for example, find that the walls, by being virtually fully covered with graphic materials of various kinds, make visual appeals to learners.

Quintus: Whew! And I thought Pulvius wanted to do so much before reading the book that the students would never get to it! Looks to me like you've really *buried* it! You ever going to have 'em read the book?

Elanchius: Indeed, Vulpius, like Pulvius, has described many possibilities. But for now should we not continue to regard them *only* as possibilities—the many from which a few may be selected? Since it is unthinkable that the teacher should attempt to use *all* that have been suggested, we shall require a principle of selection. Let us, then, seek a principle which will guide us unerringly to the *appropriate* few.

Libentia: Well, I believe the principle we are seeking is implicit in the question, what kind of background will best help the book to reach the student with its humanizing force? Is not our principle, then, that the teacher should introduce only those elements of background which are clearly and significantly relevant?

Elanchius: Relevant, by all means, Libentia! But relevant to what? To the book? To the student?—to the immediate situation in the class? Surely, one cannot properly speak of the relevance of anything until he has established the point—whatever that may be—by which relevance itself is determined.

Libentia: I should have said, *those elements of background are to be used which are demonstrably and significantly relevant to the highest purpose which the study of literature can serve.*

Quintus: Say, Libentia, what you just said about *background* sounds mighty like what we said about *arrangement*. We said the teacher ought to use a way that at least didn't hinder the purpose and really ought to help it along.

Pulvius: Well, now that the principle has been formulated, Elanchius, just what implication has it for my question? I ask again: will the facts of chronology, type, region, authorship, and so on be presented, or will they be ignored?

Empiricus: Has not Libentia answered your question? True, the principle which she and Elanchius have just stated does not point out particular elements of background that the teacher should choose, but it does answer unmistakably the more basic question, "how shall the teacher determine what particular elements of background she should use?"

Pulvius: Still, no one has yet said yes or no to my question. Will these matters be taught, or will they not?

Quintus: Really want to get that stuff in somehow, don't you, Pulvius! You scared this new principle will throw it all out? Hey! maybe that's about the way the wind's blowing, too.

Elanchius: Wait, Quintus! Surely nothing said thus far should lead either you or Pulvius to assume that the matters which are dear to his heart—and quite properly so, I may add—will necessarily be ruled out by this principle.

Quintus: Hey! You said that just in time. Pulvius was beginning to turn purple. Thought for a minute he was choking on an olive or something.

Elanchius: But why should you be so alarmed, Pulvius? We have said only that the teacher should use those elements of background which are demonstrably and significantly relevant to the highest purpose which the study of literature can serve. Would you have us suspect that those matters so important in your own scholarly approach to literature are quite irrelevant in an approach which aims at the humanization of the reader?

Pulvius: Not at all, Elanchius. They are relevant.

Elanchius: Do you mean that all of them are relevant, and *always* relevant?

Pulvius: Well, I consider all of them relevant to some purpose at some time.

Elanchius: But we are thinking of a specific purpose.

Pulvius: Perhaps I should have said that any of them might be relevant to that purpose at some time.

Elanchius: And do you agree that the teacher should make use of them when they are demonstrably and significantly relevant?

Pulvius: Emphatically.

Elanchius: And what of the converse, which is implied by our principle—that elements of background *not* demonstrably and significantly relevant to the specific purpose are better omitted?

Pulvius: Why—uh, well—

Quintus: Don't stall there, Pulvius. Do you think so or not?

Pulvius: Being a reasonable man, I trust, and no pedant, I agree that nothing which is clearly irrelevant should be introduced. But I suspect that we shall not always agree precisely on what is not irrelevant.

Elanchius: The concession that you have just made—to one who knows of your devotion to literary history—must appear truly magnanimous! And I say so in spite of the reservation you have added.

Quintus: Yeh! guess that's right. Still, I think he ought to give us a straight answer—yes or no, and no monkey business.

Elanchius: Perhaps, Quintus. But are we being altogether fair in demanding an unequivocal reply from Pulvius just yet? We have all been speaking in the abstract. Can we not be more specific? Should we not have a particular literary work before us?

Quintus: Good idea! I'd like to see just how this all works when you get down to cases.

Elanchius: Having a particular literary work before us, we shall be able to test the effectiveness of our principle as a means of selecting what is relevant and rejecting what is not. Perhaps we may even be able to demonstrate how relevance itself is determined. And I forewarn you that when we shall have settled this immediate matter, I intend to suggest a kind of approach quite different from any of the possibilities which have been enumerated. For this kind of approach it will also be helpful to have a specific literary work before us.

Quintus: Hey! After all this time are you going to tell us that *none* of this Pulvian kind of background stuff fits in?

Elanchius: Not at all, Quintus. With a literary work before us, we may well find that at least some of what you call the "Pulvian kind of background" is relevant to our purpose. But I shall thereafter suggest an approach that is not of the "Pulvian kind."

Libentia: You have whetted my curiosity, Elanchius.

Empiricus: And mine.

Elanchius: Our next task is to choose a specific work. You, Libentia, are the very one to find it for us.

Libentia: What kind of work shall it be? Long? Short? Old? New? Poetry? Prose? Native? Foreign?

Empiricus: So that we can examine it wholly, it should be short.

Pulvius: And of course of genuine literary merit!

Elanchius: If we hold to our own principles, Libentia, it should not really matter whether the work is old or new, poetry or prose, native or foreign.

Libentia: Then I shall choose a brief but distinguished work.

Vulpius: I can provide you with an extensive list of reading materials from which to select, Libentia.

Pulvius: Oh no!

Elanchius: We may safely leave the decision to Libentia's judgment. And now shall we begin our walk back to the city? During these past few minutes the air has become rather chilly.

Pulvius: It is a nipping and an eager air.

Libentia: Gentlemen, since we are to discuss not only the approach to a work of literature but also its actual presentation in the classroom, should we not meet at my school? Although the pupils will not be present, the surroundings will remind us of them.

Quintus: Good idea, Libentia. But the building's locked for the summer. You got a key?

Vulpius: I have the key to the main entrance of the plant.

Pulvius: Ha!

Quintus: What's that, Pulvius? Got to get in, don't we?

Pulvius: I had another thought in mind, Quintus. But let that pass.

Elanchius: Then let us meet tomorrow morning early at Libentia's school. Come, shall we walk?

The Presentation Sought

Persons of the Dialogue

LIBENTIA MAGISTRA

PULVIUS GRAMMATICUS   VULPIUS MATERIES

J. QUINTUS   EMPIRICUS MARTIALIS

ELANCHIUS

Scene: Libentia's classroom

Libentia: Welcome, gentlemen, to my little kingdom!

Empiricus: And a charming one it is, Libentia. Indeed, the entire school appears perfectly splendid. It is very different from the frame building in which I learned!

Quintus: Oh, we're modern, all right! Latest stuff all through. Got the best architects in the country to draw up the plans. Cost plenty, too. But nothing's too good for our kids, I always say.

Vulpius: Quite right, Quintus. And let me point out how efficiently the designers have implemented the findings of we in the profession. To instance a case, a former student of mine compiled a comprehensive report on the optimum adjustability quotient of pupil seating arrangements as a factor in the total learning environment. The findings of that report are evidenced in these highly flexible seating units. Furthermore, the designers have utilized the latest researches into light, air, and heat control, as well as optimal floor space ratio to pupil personnel. Still another aspect of the plant also deserves your attention. These classroom furnishings evidence extensive experimentation and research into optimum learning conditions. You will note that groupable tables have replaced the fixed seats and desks of the traditional school plant, thus facilitating a more democratic learning atmosphere. Also ample cabinet space has been provided so that modern learning aids can be available for frequent utilization. And finally there are the expanses of bulletin boards at various points of advantage. Here the teacher can display class-interest oriented objects and illustrations, and the pupil personnel can also post items which have caught their eye. In passing, I should add that both the bulletin boards and the equipment cabinets provide worthwhile opportunities for student committees to develop responsibility in their care and maintenance by providing a vital situation which resembles in many important aspects real-life situations.

Pulvius: Truly, this classroom hardly resembles a bare log!

Quintus: Don't get you, Pulvius. Won't find any logs lying around here.

Elanchius: Perhaps Pulvius means that education of a high character can occur in very simple settings, Quintus. However, I doubt that he would begrudge the teacher such lavish accommodations as these or deny that education of high character might occur here also.

Pulvius: It might. But if it does, it is still Libentia's doing!

Elanchius: True, Pulvius. Education of high order is unlikely to take place if mere physical equipment is mistaken for education itself.

Quintus: Never thought of that. Maybe you got something there. But this school's a real showplace, and I guess most people think because we got this new plant Vulpius helped us figure out we just automatically got the best education too.

Libentia: Well, gentlemen, I sought your help in the first place because I wished to make the quality of my teaching match that of the classroom with which the community has so generously provided me. And my hope is steadily rising that through these conversations I shall be able to do so.

Empiricus: And that, Libentia, sounds to me like a tactful request that we get on with our business.

Quintus: Yeh, let's do. Just what comes first, anyhow?

Elanchius: Well, then. You will remember that yesterday Libentia agreed to choose some literary piece to place before us.

Quintus: That's right. Found one, did you? Remember we were trying to figure out just how to get to it—just how much of that Pulvian kind of background stuff to use.

Libentia: And remember also that Elanchius promised to describe another approach, quite different from "the Pulvian kind."

Elanchius: So I shall, in good time, Libentia. But it is you who must take the lead this morning. I presume that the book you hold in your hand contains the work you have chosen. I for one am impatient to learn what it is.

Pulvius: And I, too, Libentia. In what genre is the document?

Libentia: Why, I decided that our purposes would be served best by a short poem. I hope you will like my choice. Now, just how shall we proceed?

Empiricus: Why not read it aloud to us, Libentia?

Libentia: Very well. But don't expect me to surprise you with something new and strange! You will all instantly recognize these lines, for they are among the most familiar in the language.* Here it is:

> I met a traveller from an antique land
> Who said: Two vast and trunkless legs of stone
> Stand in the desert. Near them, on the sand,
> Half sunk, a shattered visage lies, whose frown,
> And wrinkled lip, and sneer of cold command,
> Tell that its sculptor well those passions read
> Which yet survive, stamped on these lifeless things,
> The hand that mocked them, and the heart that fed:
> And on the pedestal these words appear:
> "My name is Ozymandias, King of Kings:
> Look on my works, ye Mighty, and despair!"
> Nothing beside remains. Round the decay
> Of that colossal wreck, boundless and bare
> The lone and level sands stretch far away.

---

* The reader may be startled to find that the lines quoted here are familiar to him, also! For reasons of a subtle nature, the editors have substituted Shelley's poem for that which Libentia actually read.

Quintus: Wow! That still packs a wallop!

Empiricus: I agree, Quintus. And I have never heard it read so well before.

Pulvius: Your choice is excellent, Libentia; I commend it heartily. And let me assure you that I shall have many facts to offer as the prelude to the presentation of that poem!

Elanchius: Like the others, I found myself again stirred by the poem, Libentia. It will do well for the task that is immediately before us.

Quintus: Hey, wait a minute! All of us have talked but Vulpius. What about you, Vulpius? Didn't you like it?

Pulvius: He's taken his reading lists out of his bag and is peering into them again. I think he failed to hear you, Quintus.

Quintus: Hey, Vulpius! You like this poem?

Vulpius: Hmm—I seem unable to identify any such reading in my lists compiled for adolescent youth. Who authored that piece of reading material, Libentia?

Quintus: Why, that's by Vatarius.* Anybody knows that!

Vulpius: What's that? Vatarius, you say? Hmm—I find nothing on my lists credited to such an individual. He is definitely not one of those recognized by we in the profession as having prepared worthwhile reading materials that are adapted for young learners.

Pulvius: Ha!

Quintus: What's that, Pulvius?

Pulvius: Let it pass, Quintus!

Elanchius: Now let us return to our immediate problem. We are about to consider the application of our principle that only such introductory material should be used as is demonstrably and significantly relevant to the highest purpose in teaching literature.

Quintus: Guess you mean just how much of that Pulvian background stuff do we need to make this poem do what it ought to do to the student.

Elanchius: Well, then. Pulvius, do your own students read this poem?

---

* It seemed proper to retain the name of the original poet, even though, for the reasons alluded to earlier, a work by another author has been substituted.

Pulvius: Indeed they do.

Elanchius: And what elements are included in your introduction to it?

Pulvius: Thank you, Elanchius! I am delighted to answer that question. Obviously, when we consider a poet of the stature of Vatarius, a literary epoch of such well marked characteristics as that in which he wrote, and a poetic form as dominant as this one, a vast body of historical and critical data must be reconstructed if the milieu of the document is to be adequately represented. Libentia, you were my student. Do you remember how we approached this poem?

Libentia: Why, I believe that we approached it very much as we did other important works we read. Let me see. We first examined the characteristics of the period in which it was composed.

Pulvius: Exactly. And we established the terminal dates of the period. We then enumerated the principal preoccupations of the age—the interest in nature, in the remote in time and space, in the supernatural and mysterious, in the importance of the individual, in the—

Quintus: Sounds like quite a time. Just when was all this?

Pulvius: Why, Quintus, the time of which we are speaking extended over a period of thirty-four years, the beginning date being just over a century and a half ago.

Libentia: Next, Pulvius, if my memory is accurate, we examined the—

Pulvius: Wait, Libentia. I have not finished. You will recall my admonition that no literary period should be imagined as standing by itself. Therefore we related the flowering of this age to the budding manifestations of these same preoccupations in the half century which immediately preceded. You will remember my lectures on that period's interest in picturesque landscapes, melancholy settings, and relics of the past. But I interrupted you. What were you about to say?

Libentia: That we next examined the history and the distinguishing features of the literary form in which this particular lyric by Vatarius was cast.

Pulvius: Exactly. You will recall that I described the origins

of this poetic form, which was created by one of the greatest of
the early masters some five centuries before it was employed
by Vatarius. In the interim, it was almost continuously fashion-
able, and although it was used to treat a variety of subjects and
themes—indeed as widely separated as slaughter, on the one
hand, and unrequited love on the other—it retained its essential
formal characteristics intact.

Quintus: What's that last mean, Pulvius?

Pulvius: Why, Quintus, it means that all poets who undertake this particular form of lyric follow a definite pattern of
arrangement in metrics, rhyme, and internal division. True, some
variation has occurred within the frame, but this has not affected
its essential character. If you had been my student, Quintus, you
would have learned to identify this form instantly, and to relate
it to the tradition in which it belongs.

Quintus: Have 'em learn all that, do you?

Libentia: Indeed he does, Quintus, with the authority of a
true scholar. And there is still another source of information upon
which he draws. I remember, Pulvius, that we also studied the
poet's biography.

Pulvius: Right, Libentia. The poem must be set within its
biographical frame. It can then be compared and contrasted with
other works of the poet which preceded and followed, and the
development of the poet—for example, in his predilection for
certain forms and in his preoccupation with tyranny and oppression—can thereby be seen. This having been established, the poet
can then be related to his contemporaries, and their attitudes
toward various kinds of subject matter compared. Influences
on the poet by his contemporaries as well as his influence on
them must of course also be considered.

Elanchius: Thank you, Pulvius. Have you now described the
main facts with which you surround the poem before presenting
it?

Pulvius: For many poems, a geographical frame is often
imperative also. However, you must understand that I have
named only the heads under which the factual details are
grouped. In actually approaching the poem, I would of course
go into detail.

Empiricus: It appears from your summary that your students acquire much information about a literary work. If I have followed it, your approach prepares students to view the poem as the product of three principal factors. You equip them to see it as a specimen of the *age* which produced it, as a specimen of the evolution of a particular literary *form*, and as a specimen of the work of an *author* at a particular point in his development.

Pulvius: Right.

Quintus: Sounds solid enough. But seems to me there's something wrong here, somehow.

Elanchius: Wrong, Quintus?

Quintus: Maybe I don't quite get what's been going on here, but it sounds like Pulvius has been saying the big thing to see in a poem is how it's all tied up with a lot of other things. That's not what I thought we said a poem's taught for, at all.

Elanchius: You are questioning the amount and kind of material which Pulvius introduces as background for the study of a literary work?

Quintus: Well, maybe not exactly. Looks more like Pulvius has got his background out in front.

Elanchius: The background has become the foreground?

Quintus: Background becomes his foreground! Yeh, that's the way to put it.

Elanchius: And does "foreground" here mean perhaps the same thing as "purpose"?

Quintus: Say! That's right. Looks like what Pulvius *really* wants is just to make his students learn all this stuff he calls background. He doesn't specially care whether it helps the poem hit the student at all.

Pulvius: Hold on there, Quintus! You're going too far! If what you are saying were true, I should hardly bother to teach the poem at all. But I *do* teach it—and rather exactingly, too.

Quintus: But you teach it just so the students'll be able to fit it into all this background you've given 'em! Practically said that right out yourself a while ago. So then your background gets to be your purpose, just the way Elanchius says.

Elanchius: Now, Quintus, yesterday we were concerned with

the problem of arrangement. Let me ask you whether you remember which arrangement Pulvius preferred.

Quintus: Ought to. Argued about it long enough. He wanted
books taught according to when they were written and what
type and country they were written in.

Elanchius: And do you recall why we rejected this arrangement?

Quintus: Said it'd get in the way of the book, like a wall, so
the book couldn't get through and do its job. Come to think of
it, guess what'd happen is this arrangement would turn out to be
the purpose, itself. Wouldn't *be* any other purpose.

Elanchius: Now, Quintus, do you think the kind of background that Pulvius has just described so ably would be appropriate if it were used in conjunction with the kind of arrangement that Pulvius said he preferred, and for the purpose which
that kind implies?

Quintus: Sure do. But that's not *our* purpose. Not by a long
shot!

Elanchius: And now, let me ask you the crucial question.
When Libentia read the poem a few minutes ago, your immediate remark suggested that it made a strong impression on
you.

Quintus: Strong impression! I'll say it did. Hit me square
between the eyes.

Elanchius: Now tell us, at that time were you familiar with
*any of the facts of background that Pulvius has just outlined for
us?*

Quintus: Didn't know any of 'em—except Vatarius. Heard of
him, of course. Everybody has—practically.

Pulvius: Hold on a minute! Elanchius, I am but obtuse north-
north-west; when the wind is southerly, I know what is up. Come
now, sir, out with it! I see where your conversation with Quintus
is leading. You will conclude that there is no merit whatsoever
in the historical-typological-biographical approach that I make
to a literary work.

Elanchius: No, Pulvius, I shall never be guilty of saying that
there is no merit in the kind of approach that you have sketched

so admirably. But I shall say that for Libentia to use this approach in her teaching would be quite wrong, aside from the mark which we have set. Yet do not misunderstand me. Libentia, as a teacher, will often need to draw upon the store of facts that you have classified. But *she will use them in her classroom only as they are relevant to her proper task.* That is to say, she will introduce knowledge of this kind only when it will strengthen the total impact of the work that she is to present. Or, more precisely, she will do so when it will help to release the humanizing potential which resides in that work. Ordinarily, these occasions will occur when certain facts are required beforehand to assist the student in comprehending the meaning or implications of the work. For obviously, if he does not understand what he reads, he will not be affected by its full and true power.

Libentia: What about the poem by Vatarius which I read aloud, Elanchius? Are there any facts which I should mention to students before they read it?

Elanchius: In the case of that poem, Libentia, I doubt that any circumstances of its origin need be introduced in advance of the actual presentation.

Pulvius: Hold on, there! Are you saying that Libentia should not even tell her students which literary form this poem exemplifies? Should she not even describe the period whose characteristics influenced this expression? Should she not even say that it is a typical work of Vatarius, who devoted his brief life to waging war on tyranny and oppression?

Elanchius: She should, Pulvius, or she should not, as their usefulness to her purpose must determine. We have agreed that her first concern must be with the poem itself, as an *utterance*, or to use her own term, a *totality*. Nothing else must be allowed to usurp its primary position. What is secondary must truly be kept in the background and not be allowed to become the center of interest and study. Otherwise, a poem becomes for the student, not the means of humanizing experience but a specimen product of certain historical conditions.

Pulvius: It appears to me that you have answered equivocally, I know not what—"she should or she should not."

Quintus: Yeh, don't get you, Elanchius. Don't get you at all. Seems to me you're saying Libentia *should* teach this Pulvian stuff, and yet she shouldn't. How do you figure?

Elanchius: Perhaps, Quintus, we can clarify what may seem a riddle by considering your own trade. Tell us, when you sell a pair of shoes to a customer, do you describe the process and the materials that were used in making them?

Quintus: Maybe do, maybe don't. It depends.

Elanchius: What sort of facts do you sometimes tell?

Quintus: Well, about the kind of leather—might even show him a raw piece of it. Then there's the business of cutting and stitching. And there's the design, too. People mighty conscious of fashion these days. Got to—

Elanchius: Well, then. Evidently there are many details of shoemaking that you might describe. Now tell me: are the shoes that you make *good* ones?

Quintus: Good! Best in town.

Elanchius: Then in describing the characteristics of the leather and of the workmanship which produced the shoes, you would, in a strict sense, be explaining *why* the shoes that you are offering for sale are good ones?

Quintus: That's right. Makes a lot of difference what kind of leather you use and how you cut and stitch it.

Elanchius: But at the time the sale to the customer is made, *the process of making the shoes is already complete?*

Quintus: Right! Shoes are done and sitting on the shelves, ready to go on somebody's feet.

Elanchius: And you do not make any changes in them when you sell them?

Quintus: Changes! I'd say not! When a shoe's made, it's made.

Elanchius: Then, Quintus, whatever you may say to a customer about the process by which shoes have been made, *nothing that you say will actually affect the shoes themselves?*

Quintus: Course not. Customer may want to know about it. But the shoes won't look any better or wear any longer just because I tell him how they're made.

Elanchius: Good. And now let us return to our question of introducing a literary work. Do you see a connection between what we have just been saying and Libentia's problem?

Quintus: Well, I guess a piece of literature is all done when Libentia's students read it, just like shoes when a customer buys 'em.

Elanchius: And if Libentia explains to her students *why* the particular work is just what it is—that is, accounts for its being *as* it is, by stating the conditions of its origin—will she have altered the poem itself?

Quintus: Course not. Poem's already made, just like the shoes.

Elanchius: Now you said that shoes would not look better or last longer merely because you told your customers what materials and workmanship went into their manufacture. That is to say, *merely accounting for the way in which shoes were made will not enhance their effectiveness in performing their function as shoes.* Now would you suppose that accounting in a similar fashion for the characteristics of a finished literary work will enhance its effectiveness in performing its function?

Quintus: Don't see how it could.

Empiricus: May I suggest that insistence on accounting for a poem's characteristics might sometimes even hinder the performance of its function as we have defined that function.

Quintus: By jingoes, Empiricus, I think you've got something there.

Empiricus: I remind you, Quintus, that I am not a literary man, and it may be that there is little in what I have just said. Let us leave it to Elanchius.

Elanchius: What you suggest, Empiricus, if I understand you correctly, is that the teacher's efforts to account for a poem's characteristics by describing the general circumstances of its origin may result in the poem's reaching the senses of the reader not as a potent human utterance, as we would have it do, but rather as a sample product of its author, period, and genre. Or to put it in another way, the poem as utterance will be displaced by the poem as aggregation of characteristics derived from the circumstances of its origin. Thus the poem itself, which must be the primary concern if the effect we wish it to have is to be realized, will lose its essential force, while the characteristics of the poem, which should be only secondary, will make the main impact.

Quintus: Boy, what a dud that could be!

Libentia: What you have just said, Elanchius, confirms my suspicion that the most widely used approach to the study of literature is incompatible with our purpose in teaching it! You have made clear to me what I must *not* do, and why I must not. But we have not yet determined what I *should* do. When we were speaking about arranging literature for use in the classroom, we concluded at once that some kind of arrangement was not only desirable but inevitable. Is it also true that some kind of approach to the particular literary work will be both desirable and inevitable? But what should it be? The question troubles me now more than ever. I hope the answer will be found when you tell us about the approach that you earlier promised to describe.

Pulvius: Wait, Libentia. Before Elanchius moves on to that matter, I should like to remind both you and him that I asked several specific questions—three, to be exact—long ago, to which no definite answers were given. All Elanchius said at the time was that the teacher might preface her treatment of a poem with the study of the circumstances which surround it, or she might not! You must admit that this is a rather vague answer. I do not wish to appear boorish, but do you realize that three times I have urged the importance of the historical, biographical, and typological frames, and three times you have said me nay? First, when we were defining the *purpose* of the study of literature, I argued that this purpose should be acquaintance with literary periods, forms, and major authors. But my argument was in vain. Next, when we sought the most appropriate *arrangement* for the documents of literature, I argued that this arrangement should be chronological, typological, and geographical. Again my urging was in vain. And finally, when we came to seek the most suitable *approach* to a literary document, I argued that this background should consist of the facts about the author, the form, and the age. And now again my urging has been in vain! Now I ask you:

in view of those repeated rejections, what can I conclude but that you have no real intention of paying any heed at all to these matters?

Elanchius: It is true, Pulvius, that we have not yet found an appropriate time to introduce the facts that are of so great moment to you. Nevertheless, do not yet assume that we must discard the knowledge of the circumstances of a work's origin. Remember that we have still to consider the actual presentation of literature, or what Empiricus has called "the presentation proper." Perhaps there, after all, we shall find the proper place to use this knowledge.

Pulvius: After so many rebuffs, Elanchius, I find cold comfort in that word "perhaps."

Libentia: Let me say at once that I cannot imagine myself presenting a literary work, Pulvius, without giving some attention to the characteristics of its form and the circumstances of its origin. But now, before we consider the problems of the actual presentation, let us hear Elanchius describe the approach that he has promised.

Quintus: Good idea. Been hearing about this Pulvian kind long enough. Time we got on to something else.

Vulpius: Definitely. I feel that we have allotted more thinking to Pulvius' traditional opinions than they are worth. Let's move into another area and pre-plan some worthwhile motivational activities, such as assembling materials interrelating with the project, electing committees to assume responsibilities for various aspects of the project, appointing chairmen and secretaries to assure a democratic sharing of findings among dynamic peer groups experiencing together, and apportioning among the pupil personnel—

Pulvius: Enough, Vulpius! My temper is too short just now to hear any more of such stuff. Quintus, did you want us to stop discussing *my* kind of background so that you could hear this?

Quintus: Can't say as I did. Libentia asked Elanchius to tell about his approach, and I want to hear it.

Empiricus: By all means.

Elanchius: Well, then. But let me begin by contrasting the approaches that have been suggested by Pulvius and, just now, by

Vulpius. *Pulvius, it appears to me that your approach to a literary work assumes a purpose in the study of literature other than the highest possible one. The effect of the preparation which you make is that the literary work is recommended to the reader— and accordingly received by him—as a specimen whose characteristics are to be duly related to their causes. By setting the work in its historical context, you prepare that work not to penetrate the student's being with its artistic force, but to be perceived by the student as an equation all of whose factors have been identified. If the best force of a masterpiece thus introduced does reach the student, it must do so incidentally—indeed, perhaps in spite of the introduction.*

Quintus: Might say in spite of the *teacher,* hey, Elanchius?

Elanchius: I fear so, Quintus. And now, Vulpius, although you spoke only briefly, the activities that you specified imply the essential character of the approach that you favor. *It appears to me that this approach does not necessarily relate to or require the study of a literary work at all, and in any event certainly is not calculated to further the best purpose that the study of literature can serve. The effect of the preparation that you suggest is that the literary work itself is likely to be set quite aside in favor of the machinery of doing, as though the main value resided in the mere fact of organized activity.*

Quintus: Vulpius wouldn't really have to have any books at all for his scheme, hey, Elanchius?

Elanchius: Perhaps not, Quintus.

Pulvius: Knowing the kind of books favored by Vulpius, I should think the teacher could manage very well without them!

Vulpius: But you forget, Pulvius. Each of them has a high readability quotient.

Pulvius: But nothing else worth mentioning. Readability, bah!

Quintus: At it again! Can't you boys settle that fight some other time? Want to hear what Elanchius has to say.

Elanchius: Well, then. Let us go at it in this way. Pulvius' approach directs the students' attention to the historical relations of the literary work; Vulpius' directs attention to the students' social relations. Although Pulvius is concerned entirely with literature, his approach neglects that in literature which can exercise a humanizing effect on the student; and although Vulpius is concerned entirely with the student, his approach neglects that in him which can be affected by the humanizing force of literature.

Pulvius: Neatly turned, Elanchius—even though I fare somewhat badly in the turning!

Quintus: So they both miss the boat, hey?

Elanchius: True, Quintus. So our task is to find an approach that will not "miss the boat" in either of these ways.

Quintus: Well, let's see. Seems to me when we were talking about arrangement we said the most important thing to be concerned with about a book is what the book is about.

Elanchius: That is, its theme. And with what in the *student* should the teacher be most concerned?

Quintus: Well, we said a long time ago she ought to be concerned with—Libentia, you're the one that has to know these things. What about it?

Libentia: We said that the teacher of literature must always be concerned primarily with that in the student which is uniquely human—with that which he shares with all others.

Elanchius: *Then the approach which we seek is one that will best prepare for the bringing together of that in the book which can affect the student as a human being and that in the student which can be thus affected.*

Quintus: Hey! Got to get together what's human in the book and what's human in the kid. That it?

Elanchius: You phrase it well, Quintus.

Quintus: Now when do these two get together?

Elanchius: In the actual presentation, Quintus. But it is in the *approach* that preparation must be made. Now tell me—on which of these, the book or the student, can the teacher work more effectively to prepare for their meeting?

Quintus: Well, she can't prepare the book. Fellow that wrote it already did that. All she can do with a book before she teaches it is pick it out, and maybe put it with some others—arrange it.

Elanchius: Good, Quintus. If the author has done his work well—and if he has not done so the book should not have been chosen—no further preparation of the *book* is either necessary or tolerable. Therefore, it must be the *student* upon whom her efforts at preparation are concentrated.

Vulpius: You say, Elanchius, that no additional preparation of the book should be utilized. But the findings of readability experts demonstrate that in order to achieve optimum reading outcomes, developmentalwise, it is always expedient to professionally abridge, adapt, or rewrite traditional readings in order to match them with the adolescent learner experiential and maturation level. Thus it is obviously more important to prepare the reading materials than the pupils, who need no preparation if the readings have been scientifically adjusted to their interest and ability ratings.

Pulvius: Vulpius, to rewrite a great book is to bid farewell to all its greatness. And when tinkers of the kind you have in mind lay hands on the masterpiece—ugh!

Quintus: Tinkers, hey?

Pulvius: Tinkers, indeed! That's a mild word for people who by no stretch of the imagination could be called authors in their own right. Why, it would be bad enough for one author to rewrite another; but for one of Vulpius' "experts" to do so—I can merely repeat, ugh!

Libentia: Would any of you care to see a book of the kind Pulvius and Vulpius are speaking of? I have a whole set here on the shelves—not by choice, I assure you.

Pulvius: No thanks. I once read nearly half a page in such a book. It was not "edited," but "idioted."

Empiricus: I would like to examine one, please.

Libentia: Here you are, Empiricus. Some of my more outspoken colleagues call these books "eviscerated classics."

Quintus: What's that "eviscerated" mean, Libentia?

Pulvius: Why, Quintus, have you never eviscerated a fowl?

Quintus: Can't say as I—hey, you mean did I ever gut a chicken? If you did that to a book, you'd really kill it.

Empiricus: If this book is a fair sample, I believe you are right, Quintus. In my own student days I attacked the original with insatiable hunger. I cannot imagine devouring this adaptation with such zeal! I conclude from this that Elanchius chose

his words precisely when he said that further preparation of a
great book is neither necessary nor tolerable.

Pulvius: Bravo, Empiricus.

Quintus: Hey, how about reading us a little of that?

Empiricus: I shall be glad to do so, Quintus. Here is the
adapter's rendering of the famous climactic moment. "One day
[he] received a great shock. He was walking along the beach
when he came upon the print of a man's naked foot in the sand.
There it was, just as plain as could be. He stood still and listened,
looking all about in an effort to see the man who had made it.
But there was no one in sight. He was certain that he had not
made it himself because it had been a long time since he had
passed that way. He walked along the beach and then climbed a
hill to look about over the island. He could see no one, nor was
there another footprint in sight. [He] was worried. He went back
to the footprint and looked at it again. He studied the print of the
toes, heel, and every part of the foot. How had it come there?
Who could have made it? He walked away toward his hut, turning every few steps to look behind him. He was very much
afraid."

Quintus: Hey, that used to pack a real punch. Where'd it go?
Libentia, you got it the way the author really wrote it?

Libentia: It happens that I have, Quintus. The school had
none, so I brought my own copy to class.

Quintus: Fine! Let's hear Empiricus read the same part
out of that.

Empiricus: Just a moment. Ah! Here it is. "It happened one
day about noon going towards my boat, I was exceedingly surprised with the print of a man's naked foot on the shore, which
was very plain to be seen in the sand: I stood like one thunder-
struck, or as if I had seen an apparition; I listened, I looked
round me, I could hear nothing, nor see anything; I went up to a
rising ground to look farther; I went up the shore and down the
shore, but it was all one, I could see no other impression but that
one. I went to it again to see if there were any more, and to
observe if it might not be my fancy; but there was no room
for that, for there was exactly the very print of a foot, toes, heel,
and every part of a foot; how it came thither, I knew not, nor

could in the least imagine. But after innumerable fluttering thoughts, like a man perfectly confused and out of myself, I came home to my fortification, not feeling, as we say, the ground I went on, but terrified to the last degree, looking behind me at every two or three steps, mistaking every bush and tree, and fancying every stump at a distance to be a man; nor is it possible to describe how many various shapes affrighted imagination represented things to me in, how many wild ideas were found every moment in my fancy, and what strange unaccountable whimsies came into my thoughts by the way. When I came to my castle, for so I think I called it ever after this, I fled into it like one pursued; whether I went over by the ladder as first contrived, or went in at the hole in the rock, which I called a door, I cannot remember; no, nor could I remember the next morning, for never frighted hare fled to cover, or fox to earth, with more terror of mind than I to this retreat."*

Quintus: Wow!

Pulvius: And wow again! Now, Quintus, you see what I meant by "tinkers."

Quintus: Yeh, and you see what I meant when I said "gutted."

Elanchius: Surely no more need be said.

---

* Because the leaves of the manuscript containing the original version of the passage which Empiricus reads are so defective as to be illegible, the translators have substituted what would appear to be modern equivalents of the original and the adaptation. The first version which Empiricus reads is from *The Story of Robinson Crusoe*, as adapted and retold by Frank L. Beals, Assistant Superintendent of Schools, Chicago (Chicago: Benj. H. Sanborn & Co., 1946), and used by permission of the publisher. The second is of course from the story as Defoe wrote it. It will be noted that even the narrator has been changed—from Crusoe himself to the adapter's shadowy persona. Other changes equally needless and drastic have rendered this powerful book pitifully sterile.

The reader may be interested in a portion of the adapter's "Introduction": "This story of Robinson Crusoe is taken from the original narrative by Daniel Defoe. It is, however, written from a different viewpoint, and it is considerably simplified. It is written in a modern manner for modern young people. *The tale has lost nothing of its flavor in this retelling.*

"The story was rewritten several times. Before each writing it was tried out by experienced teachers in actual classroom situations. The reactions of teachers and pupils were carefully considered in the rewriting. As the story now stands, both teachers and pupils have expressed themselves as well pleased with it." (Italics added.)

Quintus: You said a mouthful there, Elanchius.

Elanchius: Well, then. Since further preparation of the book is evidently improper, it must be the student, as I formerly said, upon whom the teacher's efforts are concentrated.

Quintus: Yeh, you said the teacher ought to get *him* ready for the *book*.

Elanchius: And remember, Quintus, his mind is to be prepared to receive the book not as a sample product of the historical forces which shaped it, but as a powerful utterance capable of affecting him as a human being.

Quintus: Well now, Elanchius, suppose Libentia here is getting ready to teach that poem she read us a while ago. Just how does she do it? We decided she shouldn't waste time with all that dynamic stuff that Vulpius said. And what does she talk about anyway? We said she shouldn't go into all that Pulvian stuff that Pulvius said. So just what's her job?

Elanchius: Why, Quintus, since she wishes the student to receive the full force of a great utterance on a human theme, *she may prepare in his mind a setting, indeed I may say a climate or environment, which will be most favorable to its reception.*

Quintus: But just what does that mean Libentia would actually do with this poem she read us? Say, hold on! Guess you already said it in a way and I didn't see it. Maybe she ought to talk about the sort of thing the poem's about, *even before she lets her students read it*. That the idea?

Elanchius: Excellent, Quintus. And not only may she talk about it herself; since she is to prepare the most favorable climate possible, she may also lead her students to discuss it and, indeed, perhaps even write about it.

Quintus: Maybe do all that before they even see the poem, hey? Now, let's see. What's that mean they'd be talking about right before they read that Vatarius poem about the oldtime big shot who had a statue made for himself?

Elanchius: Why, Quintus, in phrasing your question you have very nearly told us that yourself!

Quintus: I did?

Libentia: You certainly did, Quintus. When you spoke of an "old-time big shot who had a statue made for himself," you came very close to stating the general theme of the poem. Elanchius, may I go on with this? I think I understand your point.

Elanchius: By all means, go ahead. Perhaps you can demonstrate the very approach I have in mind.

Libentia: I shall try. Now then, Quintus, will you tell us why this man had his statue made?

Quintus: Because he was so sure he was a big shot. Wanted everyone else to know it, too.

Libentia: And what became of the statue?

Quintus: Got all broke up and lost in the sand. Just pieces of it around.

Libentia: Then the expectations of this man were vain?

Quintus: You kidding? Nothing left but a bunch of junk and all that sand.

Libentia: Now, Quintus, just what did you mean when you called this man an "oldtime big shot"?

Quintus: Well, guess I meant he lived a long time ago. But we got 'em today, too.

Libentia: Many of them, Quintus?

Quintus: Well, not so many kings, like that fellow. But just about everybody gets to acting like that sometimes. Used to put on a little myself. Got over it though. Beat out of me.

Libentia: You seem not to look very favorably upon those who haven't "got over it."

Quintus: "Look favorably!" No, sir! I'd say whatever happens to 'em, they've got it coming.

Libentia: Why do you say so, Quintus?

Quintus: Ever been around one of 'em? Hard to get along with. Don't think of anybody but themselves. Always "I" this and "I" that, and "Get outa my way." You wouldn't even think they were human, some of 'em.

Libentia: What is it exactly that makes them seem less than human?

Quintus: Well, its—its that they're just—its—

Pulvius: Vanity, vanity! All is vanity!

Quintus: What's that, Pulvius?

Pulvius: Turn away mine eyes from beholding vanity.

Quintus: Hey! Thought there for a minute that heat we had this afternoon was too much for you, Pulvius. But I get you now. Vanity! That's exactly what I was trying to say, Libentia.

Pulvius: Bravo, Quintus!

Elanchius: And bravo, Libentia!

Empiricus: You have managed the demonstration beautifully, Libentia.

Quintus: Demonstration? What demonstration?

Elanchius: Why, Quintus, you and Libentia have just demonstrated, as accurately as our present circumstances would allow, an approach to Vatarius' poem.

Quintus: But we already read the poem. Thought an approach came first, not afterwards.

Elanchius: True, Quintus, and if circumstances had permitted, that is how we should have arranged it just now. But since we could not, we shall have to imagine a little. Do you see that your conversation with Libentia on the theme of vanity, though it here *followed* and was inspired by the reading of Vatarius' poem, might instead have *preceded* the reading, having been inspired by some other means?

Quintus: That'd be easy enough. Plenty of vanity around anywhere you look. Guess we wouldn't need a poem just to get us started talking about it.

Elanchius: That is precisely the point. Any one of the abundant local manifestations of human vanity might have served to start you and Libentia thinking and talking about this theme. Through such talk—and, if you were in a classroom, even writing— would there not come to be established in your mind a special environment—a climate, I have said—*favorable to the reception of an artistic utterance on the theme of vanity?* And then might not the poem, being read in the setting thus prepared for it, strike with a greater impact than if no such preparation had been made?

Quintus: Think I get you now, Elanchius. You mean Libentia and I ought to have had our little talk about big shots, only maybe a good deal more of it—and *then* read the poem right afterwards, when our minds were on the sort of thing it was about. Say, I'll tell you what. My mind's still on that business.

I'd like to hear that same poem read again, right now!

Elanchius: Excellent, Quintus! Libentia, let us hear the poem once more. But this time, if you have an additional copy, *let Quintus hold it in his hand and follow with his eye as you read aloud.*

Libentia: Several volumes on my shelves contain the poem. Everyone who wishes can have one. Here they are.

Empiricus: Let me help you distribute them, Libentia.

Vulpius: Hmm. Just as I suspected. No attention was paid in the preparation of these reading materials to professional findings as to the optimum line length in relation to the typical eye span and number of eye jerks of adolescent learners. These volumes will have to be replaced, Libentia.

Quintus: Oh, shut up, Vulpius! Let's hear the poem.

Libentia: All ready? Then here it is:

> I met a traveller from an antique land
> Who said: Two vast and trunkless legs of stone
> Stand in the desert. Near them, on the sand,
> Half sunk, a shattered visage lies, whose frown,
> And wrinkled lip, and sneer of cold command,
> Tell that its sculptor well those passions read
> Which yet survive, stamped on these lifeless things,
> The hand that mocked them, and the heart that fed:
> And on the pedestal these words appear:
> "My name is Ozymandias, King of Kings:
> Look on my works, ye Mighty, and despair!"
> Nothing beside remains. Round the decay
> Of that colossal wreck, boundless and bare
> The lone and level sands stretch far away.

Libentia: Well, I've finished. Isn't anyone going to speak?

Empiricus: We have been moved by this, Libentia.

Pulvius: Elanchius, it occurs to me that the approach which you and Libentia have demonstrated is very like the practice of the dramatists, who prepare our minds long in advance—create a climate, as you called it—to receive the most moving and crucial utterances of their characters! All things considered, and despite the fact that we have used it here only in an abbreviated form, I agree that there is merit in this approach.

Elanchius: Your observation that this approach resembles the dramatist's practice is an astute one, Pulvius. And your admission of its merit means much.

Libentia: But I wonder why Quintus does not speak. When I read this poem earlier, Quintus, your immediate response was "Wow!" Yet now you are silent.

Pulvius: —upon a peak.

Quintus: Couldn't think of anything that seemed worth saying. Thought I knew all along what you and Elanchius meant when you were talking about what books can do to people if you handle 'em right. But I guess I never really got it at all until right now when we read that poem.

Elanchius: "When *we* read that poem." I shall remind you of your choice of that word!

Empiricus: Your reaction, Quintus, is noteworthy evidence that our claim for the power of literature is well founded.

Elanchius: The comments of all who have spoken support that evidence, Empiricus. But one of us has not spoken. Vulpius, were you, like Quintus, struck silent by the poem?

Vulpius: The findings of we in the profession demonstrate conclusively that the presentation method utilized by Libentia here cannot be effectively utilized in the classroom. In a situation involving oral reading by the teacher while the young learners attempt to follow in their reading materials, a condition results which frustrates worthwhile outcomes. This practice coerces the young learner to coordinate his eye jerks with the reading speed utilized by the teacher, thereby creating tensions. Research says—

Quintus: See here, Vulpius! Elanchius asked whether the poem really got to you. What've these eye jerks got to do with that?

Empiricus: Yet Vulpius has indirectly answered the question, Quintus. His remarks make it plain that the poem did not affect him as it did the rest of us.

Quintus: No wonder! He didn't pay any attention to the poem. He was thinking about his own eye jerks.

Elanchius: Vulpius' criticism, in any event, is directed not at the approach which we made to the poem but at its actual presentation. I remind you that the "presentation proper" is our next subject. Unless, therefore, Vulpius does wish to object to the kind of approach on which the rest of us have agreed, may we not turn our attention immediately to that crucial question?

Quintus: Oh, let's just go on.

Vulpius: Far from having a negative evaluation to offer, I tend to find my thinking in general agreement as to the approach activities provided for by your preparational technique, Elanchius. The teacher who has thoroughly acquainted herself with the available devices for stimulating group dynamics by utilizing the approach you have described can thereby create a variety of occasions for participatory experiences by individual learners in related aspects of the subject, such as collecting, cutting, pasting, speaking, listening, and sharing activities; indeed, even thinking activities can be motivated thusly. By careful pre-planning, the teacher can develop a worthwhile series of classroom experiences dealing with such real-life situations as vanity, for example, since that is the one you spoke of—although I myself would prefer such a topic as personal relationships—and relational materials of all sorts can then be utilized to develop a unit structured about them. You mentioned the poem as one type of relational material, and I should not necessarily object to the utilization of such traditional materials—where they are worthwhile. But the realistic teacher will not overlook the many other types of materials, and she will of course solicit personal opinions and accounts of experiences from each individual learner, which can then be compiled in a cooperative volume, provided with a permanent binding, and equipped with appropriate illustrations by learners whose contributions to the class activities tend to be chiefly nonverbal. I should like to develop this at greater length, as I see an endless number of possible ways of implementing such a project. However, I have probably already indicated how, in the hands of the teacher who is well versed in the findings of professional research, this approach you have advanced, Elanchius, could be implemented so that each youth, while feeling that he is making a worthwhile contribution to the group, will be kept busy.

Pulvius: What a perversion of a fine approach! We were speaking of *use*, and you make it *abuse!*

Quintus: Yeh, Vulpius! Looks like you're saying a book's mainly an excuse to keep a lot of *busy* work going. And, guess you'd say just anything that'd get the noise started would do as well as a book. Now with Elanchius, the book's the main thing. Vulpius, you'd have the tail wagging the dog.

Pulvius: There's a fine figure! I fail to see how you could improve on it unless you eliminated the dog altogether!

Quintus: Well, that's that. Now let's get on to the next job.

Libentia: May we not, Elanchius?

Elanchius: Well, then. We come at last to the actual presentation.

Quintus: Hey! Just happened to think of something. We already *had* a presentation—couple of 'em in fact. Worked mighty well, too. What more is there to do?

Elanchius: True, Quintus. Libentia did present Vatarius' poem. And she presented it well. It would indeed be pleasant to assume that our problem has thus already been solved! But we have now reached the most crucial phase of the teacher's work with literature. For though she may have been as wise in *selecting* books as we wish her to be, equally circumspect in *arranging* them, and not less so in *approaching* them, yet if she is unwise in her method of *presenting* them, she may undo all her earlier labor.

Quintus: Can't let that happen after all the trouble we've been to.

Elanchius: Therefore let us proceed with care. Now, must we not begin by posing questions that are most pertinent to a full consideration of our problem?

Quintus: Yeh, let's hear 'em. Always works fine when we do it that way. Libentia, you're always full of questions. Why don't you start us off?

Libentia: Why, Quintus, a while ago you yourself spoke of "the actual business of getting the books into their heads." Isn't our real question just *how* the teacher can best do so? There are many ways open to her. Shall she have the students read everything silently? If so, shall she have them do most of their reading at home unattended, or in the classroom under her supervision? Or should most of the reading be done aloud? If so, who should do it? The students? If so, shall it be the better readers or the poorer who read most? Should they read singly or in chorus? Or should it be the teacher who reads aloud? If so, should the students follow silently in their own books, or should they just listen?

Elanchius: I note that all your questions pertain to the *manner* in which the reading itself is to be accomplished. Are there questions of any other kind which we should have before us?

Empiricus: Must we not consider also, Elanchius, just what measures the teacher should take to make certain that her students understand the work that is read? For we would presumably agree that whatever means of presenting are chosen, adequate comprehension is essential to the humanizing effect which we hope will be the ultimate result.

Elanchius: We must consider this question, of course. It is different in kind from Libentia's, and we may find that our answer to it will help to determine our answer to hers. But now are there other questions that we should have before us?

Pulvius: At the risk of being tedious—

Quintus: Bet I know what he's going to say!

Pulvius: It should need no ghost come from the grave to tell you that, Quintus. Let me say once more that I have not yet received a straight answer to the fundamental question I have repeatedly raised. I have been advised that facts of historical period, biography, and literary form must play no part in the arrangement of documents. I have been advised that they must play no part in the approach to documents. A slender hope was held out to me that they *might* be allowed some insignificant little role in the actual presentation of documents. Now tell me. May I continue to cling to this straw, or is it, too, to be denied me? Shall I expect Libentia's students to come into my classes totally ignorant of historical and formal matters? Unable to distinguish between tragedy and ode? Between epic and idyl? Or, if they are not to be totally ignorant, when and how *are* they to be given enlightenment?

Quintus: Thought so! Still scared we'll put you out of business, hey, Pulvius?

Elanchius: Your vexation is understandable, Pulvius. And this time, without fail, we shall answer you. Now, however, let us make certain that all of the kinds of questions which we should consider have been represented. Quintus, do you think of anything further?

Quintus: I'm not forgetting how much time we spent figuring out how to *arrange* the books. Now when the teacher *presents* these books, is she going to talk about the books themselves mainly, or about those themes they're grouped under? Guess she shouldn't talk just about the themes by themselves—remember how those gray eyes of yours crackled the other day when somebody predicted it'd turn out that way.

Elanchius: I am sorry, Quintus, that I lost my temper—even for such a good reason!

Libentia: But I hope that you would lose it again for the same reason.

Elanchius: I might, Libentia; indeed, I might. But let that pass. Quintus has raised a fourth kind of question, that of the amount of attention which the teacher should pay, in presenting a particular work, to the thematic affinities responsible for its inclusion in a group of works. Now, are all the questions before us? Vulpius, have you any questions for us to consider?

Vulpius: No questions, Elanchius. But, fortunately, my familiarity with research findings has provided me with answers to all the questions which have been advanced here. I can therefore expedite this discussion by acquainting you with the conclusions made available by professional researchers as to the presentation of reading materials to present-day adolescent youths. A realistic approach to the problem involves recognition of the necessity for stimulating group activities which accommodate individual differences and which appeal to individual learner interests by providing a participatory outlet through peer-group activity. In view of empirical evidence, therefore, all presentation problems must be—

Quintus: Thought you said you were going to answer our questions.

Empiricus: Apparently, Vulpius believes that "group activities" constitute a general solution to the problems of presentation. But you might help us more, Vulpius, by considering some specific questions that have been raised.

Vulpius: I was approaching those. The teacher whose thinking has been adjusted to fit the professional pattern will utilize the most recent presentation devices based on the realities of the classroom situation as they have been determined by research. The—

Pulvius: The wheel has come full circle. Vulpius is where?

Quintus: Come on there, Vulpius! Are you going to answer Libentia's questions about getting the books into the kids' heads?

Vulpius: Definitely. As an example, suppose that Libentia has thirty students in one of her classes. By using sociometric techniques recently devised, she will divide her class into five or six groups—more if necessary—in each of which, utilizing democratic processes, a leader and a recorder will be designated. Each of these groups will be allotted a piece of reading material whose readability quotient, of course, has been adjusted to the group developmental level.

Quintus: Looks like what you're saying is that each bunch'll be reading a different book. Thought we were figuring they'd all be reading the same thing—like that poem of Vatarius', for instance.

Vulpius: That thinking has been advanced by some of you, but its validity has not been corroborated by empirical data. However, although ordinarily different pieces of reading material should be distributed according to the individual differences of the groups, it is also sometimes acceptable to utilize a reading whose readability quotient accommodates the lowest reading level found in any group. In that event the teacher will divide the whole work, giving each group responsibility for reporting to the other groups as to the contents of its portion. To illustrate, suppose that a class utilizing traditional materials wishes to become acquainted with a long poem. Group A will be assigned to cooperate in reading the first fifth of the poem. Under the direction of the leader, the members of this group—by democratic processes, of course—will decide upon the main points touched on in their segment.

Quintus: You mean they'll vote on what happened, Vulpius?

Vulpius: Definitely. Having arrived at their findings by utilizing dynamic peer-group interactivity, the recorder will summarize them in a form which makes them accessible to groups B, C, D, and E. At the same time the recorders of those groups will make accessible the findings arrived at as to their segments by similar participatory interchange. As a result, a set of common learnings will be achieved by active sharing. Each group will thus be acquainted with the points touched on in the entire poem.

Pulvius: *Vulpius, have my ears deceived me? Or is it possible that you have in fact just said that no one of the students will read the entire poem, but that each will read only a part and will depend for the rest upon summaries prepared by his fellows?*

Vulpius: Definitely. Thus the teacher, even when utilizing traditional materials, can provide opportunity for the development of outgoingness. Further, the most worthwhile benefits of reading materials can thus be—

Pulvius: Elanchius, may we adjourn our meeting soon? I feel suddenly sick at my—uh—

Quintus: Hey! Look how green he's turning! Don't say any more right now, Vulpius! You'll kill him.

Pulvius: Uh—uh—uh—

Quintus: Wait, Pulvius! Let me help you outside. Quick!

Elanchius: In the circumstances, should we not adjourn our meeting until this afternoon?

Libentia: Poor Pulvius! Do you think he will be able to rejoin us then?

Elanchius: Let us hope so. And shall we meet again here in your classroom?

Libentia: That will please me, Elanchius.

Elanchius: I shall myself, then, in the interim, call on Pulvius and inform him of our plan.

The Presentation Found

Persons of the Dialogue

LIBENTIA MAGISTRA

PULVIUS GRAMMATICUS   VULPIUS MATERIES

J. QUINTUS   EMPIRICUS MARTIALIS

ELANCHIUS

Scene: Libentia's classroom

Libentia: Welcome once more, gentlemen. But, Elanchius, what is the news of Pulvius?

Elanchius: Still pale and nauseated. I left him in his library among his books, seeking to overcome his indisposition.

Quintus: Won't he be here at all this afternoon?

Elanchius: He hopes to be able to rejoin us in a little while.

Libentia: Shall we wait, or shall we begin without him?

Elanchius: He suggested that we go ahead, and I agreed. If we begin at once, we may be able to complete our task before the day ends.

Quintus: Sort of hoping we can myself. Got to get back to my business—I mean my *other* business. Lots of work piling up in the shop.

Empiricus: According to the plan we drew up earlier, we have only one or two topics still before us. Like Quintus, I have other urgent affairs also.

Elanchius: Then let us resume our discussion at once. You will recall that this morning Libentia, Empiricus, Pulvius, and Quintus each in turn posed questions about the presentation of

251

literature in the classroom. Vulpius, although he had no questions of his own, had begun to furnish answers. It was at that point that Pulvius had a touch of nausea.

Quintus: Yeh. What do you say we have Vulpius go right on while Pulvius is away? Don't want the same thing to happen this afternoon that happened this morning. Vulpius, guess you finished answering Libentia's question. Got an answer to the one Empiricus asked, about how to make sure the students'll understand the books they read?

Vulpius: Definitely. I must reiterate that by insisting on your so-called classics you are being completely unrealistic. Now, if you utilized the reading materials from the lists compiled by our experts, there would be no comprehension problem. Our lists are graded as to developmental levels, and each individual experiences only such materials as he is able to understand without difficulty.

Quintus: Can't see that you've really answered Empiricus' question, though. All you're doing is throwing the good stuff away instead of figuring out how to read it.

Vulpius: As I was saying, since you insist on these unrealistic materials, my answer is that they should not be presented to learners in the form in which they were written—since obviously the authors had no evidence as to adolescent youth interests and reading levels. They should be altered according to scientifically prepared adolescent developmental formulae. Long works should be abridged to bring them within the typical interest-span, and difficult works should be revised as to vocabulary range, sentence length, and content maturity. Longer descriptive passages, which individual learners find uninteresting, can be eliminated, and sections which are too philosophical for adolescent readers can be rewritten from a more practical viewpoint—in those instances where they are necessary to the story at all. This scientific approach to the preparation of simpler versions has found great favor among those who have investigated the adolescent reading responses. Furthermore, its worthwhileness is substantiated by widespread utilization of specialist-compiled materials in the modern classroom.

Empiricus: Then, Vulpius, your answer to my question is

essentially this: It is preferable to use only books which have been written by "experts," but when others are used, they must be simplified by these same experts. Your answer does not truly confront the problem of overcoming difficulty, but shifts the responsibility for presentation from the teacher herself to those who prepare books that need little effort in the presentation.

Quintus: Yeh, reminds me of a story I read when I was a kid at school. This mean fellow—I forget his name—cut all his visitors down to the same size so they'd fit the bed he made 'em sleep in.

Vulpius: I fail to recognize your story, Quintus. Evidently none of our reading experts have adapted it yet. But to return to Empiricus' comment as to responsibility. The teacher should always utilize every means of de-emphasizing her need to concentrate on the materials themselves, and since, as you say, the rewriting of classic-type materials shifts the responsibility to the adapters, she will thus be freed to perform her primary function as teacher—that of directing dynamic group activities. Furthermore, by preparing stimulating study guides and questions on the reading materials, she assures that these reading groups will read purposefully, since they must understand what they read in order to answer the questions she has prepared.

Quintus: All I can say is, it's a good thing Pulvius hasn't come back yet! Well, if you've finished answering Empiricus' question—let's see, what is it comes next?

Empiricus: Pulvius, I believe, was the next to pose a question, Quintus.

Quintus: That's right. Wanted to know if the teacher'll get in any of that Pulvian kind of background while the books are getting read. Maybe Vulpius better answer that too before Pulvius gets back.

Vulpius: I welcome the opportunity to discuss the implications for the reading teacher of the numerous scientific studies in this area. To turn to Pulvius' question, research in the adolescent interest and needs fields tells us that the merely academic material that Pulvius so obstinately recommends has no worthwhile contribution to offer present-day adolescent learners. The utilization of such aspects as historical background and literary forms may have a high value quotient for Pulvius' traditionalist-type studies, but scientifically speaking, they have only a negative correlation with the needs and interests of readers such as, for instance, Libentia's students. On the other hand, research indicates that there are other types of information touched on in reading materials which the teacher can utilize effectively. For example, there are descriptions of foreign lands and of the customs and dress of foreign peoples. The alert teacher utilizes reading material presentation as an opportunity to interest students in such matters, thus aiming to achieve improved relations through better understanding of other lands and peoples.

Quintus: Just how's she go about it, Vulpius?

Vulpius: The worthwhileness of this, Quintus, is demonstrated by its usefulness for devising special projects and group activities. You no doubt remember the structured group organization I mentioned this morning. Group A in such a class could elect to do research on the costumes of the country dealt with in the reading materials. Group B could elect to investigate the courtship and marriage customs. Group C might elect to look into the weapons and other implements utilized. Other groups could undertake similarly worthwhile projects. Each of these studies would terminate in a cooperative project in which, since each member of the group had shared his findings with others, there would be a sense of participation and recognition of the worthwhileness of group activity. Such slow learners or non-verbal students as will normally be present in each group could be elected to make covers for the completed projects and to prepare illustrations for the written portions. All will thus have experienced equally in a sharing activity democratically structured, and also, the findings of each group would thus be made available to the other groups.

Empiricus: Then, Vulpius, if I understand you, literature thus presented serves to familiarize students with foreign lands and peoples—their customs, clothing, and so on?

Vulpius: That is only part of it, Empiricus. The principal value, of course, is the utilization of reading materials to stimulate worthwhile classroom activities.

Quintus: Bet if Pulvius was here, he'd make a crack about the cart and the horse.* Now if you've finished answering Pulvius' question, what do you say about the one I asked? You in favor of teaching the books, or the themes, or what?

Empiricus: I believe we know Vulpius' answer to that question, Quintus. You will recall that when we were discussing possible ways of arranging books in the program he left no doubt that for him the teacher's primary responsibility is to the unit, as he called it, the books themselves being secondary and serving mainly as implementation.

Quintus: Yeh, remember that all right. That's when Elanchius blew up. Well, looks like Vulpius has finished answering all our questions. Guess we can go home!

Elanchius: You are satisfied with his answers, Quintus?

Quintus: Just kidding, Elanchius! Used to be, but not now.

Elanchius: Why have you changed your opinion?

Quintus: Looks to me like Vulpius is just away off, somehow. Don't know quite what it is—can't put my finger on it.

Elanchius: Is it, perhaps, that in giving his answers Vulpius has disregarded some step?

Quintus: Yeh, maybe that's it. He sort of plumb missed the boat.

Elanchius: Can you tell us which step he neglected?

Quintus: Well, seems like the way he answered these questions you don't have any way of knowing what's right or wrong.

Elanchius: Is it that he neglected to pose a certain underlying question before answering others?

Quintus: Could be—but just what is that question?

Elanchius: It is one whose answer will guide all subsequent

---

* A similar reversal of emphasis appears in the catalogue description of a course for teachers of reading announced by the Department of Education at the University of California: "Education S134. Objectives, standards of attainment, types of reading instruction, diagnostic and remedial techniques, reading readiness, *place of reading in the activity program*. Introduction to children's literature, children's interests in reading, criteria for selection of content, the place of supplementary and library reading" (*Bulletin* of the Summer Sessions, 1958, pp. 53-4; italics added).

questions about the actual presentation. Let us attempt to phrase—

Libentia: One moment, please, Elanchius. I hear footsteps approaching our door. Who's there? Pulvius?

Pulvius: A piece of him.

Elanchius: Welcome back, Pulvius.

Libentia: Faithful Pulvius! But should you have come? Elanchius, does he not look pale?

Pulvius: —as my shirt, my knees knocking each other. But have no concern. Although shaken, I am now recovered, thanks to some fresh air and the restorative powers of a document or two in my library.

Quintus: Got here just in time too, Pulvius. Vulpius answered all our questions for us, and you missed the whole thing!

Pulvius: By biting my nether lip severely, I believe I shall be able to endure that deprivation.

Empiricus: You arrived just in time for another reason also, Pulvius. Elanchius and Quintus were saying that Vulpius, in answering the questions about presentation which you remember we had posed, proceeded without first defining a principle by which they can be answered wisely.

Pulvius: And have you succeeded in defining this principle?

Elanchius: We were just ready to phrase a question which may lead to it.

Empiricus: Elanchius, I believe it would be helpful first— both to Pulvius, who has just returned, and to all of us—for you to recapitulate the reasoning which has led to our decision that we cannot proceed beyond this point until we have phrased and answered this question.

Elanchius: Well, then. We have agreed that in answering all our questions as he did, Vulpius disregarded our usual practice. We have said that there exists no basis for reasoned answers to certain questions until prior ones have been answered. Thus we found that before we could properly answer any questions about the reading program, we needed to ask what the highest function is that the reading of books should serve. We have approached all subsequent questions in the light of our answer. Thus we came to conclude that only those works should be selected which have power to penetrate and enhance the nature of the reader. Thus also we concluded that an arrangement by themes is best. So also we decided that the approach to a particular work must be made not in terms of its secondary characteristics and peripheral aspects, but in terms of its primary and essential nature as an artistic utterance upon a fundamentally human theme. And now, in confronting the problems of the actual presentation of literature—what form it should take, what matters should be emphasized, what measures should be taken to insure the reader's comprehension, and so on—we must again define a principle by reference to our antecedent question.

Libentia: We agreed long ago that the teacher will not do anything wisely until she knows what she should be trying to do. Is not our initial question about presentation, then, something like this: *What is the most important function to be served by the actual presentation?*

Elanchius: Excellent, Libentia. Now, if we are to determine which is most important, we should have all the possibilities before us. Will you name some of them?

Libentia: Clearly, one purpose is to develop the student's ability to read and to understand what he reads. The presentation may also be used to give the student experience in reading aloud and thus to develop his self-confidence and poise, to improve his diction, and so on. It may be made to give experience in listening, too, and—

Vulpius: And in sharing with one's peers through dynamic group activities, Libentia. Working together for social—

Quintus: Yeh, you already told us about those groups, Vulpius.

Elanchius: These are some obvious purposes, and of course we might name many more. But let us probe a little more deeply. May I remind you that just before we phrased our immediate question, we agreed that *it must be answered in the light of our answer to the antecedent question.* Now have we, in our haste to get the possibilities before us, momentarily forgotten our agreement?

Empiricus: At least some of the possibilities just named suggest that it was forgotten.

Quintus: Don't tell us we forgot about that again! Anyhow, I know what it is. Said the teacher's biggest job with books is to make 'em humanize the people that read 'em.

Elanchius: Good, Quintus. And just where did we say the humanizing force resides?

Quintus: Said it was right in the books themselves.

Elanchius: Did we not say that it was contained in them *as a potentiality*?

Quintus: Yeh. But, you know, I never quite knew what we meant by that "potentiality" business.

Elanchius: Why, Quintus, that is said to be potential which, although possible, is not yet actual, or realized.

Quintus: Mean it's there and then again it isn't? Sounds like a riddle. Don't get it, Elanchius.

Elanchius: Empiricus, you are our authority on potentials. Please give us an illustration.

Empiricus: Let me see—Quintus, with what fuel do you cook your dinner?

Quintus: Wood, of course. Like olive branches, myself.

Empiricus: But are olive branches *hot*?

Quintus: Course not—till they're set afire.

Empiricus: And in setting them afire do you put the heat into them?

Quintus: Course not. Get it out of 'em.

Empiricus: Then it was in them, all the while?

Quintus: Guess you'd say it was there and it wasn't. Hey! Now you've got *me* doing it! But it was there all right. Had to be.

Empiricus: What was in them before they were lighted, Quintus, was the potentiality of heat.

Quintus: Yeh. Guess you'd say this heat was sort of lying there, locked in.

Elanchius: Splendid, Empiricus. And now, Quintus, when we speak of the humanizing force as potential in a work of literature, we may use your own phrase: it is *lying there, locked in*.

Quintus: Yeh, locked in.

Elanchius: And what, again, did you do to your olive branches in order to make the potentiality an actuality?

Quintus: I set 'em afire. Guess you'd say I let it out.

Elanchius: Well, then. What would you do to make the humanizing potentiality in literature an actuality?

Quintus: Guess I'd let it out, too!

Libentia: I see it, Elanchius! I see it! My task is to effect the release of the humanizing force!

Elanchius: And precisely *when* are you to do this?

Libentia: Why, in the actual presentation! *The most important function of the presentation of a literary work is to effect the release of the humanizing force that is potential in it.*

Pulvius: Bravo, Libentia!

Libentia: As the teacher, I must find and use that form of presentation which will most nearly guarantee the release.

Elanchius: You say "that form." Is there some particular form that will be used invariably?

Libentia: With every work? I doubt that any single form will always be the best one.

Elanchius: Why not?

Libentia: Because of the variety of books. The means that will best effect the release of the humanizing force locked in one may be inappropriate for another.

Vulpius: And because of the differences as to the learners. We in the profession speak of those as individual differences.

Libentia: I agree that these also must be allowed for.

Elanchius: True, Libentia. But an immediate question is suggested by your own word "inappropriate." How might a particular form of presentation sometimes be inappropriate?

Libentia: Why, it might simply be contrary to the purpose which presentation must serve. Or, though suited to the purpose, it might be inadequate, on the one hand, or unnecessarily elaborate, on the other—depending on the particular work. One form of presentation that I would consider as contrary to the purpose is that described by Vulpius this morning. I hope you don't mind, Vulpius.

Quintus: Let's hear it.

Libentia: The method Vulpius recommended involved the use of several groups of students, with each group responsible for reading and reporting on one portion of a long poem.

Quintus: Hey! Better stop right there. That's what made Pulvius sick.

Libentia: Since you recall the details, I need not go further. But will it distress you, Pulvius, if I tell *why* I find this form of presentation so inappropriate?

Pulvius: Distress me! It will delight me.

Libentia: Well, Vulpius praised this method because it gave opportunity for group activities. It is not for me to say that group activity has no value. A good deal of a student's time in school should no doubt be spent in activities in which learning to "get along" with his fellows is the main purpose. *But the moments when a literary work is being presented are not the time for that!* We have agreed that the most important function of the actual presentation of a literary work is to bring about the release of the humanizing force which, as Quintus said, is locked in it. Now obviously Vulpius' plan will not serve this purpose—for no student will even read the entire work! Instead, he must rely on his fellows' summaries for most of it.

Quintus: Ho! Bet those summaries don't have much of that humanizing force locked in 'em!

Pulvius: None, Quintus.

Quintus: Guess it'd be quite a job setting them afire, hey, Empiricus? No heat in 'em.

Empiricus: I fear not, Quintus. It is evident that whatever virtue Vulpius' method of presentation may possess, it does not possess the indispensable one; for the force that is potential in literature will hardly be released if the literature is unread!

Elanchius: But now, Libentia, suppose that each of Vulpius' groups reads an entire work rather than a mere portion—but still in the same manner, and for Vulpius' purpose of stimulating group activity. With this change, will the method serve our purpose?

Libentia: Well, of course it is better to have students read whole works than merely parts. But as long as the method of presentation is mainly designed to stimulate group activity, it will at best release the humanizing force only accidentally—and at worst the very character of the group activity will thwart the true purpose.

Quintus: Hey! We've talked several times about things getting thwarted. Looks like the teacher has a pretty tough job there. Always got to be on the look-out so the *big thing* won't get thwarted.

Empiricus: Exactly, Quintus. Since we began these conversations, Elanchius has urged the need for harmony of purpose and means. So interdependent are all the parts of the teacher's task that a failure at any point may make her whole venture useless. Do I overstate the case, Elanchius?

Elanchius: No indeed. No matter how careful she has been to *select* books that have a humanizing potentiality, if she then chooses an *arrangement* that emphasizes matters which divert the artistic force, her care in selection will be wasted. Similarly, if her *approach* to a literary work shifts the reader's concentration from the work itself to its periphery, her previous effort may again go for nothing. And now at last, unless she uses a form of *presentation* expressly designed to release the humanizing potential, her utmost care in the preceding steps will be rendered futile. So you see, Quintus, the danger of thwarting the greatest purpose in teaching literature is present all along the line, and the true teacher will always be on guard.

Quintus: Guess her job's even tougher than I thought.

Elanchius: Well, then. Let me remind you that besides describing a plan of presentation through group activity, Vulpius recommended the use of study questions to guide the students' reading. Would you think these appropriate to our purpose?

Libentia: To some purposes certainly, but not to ours. I have often seen this method used. Let me tell you how *all* the students go at an assigned poem. They begin by reading the first question on the list. Then, *with their fingers following the lines, they seek the answer!* When they find it, they write it down with an air of satisfaction, as much as to say, "Well, that's done." They then read the second question on the list, and thus they proceed until

262 DIALOGUE THE THIRTEENTH

they reach the end of the poem—or the end of the list, whichever comes first. At last, what they have gained is not an aesthetic experience, but only the satisfaction of having completed answers to questions!

Pulvius: Ha! Now who's upset about Vulpius' schemes!

Quintus: You sound plenty worked up about this deal, Libentia. But what about that experience? Does it humanize 'em?

Libentia: On the contrary. I should say that this method makes achievement of the great purpose not only unlikely, but quite literally impossible!

Empiricus: The procedure that you have described would seem truly deadly. Probably nothing so delicate as aesthetic experience could survive it. The students may even suppose that the satisfaction of completing a mechanical assignment is the experience of art itself!

Libentia: I would quit teaching rather than so misuse literature!

Pulvius: A grievous misfortune—either way!

Quintus: I'll say! Wish I'd had a teacher like you when I was in school, Libentia. Say, you oughta get a raise!

Elanchius: Well, then. So far our principle has shown that Vulpius' methods of presentation will not do. But we have yet to find what *will* do. Let us try again. You will recall that Libentia asked several specific questions about the manner of presentation.

Quintus: Yeh—about who should do the reading and when and how. Lots more, too. Maybe we can answer 'em now that we've got a lot of wrong stuff out of the way.

Elanchius: Let us hope so. Now when we ask, "What is the best form of presentation?" are we not asking, in effect, "What is the role of the teacher in the presentation?"

Quintus: You mean what she ought to *do* to make sure that force that's locked in the book gets out?

Elanchius: Yes, Quintus. Can you answer that question?

Quintus: Well, the thing she'd have to do first is find out herself what's in the book—if she didn't already know. Sure couldn't let it out if she didn't know.

Elanchius: True. The teacher must know what is in the literary work. And must the student also know, if it is to affect him?

Quintus: Well, she's got to help him see what's there so he'll know too. Otherwise, the book won't do much for him.

Elanchius: Then the task of the teacher in releasing the humanizing force is to help the student perceive the author's book in its totality. If she succeeds in that, the book itself will do the rest.

Libentia: With the help you two have given me, I believe I can now answer my own questions.

Quintus: You can, Libentia? Good. So how you going to get the books read?

Libentia: Well, there is really only one answer to all of my questions: *a work must be presented in the way that will best enable the student to perceive what is actually in it.* But the way will obviously vary. In the presentation of a relatively simple work, the teacher's role may involve hardly more than encouragement. But for the more difficult or complex work, she may find it necessary to explain meanings that are contributed by structure, for example, and to clarify allusions and images; in short, she may need to devote considerable time to explication of the work.

Quintus: Hey there! You mean after all this talk we're not going to come up with one set way the teacher ought to go at the business of getting the books in their heads?

Libentia: That is exactly what I mean, Quintus. But how could it be otherwise? Literary works are at least as different from one another as children are! No one means can be best for releasing the force that is potential in all.

Quintus: Yeh, remember before, you said we probably couldn't expect a miracle to happen. Guess the same way wouldn't do for 'em all. Still, there ought to be something alike here somewhere. If there's not, looks like we've just been wasting our time.

Libentia: No, no, Quintus! Though we cannot prescribe one method of presentation that will be right for all works, whether poetry or prose, long or short, simple or complex, yet we have found the *principle* that will determine the teacher's choice and use of her method. *Always, she will choose whatever method best serves to expose the work in its totality, so that the humanizing force is released.*

Quintus: So then the ways she goes at it can be different, but they've all got that one thing in common, hey? All trying to get the same job done. Now, all I want to see is just how this works. What about the rest of the questions you asked a while back? You said was it better to have the students read the books to themselves, or read them out loud to the whole bunch, or maybe have the teacher read 'em to 'em. How're you going to answer questions like that now?

Elanchius: But is it not apparent, Quintus, that Libentia has found the *means* of answering these questions, and so, in a sense, has already answered them? And not only these, but also those asked this morning by Empiricus, Pulvius, and yourself.

Quintus: Well, maybe she has. But if we've got these answers now, why don't we get 'em out? What about that first one—are the students going to read books to themselves, or aren't they?

Elanchius: Why, Quintus, will not that depend on whether, reading silently, they will be able to perceive what is truly in the given work?

Quintus: Yeh, guess so. If they can get it that way, let 'em. Guess what it comes down to is whether the book is the kind of book that that way will do the job for.

Elanchius: And if the work is not of that kind?

Vulpius: That would indicate that the reading material is not adapted to the individual's reading level. Obviously, what the teacher will do in that case is provide material lower down on the reading ladder.

Quintus: You mean get another book, Vulpius? That's the easy way out! But if she's picked out a book that has the real stuff in it, the way we said she should, I don't think she ought to throw it away and get another one!

Vulpius: Then let her keep the book, but rewritten by one of our experts.

Pulvius: Ha!

Quintus: Let's not go into that again! Already saw that won't do.

Elanchius: Truly it will not, Quintus! But what do you think she should do instead?

Quintus: *Keep the book and find another way of going at getting it read!*

Empiricus: Permit me to compliment you, Quintus. Your conclusion is the only rational one.

Pulvius: I agree. I can only add my profound regrets that some of those who have taken over the education of young people, whether it be that they are too obtuse by nature, or that they are too closely encased in the web spun out of their own entrails, or that they are mired in their own—uh—their own—

Quintus: Their own what, Pulvius? Stuck?

Pulvius: Let it pass. In any event, it is a sad fact that Vulpius has learned nothing from these conversations.

Elanchius: Well, then. We agree, Quintus, that if the literary work is of such a kind that the student will not perceive what it truly is by reading it silently and alone, *the teacher should choose not another work but another method of presenting it.* Now, what other method do you suggest?

Quintus: Well, Libentia mentioned some other ways herself. How about having the students read it out loud?

Elanchius: But if they cannot perceive what is truly there when they read it silently, Quintus, do you think they will do so when they read it aloud?

Quintus: Well, seems sometimes the way a thing sounds can help you see what it's all about. Student might get more out of it if he gets his ear on it.

Elanchius: That is true, Quintus. Since the sound of certain works is an integral part of the totality, to read them silently is, at least for the inexperienced reader, to leave that part unperceived.

Quintus: No doubt about it. Take that poem Libentia read us. Guess that's one where the way it sounds has plenty to do with it. Libentia really brought it out, too.

Elanchius: True—but remember that Libentia is a teacher—and a good one! Your suggestion, however, was that the *students* read the work aloud.

Quintus: Well, what's the difference? Either way, it gets out so you can hear it.

Elanchius: But does it? Reflect for a moment. What is it, again, that you want students to gain by reading aloud?

Quintus: Well, want 'em to see what's there—understand it.

Elanchius: They will not have understood it *before* they read it aloud?

Quintus: Course not. That's why they're reading it aloud—so they *will*.

Elanchius: But Quintus, if they have not understood it beforehand, do you believe that they will read it aloud very well?

Pulvius: Ha!

Quintus: What'd you say there, Pulvius?

Pulvius: Quintus, have you ever heard students read aloud lines that they do not understand and have not read before?

Quintus: Guess I must've, sometime or other.

Pulvius: It is a dreadful experience, Quintus, dreadful.

Libentia: Indeed it is, Pulvius. And when the student reads badly, his reading will not help either him or his classmates to see what is in the work!

Elanchius: And if the students fail to see this, Libentia, can it be said that the humanizing force potential in the work has been released?

Libentia: Certainly not.

Elanchius: And if it has not been released, can it have affected them?

Libentia: Hardly!

Elanchius: Then the presentation will have failed.

Vulpius: Failed, Elanchius? Definitely not. The young learners will have experienced a doing-activity in a cooperative endeavor with their peers.

Elanchius: We earlier agreed, I recall, that there can be value in such activities. *But when any method, though it serves well a secondary purpose, thwarts the primary one, it must give place.*

Pulvius: Good reasons must, of force, give place to better.

Quintus: Yeh.

Libentia: Nevertheless, before we leave the question of having students read aloud and thus seem to have condemned the practice entirely, I must say a word in its defense. Do not misunderstand me, however. I agree with Elanchius that, improperly used, it thwarts the main function of the presentation. I am convinced that a teacher who truly values a fine poem, and truly believes that it can do what we have said it must be given the best possible chance to do, will do nothing so disastrous as allow her students to hear it read *for the first time* by one of their own number!

Pulvius: Bravo, Libentia!

Quintus: Mighty strong words, Libentia. But guess you're right. No sense in the teacher going out of her way to thwart what she's trying to do.

Elanchius: True, Quintus. But now, Libentia, you were about to say a word in defense of the students' reading aloud.

Libentia: Not in defense of it as an appropriate form of the *initial* presentation. But *after* the students have come to understand the poem I would not want to deprive them of the additional experience—and, I should say, privilege—of reading it aloud. Indeed, for some works I think the teacher's task has not been completed until she has provided this opportunity, for it is a further step toward making the poem the students' own.

Empiricus: My admiration of your understanding continues to grow, Libentia.

Quintus: Mine, too. But look here. We just blasted another idea we had for getting books read the first time. You can't have the students read a thing out loud after they've got to where they understand it if you still haven't found a way to get it read so they understand it in the first place!

Elanchius: That is good sense, Quintus.

Pulvius: And quite remarkable syntax.

Quintus: Thanks. Now let's get on with the job. Say, have we got any ideas about this left? If the student shouldn't read it to himself or out loud either, then just how're we going to get it into his head, anyhow?

Elanchius: There is not yet need for alarm, Quintus. Libentia herself suggested a third possibility this morning.

Quintus: She did?

Empiricus: Not only did she suggest it, Quintus. She demonstrated it—twice.

Quintus: Well, let's see. She read that poem a couple of times. Hey! That's it. The *teacher* can read it to 'em herself!

Vulpius: Your thinking is unrealistic if you recommend such a presentation method, Quintus. If the teacher monopolizes student time by reading to them, she has not kept up with professional research findings. Unless carefully pre-planned doing-activities are utilized, there will be no worthwhile reading growth. Moreover, in this instance, since the relational rapport that is established will exist only between teacher and individual listener and not between members of a peer group participating dynamically in a group situation, the desirable outcomes implicit in the dynamics of group situations will not be achieved.

Quintus: Don't think I got that, Vulpius. Say, Empiricus, can you tell me what he just said?

Pulvius: Sift, Empiricus, sift!

Quintus: Huh? Oh—sift!

Empiricus: My impression is that Vulpius has brought two charges against the teacher's reading to her students: first, that the practice does not teach them to read; and second, that it does not allow them to participate.

Quintus: Stands to reason all right. Can't learn to read if they don't read. And they can't read if they don't even have a book in front of 'em.

Elanchius: Ah, Quintus, but suppose that they *have*?

Quintus: You mean have 'em be looking at the words while the teacher's reading to 'em?

Elanchius: To them, Quintus? *To* them?

Quintus: Well, uh—*for* 'em?

Elanchius: No, not that either, Quintus. For remember that the student will be reading, also, though silently.

Quintus: Oh, you mean *with* 'em. Hey! That's how Libentia did that Vatarius poem the second time. She read it out loud, only we read it, too!

Elanchius: So we did, Quintus, as you yourself remarked at the time.

Vulpius: No consideration of that practice is worthwhile, as the findings of specialists in the field demonstrate conclusively. You will recall that when Libentia read that material, I experienced strain in accommodating my eye jerks to her reading rate. Provision for individual differences as to—

Quintus: I want to get this *to* and *with* business settled. Mind keeping those jerks to yourself for a minute, Vulpius?

Pulvius: For a minute, Quintus? Forever!

Elanchius: I agree with Quintus that we should first differentiate reading *to* and reading *with*. Thereafter we can consider possible objections and, if necessary, make qualifications.

Quintus: That's the idea, Elanchius.

Elanchius: Having raised the two possibilities, let us determine which is better suited to our purpose.

Quintus: You mean the big job? We said the way we use to get the books read ought to let out what's in 'em.

Elanchius: True, Quintus. We called that the most important function of presentation. And let us never forget that we said so. But did we say that this is the *sole* function?

Quintus: Guess not, but we've always been saying we ought to answer our questions according to what the biggest job is the teacher's trying to get done. So it looks like whichever one of these ways gets that job done best is the best way.

Elanchius: Well, let us say, for the moment, that either by reading *to* her students or by reading *with* them the teacher may be able to release the force that is locked in a particular work. It may be we shall decide later that one way will have the edge over the other, but for the moment let us suppose that the two ways are equal in this respect. Even so, do you think of any reason why you might conclude that reading *to* the students should not be accepted as a regular, daily form of presentation?

Quintus: Don't see how that could be, if it gets the big job done. Looks like if we say anything else we're taking back what we already said.

Elanchius: No, Quintus, not at all. We shall never go back on our word there! But now let us try another tack. Tell me, will Libentia's students continue all their lives to have her, or some other teacher, to aid them in reading books?

Quintus: Course not. Even the ones that go on up to Pulvius will get through some day. Most of 'em, anyhow.

Elanchius: True, Quintus. And therefore must not a teacher of literature, in choosing a form of presentation, bear in mind that her responsibility is not only to help release the force contained in the particular works read in the classroom, but also to develop her students' power to release the force of other books for themselves when the teacher will no longer be by to aid them?

Quintus: Guess if they're going to go on reading books like these when they get out, they better learn how to do it while they're still in.

Elanchius: Then do you see why reading *to* students, as a regular form of presentation, is unsatisfactory?

Quintus: Hey! Guess they wouldn't learn to read at all, that way. Couldn't. Wouldn't even have any words in front of 'em.

Elanchius: And if they are not learning to read at all, they certainly are not learning to read with understanding and insight. Then can they be expected later in life to experience the humanizing force of the kind of books we have been recommending?

Quintus: Course not. There's still something bothers me here, though. We've been saying ever since we started talking about these things that we ought to decide whether some way's the right way to do a thing by whether or not it gets the biggest thing done that ought to be done. Now we just said this way of reading to students could maybe get the biggest job done that the presentation's supposed to do. But next we say this way has to be thrown out because it won't teach 'em how to read so they'll be able to let out what's in the book by themselves later on. See what I mean?

Empiricus: Let me commend your perception of what does appear, at first, to be a violation of our usual practice.

Elanchius: By saying "at first," Empiricus, do you suggest that it is not in fact a violation?

Empiricus: We began with the supposition that either method—that is, reading *to* or reading *with*—may effect the release of the humanizing force. Yet, even if equal in this indispensable respect, these methods are manifestly unequal in another—for it is obvious that the former can contribute nothing to the student's power to read. Now, Quintus, which method is superior? That which will result in releasing the force only of the few works read in the classroom? Or that which can result in releasing the force not only of these but thereafter of many more which the student may choose to read?

Quintus: Last one, of course. No sense killing the goose after it's laid you one egg if you can fix it so it'll keep on laying 'em.

Pulvius: The quotation, as well as the syntax, is somewhat imprecise, Quintus. But the shoe fits!

Elanchius: Well, then. It is apparent that the teacher's reading *to* students as a regular form of presentation is inappropriate. But, though we have found that one way is unsatisfactory, have we yet demonstrated that the other is the best way possible?

Quintus: Well, maybe not. Still, looks like if reading *with* 'em unlocks that humanizing force and teaches 'em to read other books by themselves too, it can't help being the best way.

Elanchius: I agree, Quintus, that if it does efficiently accomplish these two purposes, it may well be the best single way. But have we yet shown that it does accomplish both? What reasons are there to believe that the teacher's reading *with* her students is the best single means of presentation?

Empiricus: Well, first of all, as we have previously said, since the teacher is the one who has perceived and understood in advance the totality of the work, it is she who is best equipped to lead the students toward the revelation of that totality.

Quintus: I'd say that's settled, especially after the way Libentia proved it by reading that Vatarius poem *with* us. Ha! got it right that time, didn't I?

Libentia: There is a second reason why this method should serve the purpose well: it involves, in the finest sense of the word, the participation of the student.

Vulpius: Participation, Libentia? How can the individuals be participating when no doing-activities are being participated in?

Empiricus: By "participating," Vulpius, do you mean that the students must be using their voices and moving about physically? Libentia's statement implies that students can participate with their eyes, ears, and minds, and that, for the classroom in which literature is being studied, this is the best kind of participation.

Quintus: Yeh, Vulpius. That's right. You can participate without all that jumping around.

Libentia: My thought, gentlemen, was that when the teacher reads *with* her students, they too are reading—though silently. They are actively "taking in" the force and meaning of the work through their eyes and ears simultaneously. And in doing so, are they not participating with eyes, ears, and minds—as Empiricus said?

Quintus: See what you mean, Libentia. Tell you what. When you read that poem to us awhile ago—first time, I mean—it hit me pretty hard, all right. Still, maybe I didn't get the whole wallop. Second time, though, when you read it *with* us, I went right along with you. Funny thing, too—*seemed like I was doing the reading myself, all the time I was hearing your voice. Fact is, it was practically like my own voice I was hearing. Course, the way you read it made it mean a lot more—but it seemed like I was sort of getting what it had to say all by myself, too.*

Elanchius: You have penetrated the heart of the mystery, Quintus! Libentia's voice, for you, lost its identity as something existing apart from the text, even while it directed your understanding and intensified your experience of the poem.

Pulvius: As I remember, Quintus, Libentia's second reading struck you silent.

Quintus: Yeh! That's when it really jolted me.

Elanchius: Well, then. So far, we seem agreed that this form of presentation may best effect the release of the humanizing force because the teacher is the one most able to guide the student's experience of a literary work and because the student is enabled to participate with two of his senses simultaneously. Now, then, is there any further reason?

Pulvius: It may be, Elanchius, that I have one to suggest—and one which, I confess, is for me of prime importance. But first I have an observation to make and a question to ask of Libentia.

Libentia: Yes, Pulvius?

Pulvius: I noted that during your reading of Vatarius' poem you did not once pause to offer comment of any kind. Now, let me ask you this: had you been reading it to your—that is, *with* your students rather than with us, might you have done so?

Libentia: Why, yes—if the need had arisen.

Pulvius: The need? What need, Libentia.

Libentia: Oh, for explanation of some kind—an unfamiliar word, a subtle image, or an allusion. Anything necessary to make the meaning clear.

Pulvius: An historical fact?

Libentia: Why, of course, if it would help to release the force of the poem.

Pulvius: A characteristic of the genre?

Libentia: Yes, if that served the same purpose.

Pulvius: A biographical fact?

Libentia: Yes, if that were relevant.

Elanchius: Observe, gentlemen! With each of Libentia's answers, Pulvius' smile has broadened!

Quintus: Yeh, look at him now! Grinning like the cat that got the canary! What you so tickled about, Pulvius?

Pulvius: You may just possibly remember, Quintus, that I have from time to time evinced some—er—slight concern lest the facts of literary history go unrepresented. My mind has been greatly relieved by Libentia's remarks just now. Frankly, the method of presentation on which we seem to have fixed appeared at first to provide no opportunity for introducing matters of literary history and convention. However, Libentia has given assurance that the teacher will pause at points where facts of these kinds are pertinent. Moreover, it has occurred to me that by proceeding in this fashion she will have a better opportunity to perceive which matters *are* relevant to the understanding of a particular document than if she sought to introduce the entire background prior to the reading.

Elanchius: You are, then, Pulvius, content to have only those matters of background introduced which are relevant?

Pulvius: I am content.

Quintus: Guess I'm not the only one that's learned plenty from these talks. Boy, what a change you've made!

Pulvius: I'm a little startled by it, myself.

Empiricus: Your observation, Pulvius, that while she is actually reading a work with her students the teacher will be in the best position to determine precisely which historical and other facts are needed strikes me as an eminently just one. As I have often reminded you, I am neither a literary man nor a teacher of literature. Yet I can imagine how very difficult it must be for a teacher, in attempting to present all the materials of background in advance of the reading, to anticipate exactly what will prove relevant and to sort out and reject what will not be so. Reading *with* her students, however, she can let the text itself guide her. When need for explanation arises, on a word or a line, she can supply it. All this is clear to me, and therefore I applauded your observation. However, to satisfy my mind entirely, I must ask one question of you and Libentia. Will the occasional interruption of reading for the purpose of explanation impair the effectiveness of the work? I ask this because we agreed earlier that the impact of the whole is essential.

Quintus: Guess when you said impair there, you were really talking about thwarting, hey, Empiricus? Got to throw this way of teaching out quick if it's going to thwart the main thing the teacher's trying to do.

Libentia: True, Quintus, nothing must be allowed to block the student's vision of the totality. But I can assure you that it is possible to pause for appropriate explanation while one is reading without intruding between the students and the work. Although the actual reading of the text is momentarily interrupted, yet the students' concentration upon its meaning is not interrupted. If the teacher's comments are truly relevant, as they should always be, and if they are presented in a quick, inconspicuous manner, they will enhance the student's experience almost without his being aware that they have been made!

Empiricus: Thank you, Libentia. You have answered my question. And even as you spoke it occurred to me that you could have countered my suggestion of a possible disadvantage by pointing out what now appears to me a positive advantage.

Libentia: Can you give me more of a cue than that, Empiricus?

Elanchius: Perhaps Empiricus is suggesting the matter of *timing*.

Libentia: Timing? Oh, I see what you mean. In reading *with* her students, the teacher can make the comment or explanation *at the precise moment it is needed*—

Empiricus: —And thus matters of background will be introduced in a truly efficient manner.

Elanchius: —With the result that the explication can immediately aid in releasing the force of the work.

Pulvius: What is this, gentlemen? A round? Well, I confess that I find it pleasing, since you make the background carry the burden! Sorry, couldn't refrain!

Elanchius: Excellent, Pulvius. I am glad that we are all in tune.

Vulpius: See here now! The thinking of we in the profession—

Pulvius: There's the sour note. Ducdame, ducdame, ducdame!

Quintus: What's that "ducdame" business, Pulvius?

Pulvius: 'Tis an old invocation, to call fools into a circle— or into a round if you prefer, Quintus.

Quintus: Say, what's this all about? Why so gay all of a sudden?

Empiricus: Because of our sense that the job is almost done, Quintus.

Elanchius: Well, then. We have stated a third reason why reading *with* students will most nearly guarantee the release of the humanizing force in literature. We concluded that this method invites the best possible use of historical and other facts, since it enables the teacher to determine precisely which of these are needed and to introduce them at the precise moment they are needed. In short, it permits the timely use of the data most relevant to our purpose.

Quintus: Say! See why Pulvius was so keyed up just now. So some of that Pulvian kind of background's going to get in after all! I thought there for a while we were going to put him out of business. Think he did, too. But guess he's got a job left, all right.

Elanchius: Indeed he has, Quintus! And an important one. The time must never come when there will be no place or need for Pulvius—all the Pulviuses everywhere. It is only they who can equip the Libentias with a full knowledge of literature, both in itself and in the many contexts, historical and other, which can illuminate meaning and help to release the force of a work to young readers.

Pulvius: Hear! Hear!

Libentia: I agree, Elanchius. Lacking the knowledge I have gained from Pulvius, I would feel unqualified to stand before my class.

Empiricus: Might one say, Libentia, that although you may not put to direct use all that you learned from Pulvius, it serves as a *strategic reserve* upon which to draw at need?

Libentia: Strategic reserve? I shall remember that, Empiricus. It suggests both the use to which this knowledge should be put and the place it should occupy—behind the lines.

Quintus: Strategic reserve? Behind the lines? Say, that's good! that's good! We said a long time ago one of the things wrong with Pulvius was that he wanted to get his stuff out in *front* all the time. Now we've got it back behind, where it won't get in the way and will really do some good.

Elanchius: We have identified three reasons why reading literary works with students can be expected to help release their power. Are there any others?

Quintus: Can't think of any, myself.

Elanchius: But it was you, this morning, who asked whether in presenting a work the teacher should emphasize the work itself or the frame used to group it with others.

Quintus: Yeh, I remember. We said she ought to stay with the book, not just gab about themes. But how's that fit what we're talking about right now?

Elanchius: Should we not consider whether the form of presentation whose virtues we are assessing meets our demand that the *book*, not the theme, be the principal object of attention?

Quintus: Looks like we don't have to worry about that. If the teacher and the students read this book together, they're bound to have it right there in front of 'em every minute. Won't have any chance to forget about it and go off talking about themes by themselves. Hey, that could be the best reason yet!

Libentia: I agree. No form of presentation will more nearly guarantee that both teacher and students will attend to the work itself.

Pulvius: And the more faithfully they attend to it, the more likely they will be to perceive what is in it!

Quintus: Yeh, and we already said they'll have to see what's there before it can get out and humanize 'em.

Elanchius: Well, then. Having heard these arguments, we must recognize the merit of the teacher's reading a literary work *with* students as a means of releasing its humanizing force. Now let us test our second major premise: that this form of presentation helps to teach reading itself.

Quintus: Yeh, it's got to do that too if it's going to be good enough to suit us. Don't think it ought to take much figuring, though, to see why it'll do that job too.

Elanchius: That may be, Quintus. Nevertheless, let us not cease to be circumspect now that we are nearing the end of our quest. Let me therefore begin by asking Libentia, who, I know, sometimes reads with her students, whether she has found reason to believe that this method can help them learn to read for themselves.

Libentia: Why, one fact comes to my mind instantly. Each time I read with my students, the hour passes too quickly for all of us, for the experience is pleasant.

Quintus: Well, I can believe that all right, Libentia. But what's that got to do with 'em learning to read?

Libentia: Only that it makes them *want* to read, Quintus. And Vulpius himself will agree that children learn to do well what they truly like to do.

Elanchius: And continue to do what they have learned to like! Clearly, students find pleasure in the teacher's reading *with* them, especially when she reads perceptively. But even so, would you say that the pleasure derives solely from their reading together, or is there another source which we should mention also?

Libentia: Well, of course, *what* they are reading plays a part too!

Quintus: Sounds like you really mean it plays a big part.

Libentia: Indeed I do, Quintus.

Quintus: But now, look here. If *what* they read is what they like about it, then what's it matter *how* they read it?

Libentia: But, Quintus, *it is by reading in this fashion that they are able to read with pleasure the works that have greatest power to give pleasure!*

Elanchius: Excellent, Libentia! They can find pleasure in the act itself. Furthermore, they can read those works which are richest in the kind of pleasure that is capable of refining their humanity.

Empiricus: And which they would otherwise not be able to read at all.

Pulvius: And which are not the documents that Vulpius has on his reading lists! By reading *with* her students, the teacher will never have to stoop to such stuff!

Quintus: Yeh! That stuff wouldn't have any kick no matter how you read it. It'd just be a reading lesson.

Pulvius: And not even a good reading lesson, since it would not give training in the kind of reading that has genuine merit! *Libentia's job is not just to teach reading but to teach the reading of literature.*

Empiricus: I accept your logic, Pulvius. If students are ever to read for themselves works of the kind we intend, their training must be *in* this kind.

Quintus: Hey, there's not much use in 'em being able to read at all if all they can read is Vulpius' stuff! The way I get it, this stuff is not only not any good itself, it just plain won't ever teach 'em to read good stuff either!

Elanchius: Well, then. We are agreed that the very pleasure which students find in the works of literature that can be read when the teacher reads *with* the class is itself a condition favorable to the development of reading power.

Quintus: All right, then. That's one reason this way's good for teaching 'em how to read. Then there's another one that's as plain as the nose on my face. Looks to me like if the teacher's going to do a first-rate job of teaching reading she's got to be right there the minute a kid runs into trouble.

Elanchius: What kind of trouble, Quintus?

Quintus: All kinds. Maybe he can't get a word, or maybe a whole line doesn't make any sense to him. This way the teacher'll be right there to help him figure it out. Maybe even show him some things he'd have thought he didn't have to figure out in order to know what it all meant. Looks to me like if she gives him a lift just exactly when he needs it, she's really showing him how to read.

Elanchius: Your point, then, is that since this method makes it possible for difficulties to be overcome *as they arise*, it is an effective way of teaching reading. I quite agree.

Libentia: And I, too. I have already learned that there is a precisely right moment, when help will do the most good.

Elanchius: And by helping at that moment, she removes the obstacles not only to the act of reading itself but also to the pleasure which can be derived from the reading.

Libentia: Yes, and if the student is to continue to read after his school days are over, he must find pleasure in his reading at school. If the teacher does her work well, she will show him how to overcome the difficulties inherent in reading, and he will therefore be more likely to continue to read, with pleasure and profit.

Quintus: Yeh, that's right. If she shows him how to get over the hard spots, he'll like what he's doing and maybe go right on doing it. Hey, just thought of something. Even if he didn't, he'd still have had a lot of good stuff in school. Thought of something else, too. Vulpius here's been claiming all along that students can't read good books because they're too tough. But they won't be too tough by our system!

Vulpius: Our experts have contrived batteries of tests to prove that your so-called great books are not adapted to individual adolescent learner reading and maturity levels.

Pulvius: By all the toplofty deities!

Quintus: Don't think you've got a leg to stand on, Vulpius. If the teacher does her job right there's no excuse for starving 'em on that thin soup your experts dish out. Nothing's too good for our boys and girls if there's any way at all to get it into their heads!

Libentia: And not only do they deserve the best, Quintus. It is also the best that gives them an appetite for more of the same. The "thin soup" you mentioned has no such effect!

Pulvius: Bravo, Quintus! Bravo, Libentia!

Empiricus: If this issue is resolved, Elanchius—as it seems to be for the present, since Vulpius offers no reply to Quintus—I should like to suggest a third reason why the teacher's reading with her students should be effective in developing their ability to read for themselves.

Elanchius: By all means, let us hear it.

Empiricus: My point is this. This form of presentation draws together the virtues of two different and equally useful methods—demonstration and participation. We have already spoken of the virtues of the latter. And concerning those of the former I can myself testify. Though a poor demonstration may be worse than none, an able one, in my own field, provides a highly efficient means of teaching. And if I may judge by Libentia's demonstration this morning, this means should be no less effective in teaching students to read works of literature. Now a form of presentation which combines both easily and naturally two such well-tested methods should prove virtually infallible.

Quintus: Hey, you're right, Empiricus. Don't mind saying that when Libentia was reading a while back and I was going right along with her in my book it seemed like I was reading better than I ever did before! Don't think it'd be long, going at it that way, before I'd get so I could read just like Libentia herself. Quite a lot to learn just from the way she hit those words. Like to get so I could hit 'em the same way!

Elanchius: "Hitting the words" is certainly a part of the demonstration, Quintus. But when Libentia reads with her young students she may demonstrate something more, also. Am I right, Libentia?

Libentia: Yes, though I'm not sure I can explain it. I think I try to show my students, as naturally as possible, not only what they should *do*, but also, in a sense, what they might be *thinking about* as they read. When I pause in the reading for a moment, I try to suggest the many awarenesses that are involved in the full comprehension of a particular line or passage.

Elanchius: I take it, Libentia, that you attempt to suggest the fullness of the good reader's mental context at any given moment in a work of literature: his multiple awarenesses of past and future as well as present, his sense of the relation of the immediate passage to earlier passages, to the wider whole of the work, even to the still greater whole that is human experience. In short, you attempt to show your students that there is much indeed to be aware of when they read a great book.

Quintus: Sounds to me like they've really got to be on their toes. Guess the idea's to show 'em how to do it so they'll go on doing it the same way when they don't have anybody to help 'em. It's a sure thing most of 'em won't do it later if nobody ever shows 'em how. Guess the one that shows 'em really's got to know her business, too. That's you, Libentia.

Libentia: Why, thank you, Quintus. You set a high mark for me to reach.

Pulvius: You need not worry about your *reach*, Libentia. Even your grasp exceeds the reach of—er—some people.

Quintus: Reach? Grasp? What are you talking about, Pulvius? And what'd you look at Vulpius for?

Pulvius: Why, Quintus, I mean that I for one do not underestimate either the imagination or the practical ability of Libentia.

Empiricus: Nor I, Pulvius. As I said earlier, a poor demonstration may often be worse than none at all, but a masterful one, such as Libentia earlier gave us, is a powerful instrument. Clearly, in order to demonstrate the alertness and thoughtfulness required in the reading of literature one must be an *expert*.

Vulpius: So you have finally admitted it! As you will recall, I have said from the beginning that adolescent learner reading growth must be guided by the reading expert. Only this specialist, utilizing growthful reading activities, will be able to conduct the progress of young learners up the reading ladder, since he has at his instant command scientific devices for determining both the reading material readability quotient and the adolescent learner reading readiness level.

Pulvius: There's verbiage for you. Or should I say—vulpiage!

Quintus: "Vulpiage!" Say, that's good! You just buried your expert, Vulpius, under that pile of garb—er—stuff. Good place for him, too! He's sure not the kind of expert Empiricus was talking about, you can bet. Kind he meant has read a great book or so. What books've your experts read, Vulpius?

Vulpius: Why, no one is a duly credentialized reading expert unless he has fully explored the literature of the subject, that is, both the research studies in the area of reading skills development and the bibliographies of reading materials actually utilized in the realistically oriented classroom situation.

Quintus: Bet that "literature of the subject" is a whole lot different than the literature we've been talking about all along! And besides that, you mean your experts won't read anything else but books like you have on those reading lists you carry around with you? Say, who'd you say wrote those books?

Vulpius: Why, most of them were either written or adapted by our specialists in the adolescent reading field.

Quintus: You mean reading experts? Hey! That's where we started from. Your reading experts don't read anything but what they wrote themselves.

Pulvius: Ha!

Elanchius: Libentia and gentlemen, we have taken a long while to consider the merits of one method, that of the teacher's reading with her students. We have said that this form of presentation is desirable, first, because it, more nearly than any other which has occurred to us, guarantees the release of the humanizing force potential in a work of literature; and, second, because by combining conditions and practices essential to the purpose, it furthers the development of the student's ability and desire to read comparable works by himself. No objections have yet been made to this method of presentation that have not been satisfactorily met. However, we should not conclude that we have found the best method until we have considered all reasonable objections. Or if we think of no outright objections, are there dangers of abuse that we should anticipate and warn against? For surely few practices of any kind or for any purpose have ever been devised that are not subject to abuse.

Pulvius: I do not wish to state an objection, but rather a word of caution. Frankly, I shudder at the thought that the teacher—not you, Libentia—may sometimes be so in love with her own voice and diction that, instead of reading with her students in a natural and inconspicuous manner, she will, in a sort, put on a performance for them, with the result that not the work itself but her reading will be the object of attention.

Elanchius: A timely caution, Pulvius! We can only hope that every teacher will be a Libentia, who knows to subordinate her own identity to that of the work. We have agreed, you will remember, that the thing which must be revealed lies *within the work itself*. Clearly, if the teacher "performs," as you suggest, Pulvius, she will exhibit not the work but herself.

Quintus: But look here! Can all teachers read like Libentia?

Empiricus: If our reasoning has been sound and our preference in method judicious, Quintus, it is their *duty* to develop both the ability and the taste that will enable them to do so.

Quintus: I'd say they ought to make it their business. Guess you don't need to worry about that, Pulvius. All we've got to do is make sure there's a lot of Libentias—all of 'em got to be, in fact. Well, that's settled. Anybody else want to caution us about anything?

Vulpius: I can only reiterate that you are completely unrealistic. There are many real objections—not just cautions, Quintus— that all of you, in your eager acceptance of this presentation method, have neglected to explore. First of all, such a method does not permit the learner personnel to progress with sufficient rapidity to enable them to cover the optimum amount of reading material demonstrated by professional research specialists as desirable for a given developmental level or maturation grouping. Furthermore, there will be no genuine participatory activity and hence little or no sharing and doing experience. What is activized in the classroom will be only the oral presentation by the teacher, while the adolescent learners will remain inactive—some gazing out the window, some meditating on socially unapproved behavior patterns, some of them experiencing withdrawal tendencies, and none of them doing more than merely thinking about what the teacher is reading, since no doing-activity will be occurring. And furthermore, as I have repeatedly remarked, the dominance of the teacher's vocal patterns will tend to frustrate individual audial and visual responses. To finalize, the researches of we in the profession as to classroom group dynamics realities demonstrate that reading materials which make necessary the utilization of such an unprogressive and static presentation method must be determined to be unsuitable for classroom utilization.

Quintus: Whew!

Empiricus: If I understand you, Vulpius—

Quintus: You kidding, Empiricus?

Empiricus: If I follow your argument, Vulpius, you object to this method because it is slow and because it requires steady concentration on the literary work being read. And since you find the method thus unsatisfactory, you conclude that any literature which requires its use is also unsatisfactory and should be replaced by readings which require no such attention. Have I represented your view accurately, Vulpius?

Quintus: Better say yes, Vulpius. At least it makes sense the way Empiricus put it! I can tell you this much—I don't have much use for your argument. Seems to me you're saying the same old thing—want to get rid of the only books that've got in 'em what it takes to do the job, and stick in that flabby stuff put out by those buddies of yours.

Elanchius: The implication of your remarks is just, Quintus. All that we have had to say about the humanizing effect of literature presupposes that those books will be read in which this effect is potential. We must therefore reject your conclusion, Vulpius, for although the works which you wish to substitute can be read easily and rapidly and do not require a form of presentation as painstaking as the one we are considering, yet, lacking the unique power of true art, they do not satisfy our very first requirement.

Quintus: That's right. Can't get blood out of a turnip.

Pulvius: No, just turnip juice! An apt figure, Quintus.

Elanchius: Nevertheless, gentlemen, although we cannot accept the conclusion that genuine literature should be replaced by inferior matter, yet Vulpius' objection that the practice of the teacher's reading *with* her students is too slow demands our consideration.

Quintus: Think he's got anything there?

Elanchius: Clearly, Quintus, were the teacher to read every work with her students and to pause for appropriate comment and discussion, the process would not be a hasty one.

Quintus: Well, who said it ought to be done in a big hurry?

Elanchius: None of us would wish it to be done so, Quintus. Nevertheless, the question whether the progress might be *too* slow requires examination.

Libentia: Why, Elanchius, even since Vulpius spoke a few moments ago, I have been thinking about my experience last year. And I must say that I think this method in the long run, is not really as slow as he suggested.

Quintus: How's that, Libentia?

Libentia: Why, Quintus, this is what I mean. If the students are given a work to prepare by silent reading beforehand, it then becomes necessary for the teacher to take much time in the classroom to supply information about background, to make explanations, and to establish relationships between earlier and later parts of the work. In doing so, she must reread passages, or at least summarize and point out places in the text to which she is referring, so that her explanations will be clear. But even so, she will have no infallible guide in her selection of points for discussion, so that she may waste much time in explanation and comments which are irrelevant. She may even encourage the students' discussion to wander. Yet, despite all the time she gives, she can never be certain that the presentation has illuminated all the matters that require it. On the other hand, by reading the work *with* her students, she can detect what needs illumination and can therefore make all the necessary explanations on the spot. Thus, the likelihood of the students' comprehension is much greater, and the efficiency of her teaching is greatly enhanced. It all comes down to this, I believe. Although reading aloud does require more time than reading silently, yet since the text itself will always be before her students as she reads with them, it is the literary work itself which will serve to concentrate attention, facilitate explanations, and guard against irrelevant and merely tangential discussion. In short, this method may better be characterized as efficient and time-saving than slow!

Elanchius: A method that is truly efficient in accomplishing its task may never properly be called slow. Let us suppose that a machine were devised which in a single sweep through the field would cut down the corn,* beat out and blow away the chaff, discard the straw, and pour into a box all the clean grain. Now, though the forward motion of the machine were less rapid than that of another which merely mowed, could we reasonably characterize it as slow, when it did the entire task in a single sweep?

Quintus: I'll say not! Boy, I could use a rig that'd make a pair of shoes all at one swoop!

Empiricus: Your analogy, Elanchius, is both apt and instructive. Yet I remember we earlier agreed that no one method would necessarily be best for all works. I now see clearly why the method of the teacher's reading *with* her students can be highly efficient. But is it possible that for some texts this method is excessive—more painstaking than is needed to release the force they contain? Will there not be shorter pieces, perhaps of a lighter nature, which students can read for themselves silently and rapidly, and for which little background or discussion is essential? And will there not also be, in longer works, some parts which the students can safely be trusted to read appreciatively by themselves? If so, the progress of the class, though painstaking when necessary, can at other times be greatly speeded.

Libentia: One might think you were a teacher of literature yourself, Empiricus! There are indeed many short, light works— masterpieces nonetheless—which the students can read for themselves silently and quickly with little assistance from the teacher. And certainly parts of some longer works can be read quickly.

Elanchius: True, Libentia. But are you aware that just now you have raised a new and subtle question, which we cannot properly pass by without answering?

Quintus: Hey, cut that out, Libentia! Want to make us stay here all night?

Libentia: I'm sorry, Quintus. Elanchius, I had thought I was merely replying to Empiricus.

Elanchius: Then permit me to phrase the question. We have agreed that some works of the kind we wish students to read will

---

* Wheat.

require the teacher's reading *with* her class. For others, as you have just pointed out, this method will be superfluous. Must we not then inquire which works should be given greater representation in the reading program—those that will require the teacher's steady assistance, or those that the students can read by themselves?

Quintus: But look here, now! We said *all* the books they read ought to be able to do what's got to be done—humanize 'em. So I don't see it makes much difference.

Elanchius: Agreed, Quintus. All books which deserve a place in the reading program must have a humanizing potential, but that force can be more readily released—or unlocked as you once put it—from some books than from others. But our question is that of determining the proper emphasis: which kind deserves preference in the reading program?

Quintus: That's easy. The kind that's too tough for 'em to unlock by themselves.

Elanchius: Unquestionably, the greater part of the *teacher's* time should be given to reading with her students books that require such treatment. This would seem the most justifiable use of her time and of her superior understanding of books.

Quintus: That's right, the teacher really knows her stuff about books, and she ought to use it. Say! It just hit me—you know what we just came up with here is just the opposite of what Vulpius was trying to put over a while ago. He said if a book's the kind that means the teacher has to read it with her students it's the wrong kind of book for 'em. But now you know what we just said? We said maybe the best kind of book for 'em is the kind the teacher *does* have to read with 'em, so if it's not that kind it's the wrong kind!

Elanchius: You have accurately discerned the basic opposition, upon this point, between our view and that expressed by Vulpius. I applaud your statement. Nevertheless, your expression of the opposition does, in a sense, overstate and misrepresent the case. As we have said, the greater part of the *teacher's* time should be devoted to reading with her students works of great potentiality which they would not, or could not adequately, read for themselves. Yet we have not intended to say that the *students'* whole time should be given to difficult and serious works of literature. Part of their time should be given to works that can be read with a minimum of assistance.

Quintus: But not that stuff on Vulpius' lists, eh?

Elanchius: Except that it consumes precious time, reading those works will do no great harm; yet, since their chief virtue is their adaptation to progressive degrees of difficulty, they serve at best only to develop skill. But we have required that works given a place in the students' reading program provide not merely practice in reading but much more.

Quintus: Looks to me like this is kind of a complicated business we've got into right here, Elanchius. Let's see if I can get it straight. The teacher ought to spend most of her time on books the students can't do a good job of reading by themselves, because that's what she's for. But the students ought to read quite a lot of other books, too, mainly all by themselves, only these other books have to have the real stuff in *them,* too. Guess the thing is to be sure these are all written by real writers and not by Vulpius' "experts." But now, see here. Let me ask you one thing straight out, Elanchius. Even if some of these books the students can read by themselves *have* got the real stuff in 'em, do you think they've got *as much of it* as the ones the teacher'll have to read *with* 'em? What I'm getting at is that maybe the students shouldn't waste any time at all on the kind of books they can read by themselves, but ought to spend it all on the kind the teacher has to help 'em with, if that's the kind that'll do 'em the most good.

Elanchius: Ah, but Quintus! Can we weigh and measure the force of individual works of art? If lighter and simpler pieces, which students read silently and quickly, and with pleasure, may lack, as single works, the profound depth and inexhaustible potential of their monumental kin, yet as true works of art they partake of the same quality as these. And even the gleam of this quality is to be prized. No, Quintus! let us not permit a momentary fault in our logic to make us, at last, extremists. By all means, let the teacher read with her students the great tragedies and the intricate comedies, the magnificent odes and the complex narratives of great actions; but let her also induce them to read for themselves and to value other works in which, nevertheless, the perfection of true art shines: the lighter tale that makes them roar with laughter, the stirring narrative whose very simplicity moves the heart,* and the sparkling poem, though it be only four lines of verse, crystal clear.

Pulvius: Bravo, Elanchius! Quintus, you are put down.

Quintus: Hey! Don't get me wrong, Pulvius! Last man I'd ever feel like arguing with is Elanchius. I just wanted to get things straight. Sure did, too!

Elanchius: Well, then. We have been considering the arguments which might be brought against the teacher's reading *with* her students as a method of presentation. Have we omitted any possibilities?

Quintus: Don't hear any, Elanchius. Guess nobody has any others.

Elanchius: Then we are agreed. We have advanced many compelling reasons for—

Libentia: Pardon me, Elanchius. I should have spoken earlier, but I have been hesitant. I cannot tell you how glad I am that we have decided upon this as the best single method of presentation. The truth, I must now confess, is that I have had all along a personal reason for preferring it! My reason is really a selfish one, and I would never have mentioned it had not other, more objective arguments already determined our decision. And even now—

Quintus: Aw, come on, Lib. Out with it!

Libentia: Well—promise me you won't make fun of me, now! We have said almost from the beginning that the supreme value of literature lies in the humanizing experience it gives the reader. As a teacher, I have found no warmer satisfaction than that of being present in the very instant that the experience occurs, when the vital force of the work touches the innermost being of the student! The satisfaction of this experience alone is sufficient to make me a teacher of literature all my life. I suppose that it is

---

* Elanchius' words here recall Sidney's: "I never heard the olde song of *Percy* and *Duglas*, that I found not my heart mooved more then with a Trumpet."

something like the pleasure the poet or the painter feels, upon putting the last touch to a work which seems fully to embody the image held in his mind; or perhaps, like the relief of the mariner who, after an extended and difficult voyage, at last safely steers his pinnace into its native harbor, carrying the seamen home. And it is only by reading with the student that I can be sure of being present when this experience occurs. Well, now I've confessed it. Should I be embarrassed?

Elanchius: Never, Libentia. Your confession is final proof of your devotion—both to literature and to your students.

Empiricus: You have almost made me wish that I had become a teacher of literature too, Libentia. Or at least that I were one of your students, to have this experience with you!

Quintus: See what you mean, Empiricus. I could use some of that experience myself. Don't get anything like it selling shoes. What about you, Pulvius? You get any kick like this the way you teach?

Pulvius: Let us say that I shall seek it more often hereafter, Quintus.

Elanchius: Now, Libentia and gentlemen, before we end these conversations, let me remind you that when we began to consider which of several possible forms of presentation will best serve the ultimate purpose of the study of literature, some of you raised particular questions. You, Libentia, asked several. Have they now been answered?

Libentia: All of them, Elanchius.

Elanchius: And yours, Empiricus?

Empiricus: I was concerned, you will remember, Elanchius, with the students' comprehension. My question has been answered.

Elanchius: And yours, Pulvius?

Pulvius: I am confident that the knowledge with which I attempt to equip successive generations of Libentias will continue to be indispensable.

Elanchius: Yes, as a strategic reserve, Pulvius! And your question, Quintus?

Quintus: I just wanted to be sure whether the teacher was

going to teach the books mostly, or the themes, too. That was settled a long time ago.

Elanchius: And you, Vulpius.

Vulpius: I had no questions to ask.

Quintus: That's right, Elanchius. Vulpius just had a bunch of answers.

Pulvius: Taunt him no more, Quintus. For even now he may be plotting how to be revenged on the whole pack of us!

Elanchius: Ah, Pulvius! But now are we ready to depart?

Quintus: Glad we got everything settled. Wanted to stay until we did, but I don't mind saying it's high time I got back to my shoes.

Libentia: As we are walking out of the building, I shall try to say how grateful I am for the help and encouragement you have all given me these past few days. But I know I shall not be able to say all that I should like.

Quintus: Don't mention it, Libentia. Say, we don't want to forget to lock this place up, too. Vulpius, you're the one that's still got the key, aren't you?

Vulpius: Yes, Quintus. The key is still in my pocket!

Concluding Dialogue

Persons of the Dialogue

LIBENTIA MAGISTRA   J. QUINTUS

ELANCHIUS

Scene: The home of Elanchius

Quintus: We about there, Libentia?

Libentia: As soon as we have passed through this olive grove, Quintus, we shall be in sight of Elanchius' door. Ah! There it is now.

Quintus: Hey, quite a door! Looks like a shield on it. And what's that thing in the middle? Some kind of a head, with snakes instead of hair.

Libentia: Surely, Quintus, you recognize—but here is Elanchius!

Elanchius: Welcome, Libentia and Quintus! I am happy to see you both. Come right upstairs to my study. Well, Quintus, I hardly expected to meet you again so soon. When we parted a few hours ago, you were hurrying back to your place of business.

Quintus: Yeh, I was, Elanchius. Found things getting along pretty well at the shop, though. A little swamped with orders for new shoes, but I'll catch up pretty quick.

Libentia: Quintus is being somewhat coy, Elanchius. The fact is that he is deeply concerned about the subject we have been discussing these past few days. When he came to see me this evening, he reminded me that we had ended our conversations immediately after agreeing how the teacher should choose the best form of presentation, but that we had said nothing about what the students should do next, or indeed whether anything at all remained to be done. After we had talked for a while, he himself suggested that we come to you for advice, not only about

292

these matters but about another, the exact nature of which he didn't reveal except to say that it was a "big one" that he thought was of great importance to me.

Quintus: Yeh, that's right! After we've gone to so much trouble to make sure everything gets done just right, it seems to me we oughtn't to take any chances that anything else that's got to be done will get done wrong. So all I wanted to know is after the students've got the books in their heads, what comes next? Looks to me like there's quite a few things along that line that've still got to be figured out. Besides that, like Libentia said, I've really got a big question I want to ask you right out, Elanchius, and I'd like to know what you think about it without pulling any punches.

Elanchius: Shall we make ourselves comfortable here by the fire? I am pleased that you came to me, Quintus, and I shall give you any help I can.

Quintus: Know I can count on you, Elanchius. You know, since we've had these good talks, I've got the idea pretty strong that shoes aren't my *only* business. Any business has got to be run right or it'll go to pieces, and now that I've finally seen why the schools are my business too, I want to see they're run right.

Elanchius: Your concern is laudable, Quintus, and more than that, indispensable if the schools are to be "run right." And if they *are* run right, they can be as effective in turning out young people who recognize and value their human potentialities as is your shop in turning out admirably made shoes.

Quintus: They've got to be, I'd say. And young people are a lot more important than shoes, too! Why, just last week a poor fellow staggered into my shop one night bleeding all over. He said a bunch of young kids had beat him up and taken all his money. Said he had quite a lot on him, too, because he'd just been paid off. Now don't get me wrong! I know the schools can't do everything. But I'll bet if those kids had got some of that humanizing experience like Libentia can give her students, they'd find better things to do.

Libentia: I shall always believe so, Quintus. Although perhaps your expectation of what the teacher can accomplish unaided is too high, I believe that, above all, she must strive to help her students realize their full human stature and make their actions accord with it.

Quintus: Like the way you said that, Libentia! If the teacher doesn't get at that business, she's not really doing her job—and that's a fact. If all she has her student do is fiddle around with this and that and pretend they're grownups and not find out how to be grownups, they might as well stay home and play dolls. That's playing you're a grownup too.

Elanchius: I see, Quintus, that you equate being a "grownup" with realizing one's human potential. Excellent! We must add at once, however, that this goal is not one to be sought only by adults—as your use of the word might suggest. The young should also be encouraged to esteem and enlarge their humanity, for the road to perfection is long indeed! Nevertheless, we must also add that although the progress toward it must be deliberate, it must not be unpleasurable. *Education must deprive no child of his childhood.* Indeed, I should go so far as to say that unless education is pleasurable, it will never affect the student deeply enough to be reflected in his conduct. If his education fails to be so, either its substance has been determined erroneously or his teacher is failing in her task. I have known many zealous and truly excellent teachers, and I have reason to believe that when the teacher fails in her highest function the substance, more often than her efforts, is at fault. I would go even further, Quintus. After a long lifetime, looking back upon this past half-century, I should say that wherever the substance is found to be at fault, there it will also be found that those who have determined this substance have so misled the teacher that she cannot possibly reach her highest goal. Instead of being a teacher, she becomes little more than a manipulator of techniques, a temporary guardian, an entertaining hostess, and a record clerk.

Quintus: Misled, eh? That's just about what I thought. But can't somebody do something about it, Elanchius?

Elanchius: Perhaps, Quintus. Perhaps. Especially since you yourself are now disturbed.

Quintus: Me? Well, I'll do all I can. But I wouldn't know how to run a school, myself. Just want to see it does what it ought to. What do you think I should do, Elanchius?

Elanchius: Ah, Quintus! Is this question the "big one" you said you had in mind?

Quintus: Guess it is. But that's not exactly the way I meant to put it.

Elanchius: But you had other questions also. Which do you think we should consider first?

Quintus: Hate to put off the big one, but first things first, I always say. So let's get at the little ones—things we didn't get around to before, when we had so much that had to be talked about. One of 'em is this. Now we've talked a lot about how to pick out books for students to read, and how to decide which ones to put together so they'll be read about the same time, and how to get 'em read. I was wondering what'd happen after that. After the students read 'em, will they do anything with what they got out of 'em? Of course I know they're supposed to humanize 'em—I won't ever forget *that* after all we said about it, but I guess you might say that happens inside 'em. Is there anything that goes on—uh—sort of outside 'em? Anything special they ought to be doing?

Elanchius: You are asking about possible activities which may accompany or immediately follow the reading of a work of literature. Do you have in mind such an activity, for example, as writing?

Quintus: Yeh. Remember I did quite a lot of writing when I was in school. Say, just happened to think of something. We've been talking about *literature* every time we got together. Never said a word about *writing* until now, as far as I can remember. What about that? That's part of Libentia's job too, isn't it?

Elanchius: It is indeed, Quintus, and a highly important part. I assure you that its omission from our conversations has been no accident. The subject is large and complex. Furthermore, writing—or perhaps we might more appropriately say *composition*—is a creative act which, like the study of literature, makes special demands upon both student and teacher. Therefore it deserves an examination no less comprehensive than we have given to the subject of literature. If Libentia and the other members of the group wish, perhaps during her next summer vacation we can turn our attention to the subject of grammar and composition.

Libentia: Oh yes, Elanchius! And I'm sure Pulvius will be glad to join us.

Quintus: Yeh, old Pulvius is all right. And you can count me in, too. Wouldn't miss it. I'll bet Empiricus'll come too. You know, it really struck me how he was really on our side all the time. First it seemed like he couldn't see any kind of an education except what'd get people ready to live in a dog-eat-dog world. Next thing I knew he was working on the idea that if you *could* humanize 'em the world wouldn't have to be like that.

Elanchius: We shall always need his support, Quintus—now more than ever. Perhaps, having seen what he has of the world, Empiricus perceives more clearly than most the urgent necessity for humanization.

Libentia: I am sure that he does, Elanchius, for on the way home this afternoon he asked if he might see me later this evening—to talk further of the matter. I look forward to his coming.

Elanchius: Good, Libentia. For the present, then, let us say only this about composition: that *all writing activities chosen to accompany the study of literature should be of a kind that will help to consolidate the humanizing force released through the study of literature.*

Libentia: Must we not say the same of all activities which the teacher may use in connection with the study of literature, Elanchius—the discussion, for example, that may follow the reading of a particular work? Also the dramatization and the memorization, if these are used?

Quintus: Yeh, that's it, Libentia. Those are the things I had in mind when I asked what the students would do after they got a book read. Did things like that when I went to school. Think it's a good idea to have students do 'em?

Libentia: Indeed I do, Quintus. Discussion and writing *stimulated by literature* can be means of expanding the opportunity for literature to have its greatest effect. Dramatization also provides such an opportunity, especially for some students who have not yet learned to visualize what they read. However, dramatization as an activity in the classroom may easily be abused.

Quintus: How's that, Libentia?

Libentia: Why, I mean, Quintus, that the teacher and students may come to regard the dramatization as a performance, to be valued in proportion to the skill of the actors, rather than as a means of increasing comprehension and heightening the effect of the work.

Quintus: Yeh, follow you there all right. Got to see first that they're good human beings and not whether they're good actors. Well, how about that other one—memory work? Do you think they ought to do any of that?

Libentia: If Vulpius were here, Quintus, he would advise you emphatically that memorization of literary passages does not fit the pattern of the modern school.*

Quintus: From the way I've got Vulpius sized up after these talks we've been having, I'd say that's about the best kind of argument for having 'em learn a lot of good stuff by heart! What's Vulpius got against it, anyhow?

Libentia: I have heard him say that—

Quintus: Wait, Libentia. Don't tell me. Bet I can hit it pretty close myself. He'd start off by giving us that line about social this and social that and all that business about *doing* things— what'd he call 'em, where there's all that hustle-bustle and moving around?

Libentia: "Group dynamics?" Or "dynamic group processes," Quintus?

Quintus: Yeh, those things. Well, he'd say this memorizing doesn't fit in there. It's too—uh—sort of *lonesome* the way a student's got to go at it, sitting there and doing it all by himself. Am I right so far?

Libentia: What I have heard Vulpius say is not essentially

---

* And not only Vulpius. The reader may be interested to learn that the authors of *The English Language Arts*, prepared for the Commission on the English Curriculum of the National Council of Teachers of English, evidently did not consider memorization important enough to be mentioned.

different from that, I think, although he required more time to say it.

Quintus: Yeh, that's what I mean—that's how he'd go on for quite a spell. Course, though, there's one way Vulpius'd be right about this.

Libentia: How is that, Quintus?

Quintus: Well, he wouldn't even be thinking about the kind of books we want 'em to read and maybe memorize parts of. He doesn't even want 'em to *read* those books. So he'd be thinking about having 'em memorize the kind of stuff he thinks they ought to read. And that's where I'd agree with him. Don't mean I'd agree that's what they ought to *read*. I mean I'd agree they shouldn't memorize it. No use memorizing stuff that there's no use even reading.

Elanchius: You believe, however, that memorization of works which *do* deserve reading may be appropriate?

Quintus: Yeh, guess I do. Only if you and Libentia say no, I've got enough sense to say no, too.

Libentia: I do have an opinion, Quintus. But, like you, I am willing to change it if it conflicts with Elanchius' judgment.

Elanchius: You are kind, Libentia. But why are you reluctant to speak?

Libentia: Because I have been laughed at, Elanchius, and once even reprimanded. To my administrative superiors and to some of my colleagues the very mention of memorization is—well, it is as though one were to resurrect some old bones long ago buried and forgotten.

Quintus: That bad, eh?

Libentia: I am afraid so. The subject is not merely unde-batable; it is unthinkable.

Elanchius: However, Quintus, you know from your own experience that this attitude has not long prevailed. A few short years ago—

Quintus: Don't have to tell me who changed things. Vulpius!

Elanchius: Not any of the rest of us, Quintus! Well, then. All three of us have admitted some liking for the memorization of literature. Now let us see whether there is a firm basis for our liking. And if we find that there is none, what shall we do?

Quintus: Why, be honest and change our minds.

Elanchius: But if we find that there is a firm basis, what then should we do—or, more precisely, what then should Libentia do?

Quintus: That's easy. Be honest and stand up for what's right.

Libentia: And with your support, Quintus, I shall!

Elanchius: Quintus, a day or two ago you spoke of hauling materials in a cart—remember, the one that became stuck in the mud?

Quintus: Remember that, all right. But what are you up to now? What's this got to do with whether Libentia ought to have her students learn things by heart?

Libentia: Patience, Quintus!

Elanchius: I presume that during your younger days, when you were building up your business, you spent a considerable amount of time in that cart.

Quintus: I'll say I did, summer and winter. All alone, too. Did just about everything by myself in those days—hauling leather and delivering shoes up the country. Plenty rough going sometimes!

Elanchius: I am interested in those cart trips. Unpleasant, were they?

Quintus: You can say that again! In the spring the roads were muddy and you got stuck. In the summer they were hot and dusty and you roasted. And in the winter—boy, the winter!—you just plain froze. Finally licked that, though.

Elanchius: Will you tell us how you did so, Quintus?

Quintus: My feet used to get so cold they nearly dropped off. Got so I'd sit in the shop with 'em in the oven just before I started out. Trouble was, that didn't help a whole lot. Feet'd be just about cooked when I'd start, and before I got out of town they'd be frozen stiff. Guess I wouldn't have any feet left at all if I hadn't got an idea.

Elanchius: Perhaps it is just this idea that Libentia and I want to hear about, Quintus. What did you do?

Quintus: Heated me a couple of orichalcum* bricks real hot and put 'em in a box in front of my cart and put my feet on 'em. Kept me warm the whole trip.

Elanchius: *Kept you warm during the whole trip!* You have answered our question, Quintus, succinctly and eloquently.

Quintus: How's that? What question?

Libentia: Why, don't you see, Quintus, that you have provided us with a basis for our belief in memorization?

Quintus: Basis? You mean those hot bricks I put my feet on?

Libentia: In a manner of speaking, yes, Quintus. But, you see, the point is that you learned it was not enough to heat your feet in advance, no matter how thoroughly. You found that *you must carry the heat with you,* if its effects were to last as long as you needed it.

Quintus: I get you! We said the teacher ought to read the books with 'em so as to make sure the effect really gets to 'em. That's like getting myself hot clear through before I started out. Now we're saying the students ought to learn some of these books by heart so the effect'll always *stay* with 'em! That's like me hauling those hot bricks to keep my feet on. That makes sense—good sense! Libentia, don't you ever let anybody tell you anything different.

Elanchius: I find it significant that the three of us have so readily agreed on the value of memorizing passages of great literature. Despite its present unpopularity as a means of teaching, memorization, by prolonging the period of the aesthetic experience, can extend the opportunity for the humanizing force of literature to exercise its effect upon the student. Thus, like writing, discussion, and dramatization, it is capable of helping literature to fulfill its highest function.

Quintus: Yeh, that's the teacher's big job!

Elanchius: True, Quintus. *And in using these and other activities the teacher must therefore subordinate them to this*

---

* It has been a matter of scholarly interest to the translators, as having a possible bearing on the origin of the manuscript, that the term here used so familiarly by Quintus occurs in Plato's *Critias,* in reference to the lost continent of Atlantis.

purpose and not let them become ends in themselves. Otherwise, they may lead her quite astray.

Quintus: I get the idea, Elanchius. The students have got to go at it from every angle, so they've got the best chance to get the best thing that's in it—and so it'll stay with 'em, too. Now how about my other question?

Elanchius: Let us hear it, Quintus.

Quintus: Well, first I'd like to say that before we started talking about the school and books and what was the teacher's business and such, the only person I'd ever talked to about 'em was Vulpius, and he always had the answers. Didn't always get everything he said, but since he's supposed to be an expert on such things, I figured he was right. Fact is, I figured what Vulpius was always saying was what everybody else would say that knew anything about the schools. Took it for granted. But then you and Libentia and Pulvius started talking too, and I found out you don't agree with him at all! Right away I saw he was really off all by himself. And not only that—he didn't even begin to stack up with the rest of you. Tell you the truth, I didn't always like what Vulpius was saying—what I understood of it anyway. So I'm really glad we got together on this business.

Elanchius: If everyone were as much interested and as perceptive, Quintus—but I am interrupting. You were about to ask a question.

Quintus: Yeh! the big one that's been on my mind. Just how come this Vulpius ever got such a hold on how Libentia does her job?

Elanchius: Just hers, Quintus?

Quintus: How's that, Elanchius? You mean he's got his hands on teaching other things too—things like history?

Elanchius: History? If reports are accurate, Quintus, the teaching of what has come to be called "Social Studies" is even more completely under his dominion than is the teaching of literature—and at least as desperately in need of rescue! Furthermore, no subject has escaped his influence.

Quintus: Hey! Thought I had my eyes open already. Guess I was mistaken. Wonder if he's as wrong about those subjects as he is about teaching literature. Bet he is, too.

Elanchius: In any event it is certain, Quintus, that Vulpius stands no higher in the regard of the historical scholar and the scientist than in Pulvius'.*

Quintus: You don't say. That's worse than I thought. Why, these fellows are the ones that know what their subjects are all about. How come the teachers don't go to them when they want help, instead of letting Vulpius tell 'em?

Libentia: I would feel unprepared to stand before my class except for what I learned about books under Pulvius' direction. Even so, perhaps Pulvius and his fellow scholars are themselves partly to blame, Quintus. For although they have provided the teachers with a thorough education in subject matter, thereafter they have too often held themselves aloof from the problems which confront their former students as teachers. As they have removed themselves from the scene, Vulpius has advanced into the breach and has come to be thought of as indispensable.

Quintus: Muscled in, eh? Still, looks to me like you teachers could get together for some meetings to figure out how to get your job done best and call on Pulvius and the others to help out when you needed them.

Libentia: You are still underestimating the extent of Vulpius' dominion, Quintus! We do have meetings—many, many of them. But these, too, are largely controlled by Vulpius, directly or indirectly. The result is that, although we are properly teachers of literature and composition, too often it is *not* literature and composition that we discuss, but such matters as group processes, evaluating mass media, "ideas that work," "the otherwise gifted," using special aids and techniques, sharing "growthful experiences," listening activities, and so on—and naturally, the speakers

---

* There are interesting modern parallels. For example, the views of the historian, Arthur Bestor, which are well known; and those of a famous scientist, who recently spoke as follows: "It is understandable that school officials who have never had any intellectual experience in their lives should try to compensate for this by denying the reality of intellectual discipline, but such persons should not be determining educational policies. They should be replaced by educated men and women" (Joel H. Hildebrand, in his presidential address to the American Chemical Society, September 12, 1955).

are "specialists" in these fields.* When literature and composition are included in the program, they are likely to be relegated to an obscure place and slightingly referred to as "traditional content," or they are discussed by speakers who are followers of Vulpius. All too seldom is a speaker invited who, like Pulvius, could speak from his profound knowledge of literature and composition. Thus, much of the program often is dissipated by concentrating on matters other than the teachers' real task, and the very tone of the program is one which discourages a discussion of the central values and issues.

Quintus: Didn't know things were that bad! Won't even let you run your own meetings, eh?

Elanchius: Nor does his dominion end even there, Quintus, as I am sure Libentia well knows.

Libentia: I do know, Elanchius. And you should know, Quintus! Almost all our administrators were trained by Vulpius. The legal authority from which we secure our license to teach is directed by Vulpius! And, increasingly, our young teachers themselves have been conditioned in advance to think like Vulpius, for the greater number now are trained in a kind of institution where the administrators and faculty are predominantly Vulpius' "experts." These institutions have no Pulviuses, Quintus, or if there may be one or two holdovers from the past they have been pushed aside from the main streams so that they can have only negligible influence on the preparation of teachers! Moreover—

Quintus: Hey! So in places like that Vulpius practically runs the whole show, eh? Know what? Looks to me like we'd have better teachers if they never went near Vulpius.

Libentia: But they must, Quintus, if they are to be allowed to teach! And unfortunately the necessity of taking extensive

---

* Libentia might almost be describing a typical conference of English teachers. Cf., for example, the following excerpts from recent programs: "What are the Values of Unit-Type [sic] Teaching?" "Using the Mass Media," "Teaching Mass Communication," "Network Television as a Springboard to Children's Reading," "The English Teacher Has Effective Appraisal Techniques," "Group Process," "Individual Differences," "Curriculum Construction," "Discussion Techniques," "Unit Method," "Traditional Content," "Using Current Materials," "Attitudes Toward English," "Learning Process."

training under Vulpius drives away many highly capable persons who might have become excellent teachers.

Quintus: All because they couldn't stomach Vulpius' stuff, eh? Now let's see if I've got this straight in my head. Even the brightest fellow ever graduated from Pulvius' school couldn't teach in yours if he hadn't served his time under Vulpius. That how it is?

Libentia: Why, Quintus, Pulvius himself could not teach in my school! Nor could Empiricus!

Quintus: You kidding me, Libentia?

Libentia: No indeed! Both Pulvius and Empiricus would have to be trained by Vulpius before they could teach their subjects in my school!

Quintus: Boy! What an empire! Looks like he's got you coming and going. Say, why hasn't anybody told me these things before?

Libentia: Perhaps, Quintus, because those who are most fully aware of the facts have been hesitant to speak up.

Quintus: Oh, that's it! You know, you've just cleared up one thing I've been puzzled about, Libentia—a lot of things, for that matter, but this one in particular. All along I've noticed how you'd keep yourself from telling Vulpius right off he was just plain wrong about something he'd said. Wondered more than once why you kept quiet. But what you just told me about this big web he's got you caught in lets me know what the score is. Don't blame you for going kind of easy with him! He's got everything sewed up. Guess you've either got to fit the picture the way he sees it, or else.

Elanchius: Or else, Quintus?

Quintus: Or else she's out on her ear, that's what. And that won't do. Say, what about this fellow anyhow? Can't let him keep running the whole business, that's for sure. You think there's any place for him at all, Elanchius?

Elanchius: It would be a shame, Quintus, if his attributes were to be wasted entirely, for they are valuable ones when they are under proper control. He is industrious, ambitious, aggressive, ingenious, and remarkably skillful in weaving intricate designs.

Quintus: You can say that again. Hey, look how late it's

getting! Hate to break this up, but I promised to meet a fellow about a big order—another big order I mean.

Libentia: I shall have to leave also, Elanchius, if I am to be at home when Empiricus arrives.

Elanchius: Well, then. We'll go downstairs together.

Libentia: As we go down, Quintus, notice the tapestry hanging there on the wall. It represents the birth of the goddess fully armed.

Quintus: Say, that's real nice! And those other things further down, too. Say, look at that big owl! You're quite a collector, Elanchius.

Elanchius: Some of these are thought to be rarities, Quintus.

Quintus: I'll say. Look at that helmet and that gold spear. Fit for a *palace*, I'd say.

Libentia: Here's a rarity, certainly! Is it new, Elanchius? I have not seen it before. A superbly wrought iron box containing a spider. See how busily he spins!

Quintus: He's a big one! Never saw one quite like that. Real lively, too, like he'd just been put in there.

Elanchius: So he was.

Quintus: Well, here's the door. Thanks for everything, Elanchius. But before I go I just want to say I know a lot more about the school business than I did a few days ago. Thanks again, Elanchius. Big job to do all right, and looks like it'll take plenty of doing.

Elanchius: It will indeed, Quintus! But if we are not eventually to lose all sense of what man is and of what he might become, it must be done. It depends most of all on you yourself, Quintus. Yes, at beginning and end it depends on you. But it depends also on you, Libentia, and on Pulvius.

Quintus: Thought at first he was a queer duck, that Pulvius. But I've got to hand it to him. He knows books, and I guess in the long run he wants about the same things we do.

Elanchius: He is a learned man, Quintus. Respect him! Without its Pulviuses, the world would not long continue literate or humane. Yet he must do even more in the future than he has done in the past. It is not enough that he educate the Libentias while they are students. He must also become less remote from their problems and quicker to heed their call when they are teachers.

Libentia: And my part, Elanchius?

Elanchius: Yours I need not define, Libentia. You know as well as I or anyone where lies your proper course, and you have the will to be faithful to your own best and most thoughtful judgment.

Quintus: Don't need to tell *me* what I've got to do either, Elanchius—not any more you don't.

Elanchius: So, Quintus?

Quintus: Remember today Vulpius let us in the school and then locked up again when we left?

Elanchius: I do, Quintus.

Quintus: You know what I'm going to do first thing tomorrow? I'm gonna get that key.

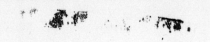